RETAILING MANAGEMENT

SUJA R. NAIR
B.A. (Hons.) M.B.A.,
Consultant Educe, Micro Research, Bengaluru.

FIRST EDITION : 2011

Himalaya Publishing House

MUMBAI • NEW DELHI • NAGPUR • BANGALORE • HYDERABAD • CHENNAI • PUNE • LUCKNOW • AHMEDABAD • ERNAKULAM • BHUBANESWAR • INDORE • GUWAHATI

First Edition : 2011

Published by : Mrs. Meena Pandey for **Himalaya Publishing House Pvt. Ltd.,**
"Ramdoot", Dr. Bhalerao Marg, Girgaon, **Mumbai - 400 004.**
Phone: 022-23860170/23863863, Fax: 022-23877178
E-mail: himpub@vsnl.com; Website: www.himpub.com

Branch Offices :

New Delhi : "Pooja Apartments", 4-B, Murari Lal Street, Ansari Road, Darya Ganj, New Delhi - 110 002. Phone: 011-23270392, 23278631; Fax: 011-23256286

Nagpur : Kundanlal Chandak Industrial Estate, Ghat Road, Nagpur - 440 018. Phone: 0712-2738731, 3296733; Telefax: 0712-2721215

Bengaluru : No. 16/1 (Old 12/1), 1st Floor, Next to Hotel Highlands, Madhava Nagar, Race Course Road, Bengaluru - 560 001. Phone: 080-32919385; Telefax: 080-22286611

Hyderabad : No. 3-4-184, Lingampally, Besides Raghavendra Swamy Matham, Kachiguda, Hyderabad - 500 027. Phone: 040-27560041, 27550139; Mobile: 09848130433

Chennai : No. 85/50, Bazullah Road, T. Nagar, Chennai - 600 017. Phone: 044-28144004/28144005

Pune : First Floor, "Laksha" Apartment, No. 527, Mehunpura, Shaniwarpeth (Near Prabhat Theatre), Pune - 411 030. Phone: 020-24496323/24496333

Lucknow : Jai Baba Bhavan, Church Road, Near Manas Complex and Dr. Awasthi Clinic, Aliganj, Lucknow - 226 024. Phone: 0522-2339329, 4068914; Mobile: 09305302158, 09415349385, 09389593752

Ahmedabad : 114, "SHAIL", 1st Floor, Opp. Madhu Sudan House, C.G. Road, Navrang Pura, Ahmedabad-380009. Phone: 079-26560126; Mobile: 09327324149, 09314679413

Ernakulam : 39/104 A, Lakshmi Apartment, Karikkamuri Cross Rd., Ernakulam, Cochin - 622011, Kerala. Phone: 0484-2378012, 2378016; Mobile: 09344199799

Bhubaneswar : 5 Station Square, Bhubaneswar (Odisha) - 751 001. Mobile: 09861046007

Indore : Kesardeep Avenue Extension, 73, Narayan Bagh, Flat No. 302, IIIrd Floor, Near Humpty Dumpty School, Narayan Bagh, Indore - 452 007 (M.P.). Mobile: 09301386468

Kolkata : 108/4, Beliaghata Main Road, Near ID Hospital, Opp. SBI Bank, Kolkata - 700 010, Phone: 033-32449649, Mobile: 09910440956

Guwahati : House No. 15, Behind Pragjyotish College, Near Sharma Printing Press, P.O. Bharalumukh, Guwahati - 781009. (Assam). Mobile: 09883055590, 09883055536

DTP by : HPH, Editorial Office, Bhandup (Shubhangi)

Printed by : **7 Hills Offset Printers,** Hyderabad.

PREFACE

In the early 2000s, the first phase of organised retailing revolution started. It was felt by market analysts then that since the retailing industry comprised of only 2 per cent of organised retailers there was a lot of potential in retail, if one could put into practise some of the Western retailing strategies in India. So, over the period of last 9-10 years one has been witness to changes occurring in the retail landscape with the emergence of many malls, specialist retailers, exclusive retail outlets, supermarkets, hypermarkets, etc. Simultaneously, the consumer behaviour has also been evolving with men and spouse both taking to work, the emergence of nuclear households, with high disposable income in hand, global travel, change in lifestyles, etc. Today, facing paucity of time the consumers are seeking retail destinations which offer convenience, quality merchandise, entertainment, additional services like free home delivery, etc. Yet the fact remains that the average Indian consumer prefers to purchase grocery and everyday necessities from the neighbourhood kirana shop, use shopping list for everyday purchases and so on. The recent economic slow down led to a slump in the retail sector with the need to re-do some of the strategies and revising product offerings and value-added services so as to inculcate positive shopping behaviour among consumers.

Thus, the area of 'Retailing Management' is not only challenging but interesting too. In this context this textbook on *'Retailing Management'* will be useful to all those students pursuing this course and especially for those undergoing M.B.A. course with the Jawaharlal Nehru Technical University (JNTU) Hyderabad. This book is divided into six units, where the chapters covered under the first five units (Chapters 1-12) are related to the various facets of retail management and are as per the syllabus prescribed by the JNTU, Hyderabad. This comprehensive textbook on Retailing Management is based on materials drawn from various books, magazines, periodicals, company websites and other secondary sources so as to make the text easily readable, enjoyable (as examples are co-related to Indian retailers) informative and easy to understand.

Main features of the book:

- Text material is supported by real Indian examples.
- Each chapter commences with learning objectives, 'Introduction', 'Subject matter', 'Summary', 'Chapter questions for discussion' and ends with an 'Activity' to enable the student get a feel of the practical aspects of the subject.

Acknowledgements

I am once again thankful to Himalaya Publishing House, especially Mr. Anuj Pandey, Mr. Niraj Pandey and Mr. Vijay Pandey for their continuous support and confidence in me. I am indeed very happy to write this textbook on the emerging and challenging area of Retailing Management. My sincere appreciation and thanks to Mrs. Nimisha, Mr. Adiga and all the staff of Himalaya Publishing House for providing all the administrative help.

Wishing the students 'All the Best'.

Suja R. Nair

CONTENTS

UNIT - IV LOCATION STRATEGIES

UNIT - V RETAILING IN INDIA

UNIT - VI CASES

UNIT I

INTRODUCTION TO RETAILING MANAGEMENT

1 BASICS OF RETAILING

LEARNING OBJECTIVES

After going through the chapter, you should be able to understand:

- The reasons behind the growth of the retail industry
- Learn about the differences between 'retail' and 'retailing' and the functions involved in retailing
- Differentiate between retailers and wholesalers functions.
- Briefly throw light on the various types of retailers.

STRUCTURE:

- Introduction
- The Advent of the Retail Environment
- Reasons Behind the Growth of the Retail Industry
- Meaning of 'Retail' and 'Retailing'
- Differences between Retailers and Wholesalers
- Functions of Retailing
- Types of Retailers
- Summary
- Chapter Questions for Discussion
- Activity

INTRODUCTION

Retailing is not only an important aspect of the economic structure but very much a part of our lives. Although trading of goods have been in existence since the olden days, it is only in the recent past that the buying and selling of goods have become more of a formal and a brand dominated activity. In fact, today retailing is evolving into a global, high-tech business. Nevertheless, the traditional forms of independently owned small businesses coexist along with the organised retailers like department stores, Speciality stores, shopping complexes, malls, large-scale multiple chains, etc.

Can you guess an industry which is considered almost as the single largest industry in many of the country's, though it employs less than 10 per cent of the labour force in the world? Well, it is the 'Retail Industry'. Do you find anything similar in the operations of *Tesco, Big Bazaar, indiatimes.coms, and neighbourhood grocery shop?* Yes, they are all involved in performing the retailing functions.

All the goods which are produced by the manufacturer reach the hands of the ultimate customers through the retailers. Retailing is the last function carried out in the marketing chain before the product (or service) finally reaches the target consumers.

This chapter begins with giving a brief description of the advent of retail environment, meaning of retail and retailing, the functions of retailers, differences between retailers and wholesalers and concludes with a discussion on the different types of retailing.

THE ADVENT OF THE RETAIL ENVIRONMENT

Marketing Guru, Philip Kotler had long back defined Marketing as *"Human activity directed at satisfying needs and wants through exchange processes"* (Philip Kotler, 'Principles of Marketing' 1985). This definition talks of marketing as a human activity which takes place involving an exchange process, so as to satisfy (human) wants and needs. Thus, the entire marketing process is evolved around human activities which take place at the markets. For the exchange processes to take place, on the one hand, the sellers have to search for their target buyers, identify their unmet needs, develop appropriate products (or services), promote them, store and transport them, enter into a relationship with suppliers who will interact with the final customers, and so on. On the other hand also, the buyers (or consumers) also will be carrying out marketing activities. She will also search out for the required product (or service) at retail outlets at a price suitable to her budget. Although, the marketing concept focuses on the "Customer" as the driving force behind all the related activities, a lot depends on the what, when, how and where decisions taken by the retailer during the course of his interaction with the buyers.

In the long run, marketers have realised that retailers play a big role in establishing , creating and keeping **profitable** customers relationship. Today, retailing occupies a prominent position in the economies across the world. The retailing sector is also witnessing constant changes at an increasing pace, forcing marketers to seek innovative ways to attract, woo and ensure commitment from the customer.

The Indian retail market comprises of both unorganised retailers as well as the organised players. It is reported that India has more than 12 million retail outlets, of which organised retailers account for only around 2 per cent of the business (Rajan Saxena, Marketing Management 2006). Nevertheless, in the past few years, we have seen the emergence of various forms of retailing to take care of the changing demands of the consumers at the marketplace. In fact, marketers are trying out various ways to segment the market with retail formats specifically to focus on the needs of the particular target consumer groups.

Along with the traditional forms of small independently owned businesses, today the retail sector is characterised by the emergence of shopping malls, chain stores, departmental stores, fast food outlets, food courts, automated retailing (ATMs, fast food outlets) and so on. Retailing is considered as an funfilled experience for the whole family, where each family member looks forward to an enjoyable shopping experience. To cater to the needs of the target customers, the retail sector has increased in the size and different formats — all in search for newer ways in which to grow their businesses. All this indicates that retailing is a dynamic and vibrant industry.

REASONS BEHIND THE GROWTH OF THE RETAIL INDUSTRY

Figure 1.1 illustrates the typical marketing chain and the position of the retailer in this. As shown since the retailer provide the vital link with the ultimate consumer and plays a very dominant role in the brand-building exercise. With an increase in the size of the retailers and the intense competition at the marketplace have prompted them to move away from the traditional format and opt for newer forces of retailing.

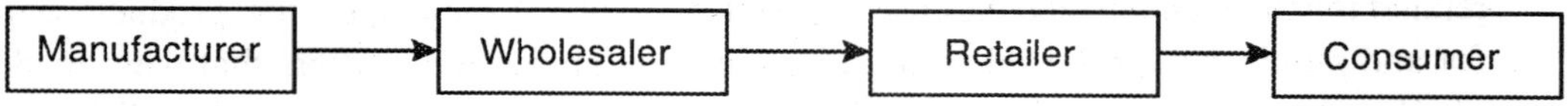

Figure 1.1: The position of the retailer in a typical marketing chain

Retailing has been integrated into the economic structure of every country and has been in vogue since the earlier times when the barter system used to be practised. It can easily be said that retailing not only shapes but is also shaped by the way of living of the people at a particular place. Although the exchange or trading of goods (and services) has always been a part of our traditional societies, along with the pace of development of the economy, retailing today has become more of a formalised brand-building activity.

Till sometime back, manufacturers did not give much importance to the retailers who were operating towards the end of the marketing chain. More emphasis was given to the manufacturing aspect, with the manufacturers taking decisions on products and prices at which the retailer has to sell the stock, his (dealer margin), distribution network and so on. The retailer was at the receiving end in case of disputes, the manufacturer would not hesitate to discontinue the relationship and seek a new distributor. However, since a decade or so, the scenario has changed and now 'Retail' is recognised as a separate function by itself. This change is visible in the coexistence of the kirana shop, mom-n-pop stores, supermarkets, exclusive outlets, retail chain, malls, etc., all forming a part of the emerging retail environment. Some of the reasons for this change could be:

- **Increasing awareness and growth of consumerism**

  Today's consumers' are more knowledgeable, understanding (more clarity with regards to their specific needs) and demanding. Retailers are existing in a dynamic world and have to acknowledge the active role of their target consumers and try to meet the latter's demands and expectations through suitable formats and product or service offerings. The proactive consumer of today seeks convenience of time and place while shopping. In order to woo the target consumers and induce in them a pleasant shopping experience has led to the use of the various formats (supermarkets, malls, speciality store, etc.), in the retail industry. Retailers have also been working at ensuring ethical consumer approaches so that the latter feels his 'consumers rights' are being taken care of, while shopping at the various outlets.

- **Ability to develop a close contact with the customer**

  In this age of e-technology, the retailer though his exclusive outlet is trying to develop a close contact and relationship with his customer. Every category of retailer will have their own policies and procedures to enable them to enter into a relationship with their customers. The retailer will organise his stock based on the requirement of his customer. Since we are living in a virtual world, the retailer is able to retail his products to various regions across the world by operating via the outlet format suitable to the particular target market.

- **Technology benefits**

  Today's tech-savvy retailer makes increasing use of technology for his day-to-day operations. With increased usage of the point-of-sale scanning systems, RFID technology, bar code, etc., the retailer has access to a lot of information. With the help of such information, the retailer is able to understand his customer better – their (customers) profile, products searched for and purchased, preferred price ranges and the promotional offers that were made use of. Retailers are even able to develop their loyal customer cards which will help them (retailer) to gauge an understanding of the shoppers and also keep a track of the purchases made. This in turn will help them to create and stock products targeted at specific customers.

  Internet has also helped the retailer reach out to a wider target customer base (cutting across geographical boundaries). Even the traditional retailer is setting up his own online retail operation. In order to develop an effective business operation, many retailers are trying to integrate both offline and online shopping.

  With the world becoming a global village, international retailing has been made possible due to the advances in technology. When wanting to enter global markets, the domestic retailers have opted for mergers franchisee partner, etc., with foreign firms. Such moves have benefited the concerned retailers for usually a large number of retailing firms (across the world) share, important information with their manufacturers and vendors so as to facilitate the availability of the right product at the right place and time till it reaches the hands of the final consumer.

  For instance, *Impact Retail* (West Asian Retailer) had established a franchise and Original Equipment Manufacturer (OEM) relationship with *Alghanim Industries* (a Kuwait based organisation, dealing in consumer electronic retail, auto retail and manufacturing) to set up stores under the *Xcite* brand name, and enter the consumer electronics retail market in India.

- **Changing consumer demographics**

  Even the consumer profile of today's consumers is changing. They are educated, young, earning handsome-salary with a high disposable income, often a part of double income household, growing aspirations and vying to adopt a global lifestyle. Manufacturers are dependent upon their retailers to provide them vital inputs on the needs and motivations of the ultimate consumers, in order to gain competitive advantage. This is very true to exist in the competitive retail environment. Thus, the manufacturer can improve his product(s) success rate by creating retailer value as well as consumer differential advantage. Based on their interaction with the customers, retailers want to optimise sales within the limited shelf-space (will vary depending upon the retail format) and displaying a portfolio of brands for the target buyers to choose from.

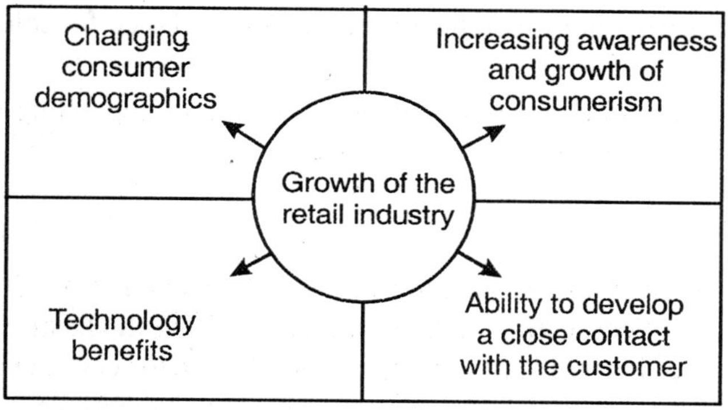

Figure 1.2: Reasons behind the growth of the retail industry

MEANING OF 'RETAIL' AND 'RETAILING'

Although there are many approaches to understanding and defining retailing, more often, emphasis is on retailing as a business activity of selling goods or services to the final consumer.

Retail

David Gilbert has defined *retail* as *"any business that directs its marketing efforts towards satisfying the final consumer based upon the organisation selling goods and services as a means of distribution"*.

As per the above definition, the final consumer is a key concept within the distribution chain, especially since the retailers are at the end of the chain and directly interact with the ultimate customer. Moreover, the final consumer is presumed to be the final user of a purchase unlike a customer who may have bought the goods for his own use or as a present or as a part of his own business activity. Retail transactions include more than the sale of tangible products, services such as financial services, beauty care saloons or dry cleaning.

Retailers are referred to as middlemen or intermediaries because they occupy a middle position in the distribution channel. They receive goods from producers and wholesalers and pass it on to customers. The retailers are able to accomplish this through the store/retail outlet located at a convenient place and also by ensuring that the customer is a focal point for the selection and display of stock.

It is said that the term retailing is derived from the old French word 'retailler' meaning 'a piece of' or 'to cut up'. This can be applied to the functions carried out by the retailer – acquiring whole stock of goods which they divide into smaller amounts which are sold to individual consumers.

Some of the *specific functions* carried out by retailers are given below:

- The interface between the retailer and customer is predominantly service-oriented.
- Retailers sell small amount of goods to customers, on a frequent basis.
- Retailers try to provide customers service through convenience in terms of suitable location, payment (or credit) facilities, range of merchandise, after-sales service, etc.
- Retailers offer an assortment of merchandise to facilitate choice for selection of goods to consumers.
- Retailers attempt to use a pricing policy which is modified depending upon consumers' demand, level of competition, etc.

Retailing

Simply said, retailing involves various activities of shopping, such as purchasing through the internet, dealing in financial services, eating at the restaurant, visiting the beauty parlour, etc. This indicates the complexity involved in retail marketing operations. Due to the constant changes occurring at the marketplace, the term retailing also has undergone changes. Nevertheless, *Retailing can be referred to all the activities involved in the marketing and distribution of goods and services.*

Retailing is carried out by *retailers* who try to satisfy consumer needs by providing the link between them and the wholesalers.They help the manufacturers to sell their merchandise by providing the *right market* and ensuring that the *right merchandise* is available at the *right price* and at the *right place* to satisfy the needs of the consumers.

Thus, *retailing is the set of business activities which adds value to the products and services sold to consumers for the personal or family use* (Michael Levy, Barton A. Weitz, 2003). Therefore, all retail operations requires the retailers to have a keen understanding on how to serve the needs of their customers.

Importance of retailing

Retail, in simple term implies 'a first hand transaction with the consumer'. So, retailing will involve a direct interaction with the customer and the coordination of business activities right from the concept (or design stage) of the product or service offering to its delivery and post-delivery (or after-sales) service to the final consumer.

Retailing occurs almost everyday in our lives and thus is often taken for granted. Generally, customers may not be aware of the sophisticated business decisions which the retailers have to make and use technologies to assure that customers receive the products and services desired by them. Yet, what is learned in the basic marketing class is to be practised by retailers in their everyday decisions.

The retailers require considerable skill and knowledge to work in a highly competitive and rapidly changing environment. The retailer has to perform many activities right from identifying the store location to achieving efficiencies in retail operations. Table 1.1 gives a brief on the activities involved in retailing.

Table 1.1: Activities involved in retailing

- Selecting the store location
- Sourcing/buying/vendor partnership/SCM (Supply-chain Management)
- Merchandising and category management
- Visual Merchandising
- Store positioning and building the 'Store brand image'
- Sales Promotion
- Store Operations
- Information Technology usage
- Inventory Management
- Handling Shrinkages/Theft/Security issues
- Real estate development
- Working towards achieving efficiencies in retail operations

If one were to think: why should we purchase products from the paricular retailer? Will it not be more easy and economical to procure products directly from the manufacturers? The answer will generally not be easy or a clear one. Although in case of certain products like vegetables and fruits it would be easier and cheaper to directly purchase the same from the farmers. Usually for most of the products retailers carryout important functions which will increase the value of the products and services they sell to consumers. Thus, the role of the retailer is a be very important one as they facilitate the distribution of the products and services for the manufacturers who produce them.

FUNCTIONS OF RETAILING

We will briefly discuss about the major functions carried out by the retailers.

Selecting the store location

Identifying the store location is a major decision area in retailing. This is relevant whether it is a standalone store retailing or operation of a chain of retail outlets. Typically, three attributes are looked into for selecting the retail store location:

- Attractiveness of the outlet
- Convenience of the store location
- Proximity

While the location decision for a standalone retail store may be relatively easy, in case of a chain of retail stores, three more aspects may have to be considered:

(a) Select the city in which the stores have to be located
(b) Within the identified city, decide on the areas where the stores have to be located
(c) Decide upon the exact location (or premises) of the store within the chosen area in the chosen city.

For instance, we can have a look at the criteria followed by the *Pantaloon Chain* of stores. For the Pantaloon outlets, the study for selecting the store location starts with conducting a study on the city to understand the city's propensity to spend and acceptance of the departmental store concept. Then it carries out areawise specific checks to see if area matches the image Pantaloon desires of its stores. Thereafter, a number of households in the various strata of the society in a given area are met to know their preferences for shopping in a departmental store in their city. Then finally the actual premises of the store is selected based on the catchment area analysis, foot falls analysis, impeditive analysis, adjoining business analysis, infrastructure analysis and traffic analysis.

Sourcing and buying

Sourcing and buying are major tasks in retailing, wherein vendor partnership and supply-chain management are integral parts of this task. A very important key to the success of the retailing format is to buy in bulk at the lowest possible prices (enabling the store to make a huge margin), and pass on the benefit to the consumer in the form of low prices. Such moves will motivate the consumer to come back again and again to the store and buy more, too in the process. For instance, *Food World*, for purchase of products like vegetables, rice, and other pulses, directly approach the large farmers to purchase the products in high volume. The produces are directly transported from the farm to their (Food World's) warehouses where it is appropriately packed for their different stores. Since the whole chains of middlemen are eliminated, Food World is able to get the produce from the producers (farmers) at very attractive prices.

Supply-chain management (SCM) is thus a very important aspect of retail management. Although SCM is being addressed to by many well known retailers, a very common problem is the lack of proper transport infrastructure facilities and inadequate storage set-up, especially in case of food products and perishables. Moreover, a large number of intermediaries could result in inconsistencies in the quality of perishables (losing its freshness). Finally when there are a large number of middlemen at various levels it could lead to lower margins.

Sales promotion

Retailers have also to adopt sales promotion measures to attract and retain customers. Sales promotions can provide extra value and incentives to customers to visit outlets or purchase merchandise during a specific period of time. For instance, the sales promotional offers from retailers like *Viveks* (during New Year and important festivals), *Bhima Jewellers, Khazana Jewellery* (special discounts on certain stock of jewellery for a limited period). Other sales promotions could take the form of special events, in-store demonstrations, coupons and contests. Sales promotions are short-term measures to increase store traffic as well as increase in customer loyalty towards the retailer's brand.

The growing importance of retailing can be summarised by saying that today it has become an integral part of our economic structure, which not only shapes but is also shaped by our way of life. Although trading of goods has been in existence since the bygone days when the barter system had been in vogue, in the recent times, the buying and selling of products has become more formal and a brand dominated activity. In fact since the past few years, retailing has taken a big quantion jump with the retailer's expectations of profits increasing and retail chains going for 'positioning' and 'branding' of the store. Simultaneously, there has been a spread of supermarkets (*Food World, Spencers*) Department Stores (*Kids Kemp, Raymond's*) Shopping malls (*Forum* (Bangalore) *Spencer Plaza* (Chennai), *Garuda Mall, Central Mall* (Bangalore)] retail chains (*Spencer Chain, Shoppers' Stop Chain, Westside Chain, Globus Chain, IOC Retail Chain, HPCL Retail Chain*) and Industrial Houses taking to set up Retail Chains [Reliance (*Reliance* Fresh, Reliance World), *Spencer Chain* (RPG Group), *Tatas* (Westside)]. The retailing sector is increasingly being accepted as an important activity in the economy and it is said to be having a positive impact on the society in general. There are a number of factors, which have given rise to retailing becoming popular, but the acceptance of its importance is a reflection of many features such as:

- Retailing accounts for a significant proportion of GDP.
- It helps to provide employment to a large proportion of the workforce.
- Retailers are considered to be running among the largest and most sophisticated of organisations.

TYPES OF RETAILERS

It is said that in spite of being a growing industry, organised retail sector accounts for close to only 2 per cent of the retailing industry in India. So, the organised retailers are trying/innovative models and formats to woo the customers. Consumers are seeking variety, convenience and quality while shopping, be it for grocery, clothes, food, music or even books. To match the consumer needs and demands, the retailers have come out with various store or retail outlet formats such as – convenience store, chain stores, franchise, departmental store, speciality store, supermarket, shopping centre, hypermaket, discount store, factory outlet (or factory seconds showroom), kiosk and shopping malls. Table 1.2 gives a brief explanation on the various store formats.

Table 1.2: Types of store formats

Type of Retail Format		*Description*
Convenience Store	:	Ideally located close to residential areas to enable target customers have easy accessibility and select convenient merchandise such as – beverages, ready-to-eat snacks, grocery, etc. For instance, the friendly neighbourhood grocery stores.

Chain of Stores	:	A single retailer establishes a chain of stores with its exclusive-store design, synergistic merchandising plan, promotion and service strategy and so on. For instance, *Raymond* chain of stores, *Khazana Jewellery,* etc.
Franchise	:	Retail stores owned and operated by individuals on behalf of, and licensed by a big supporting organisation. For instance, *Pizza Hut, Baskin Robbins, Aptech, NIIT, Nirulas, McDonalds,* etc.
Speciality Store	:	Retail shops displaying merchandise which have narrow product-lines, specialising in a particular type of merchandise and offering specialised services to customers. For instance, *Carbon* from Peakok Jewellery, has its own exclusive stores selling fashion accessories and jewellery. Or *Park Avenue;* from Raymonds is a men's speciality store.
Departmental Store	:	A store having several departments such as clothing, personal care and cosmetics, books and stationeries, house-ware goods, electronics, etc., all under a single roof, although individually functioning as a Strategic Business Unit (SBU). These stores are large in size (or area) more often owned by large or national chains. For instance, *Life Style, Shoppers' Stop, Pantaloon, Westside, Ebony,* etc.
Supermarket	:	A store which is departmentalised, with self-service offering groceries, limited non-food items such as health and beauty related items and general merchandise. For instance, *Food World* outlets, *Nilgiris* (in the South), etc.
Hypermarket	:	Hypermarkets are very large in size, carry grocery, hardware, appliance and other general merchandise, with self-service facilities, usually located in warehouse type structures with large parking facilities. For instance, *Trent's* (a Tata Enterprise) *Star India Bazaar, Giant* (RPG Group) and *Big Bazaar* (Pantaloon Retail India).
Shopping Mall	:	A shopping mall is an arrangement of retail stores and providing the right mix of shopping, food courts and entertainment and parking facilities. The retail space is shared by an anchor stores and other retailers (tenants), who will pay the developers of the mall – rent or lease payment for putting up the shop within the mall premises. For instance, in Bangalore – *The Forum, Central, Sigma Mall,* etc.
Shopping Plaza	:	The shopping plaza will be a configuration of many tenants using space of 1,000 sq. ft. or so for putting up stores within a single building. For instance, *Fountain Plaza (Chennai), Modi Arcade Plaza* (Bangalore), etc.

Discount Stores	:	Discount stores retail a broad variety of merchandise, offer limited services and at low prices. For instance, *Margin Free Supermarket.*
Factory/Seconds Outlet	:	The factory stores are owned and operated by the manufacturers who sell discounted merchandise or factory seconds or cancelled orders to consumers at low prices. For instance, the *Bata factory Outlet, Indigo Nation/Peter England* factory outlet, etc.
Kiosk	:	Kiosk as a store, often, it is a concession format store placed within a mall/shopping centre, a bus station, airport, etc. It is a free standing pavilion open on one or more sides. For instance, in a bookstore kiosk, customers are provided with online catalogue service to help them to identify titles and read reviews before making a purchase decision.

Table 1.2 gives an overview on the popular retail store formats which form a part of the retail industry. Of course most of the organised retail formats have set up shop in India in the post-liberalisation era. Although different types of retailers or retailing have emerged, the successful ones are those who have been able to attract and maintain a significant customer base. The retailer must take care while developing a suitable retail strategy and also have a suitable retail mix elements. The important elements in the retail mix include:

- Store design and display.
- Customer-service.
- Communication mix elements.
- Pricing method or strategy.
- Merchandise planning and assortments.
- Location.

The above are the key retail mix elements which can be used by retailers to attract and maintain a significant customer base.

For the purpose of classifying retailers, typically, four elements of retail mix are used:

(a) The type of merchandise sold.

(b) The variety and assortment of merchandise sold at the outlet.

(c) The level of customer service offered at the outlet.

(d) The price or cost of offering the merchandise.

The *type of merchandise* could be categorised as furniture and home furnishings, food and beverages and vegetables, clothes and clothing accessories, restaurant (food service) and bar, fashion, jewellery stores, luggage and leather goods, etc.

Variety refers to the number of merchandise categories a retailer offers. While, *assortment is the number of different items in a merchandise category.* The different item(s) of merchandise is referred to as a SKU (Stock Keeping Unit). Depending upon the type of retailer, there will be variations in the variety and assortment of merchandise. The variety is often referred to in terms of the breadth of merchandise and assortment as the depth of the merchandise.

Customer-services will vary from retailer-to-retailer. Some of the services expected by customers include convenient and long store timings, parking facilities, attentive salespersonnel, etc. Some retailers may offer free home delivery *(Food World)* and gift wrapping services.

The cost of offering a good assortment and variety of merchandise to the customer means that the retailers should have many SKUs. This means inventory investment increases, with the retailer required to have back-up stock for each SKU. The other costs incurred by the retailer will be towards having a good and efficient salespersonnel, providing for restroom, offering credit and instalment payment facilities, etc. All this will require a financial investment which otherwise could have been used to buy more merchandise.

DIFFERENCES BETWEEN RETAILERS AND WHOLESALERS

According to S. Brown the term *retailing* is said to have been derived from an old French word *Retailer,* which mean 'piece of' or 'to cut-up' (S. Brown, 1992). This could be with reference to the breaking of the bulk fraction carried out by the retailer. This mean that the retailer receives large amounts of products (or stock) to sell and in turn this is divided into smaller amounts (of stock) to be sold to individual customers.

We, as consumers purchase different products and services for our personal consumption from different retail outlets. And *retailing* will include all the activities carried out by the retailer to sell products and services to the ultimate consumers for their personal consumption. Hence, the retailer is required to focus on understanding the needs of his target buyers, make it available to them at his retail outlet and thereby make the buying experience a very satisfying one.

The purpose of *wholeselling* is very much different from that of the retailer. Wholeselling is concerned with selling of goods and services to individuals and organisations for their business purposes. Thus, the nature and purpose of functions carried out by retailers and wholesalers are distinct and different.

Some of the specific differences between the retailers and wholesalers are given hereunder:

1. The *retailer's* interface with the ultimate consumer is service- based involving social interaction and personal selling techniques. The wholesalers work technique involves using sophisticated computer-based ordering, stocking and transaction systems.
2. The retailer sells small quantities of items, more frequently to their customers. The wholesalers will sell goods in bulk and on a less frequent basis to their buyers.
3. Retailers locate their outlets at places so as to facilitate convenience in time, place, payment facilities, after-sales service, etc., to their consumers. The wholesaler sells in bulk to many customers, so exclusive convenience for every customer may not be possible.

4. Wholesalers may stock a broad assortment of merchandise based on the demands of their target customers. Retailers provide an assortment of merchandise to the customers, to choose from.
5. The retailer may charge higher unit price for goods sold to customers than a wholesaler would.
6. The retailer's pricing policy will be simpler and based on the MRP (Maximum Retail Price), while the wholesaler's pricing policy will involve a discounting structure.
7. The retailer has to carry a different type of risk when compared to the wholesaler and the manufacturer.

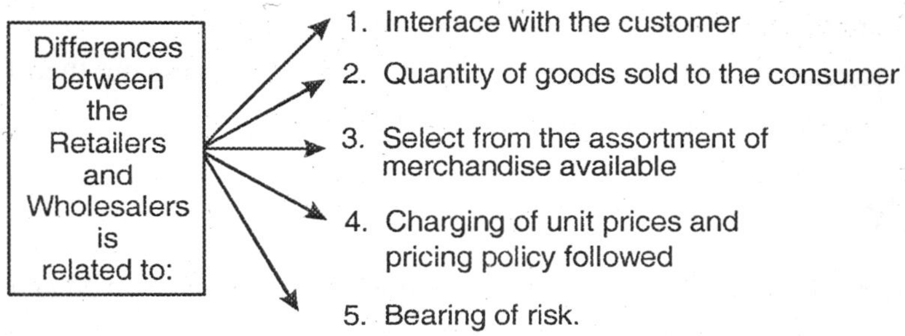

Figure 1.3 Differences in the functioning of retailer and wholsaler activities

SUMMARY

Philip Kotler defines marketing as a human activity directed at satisfying needs and wants through exchange processes. Although the marketing concept focuses on the 'customer' as the driving force behind all the related activities, a lot depends on the what, when, how and where decisions taken by the retailer during the course of his interaction with the buyers. Along with the traditional forms of small independently owned businesses, today the retail sector is characterised by the emergence of shopping malls, chain stores, departmental stores, fast food outlets, automated retailing and so on.

Retailing has been integrated into the economic structure of every country and has been in vogue since the earlier times when the barter system used to be practised. The many reasons behind the growth of the retail industry can be attributed to: (a) changing consumer demographics, (b) increasing awareness and growth of consumerism, (c) ability to develop a close contact with the customer, and (d) technology benefits.

Retail is defined as any business activity that directs its marketing efforts towards satisfying the final consumer based upon the organisation selling goods and services as a means of distribution. While retailing refers to all the activities involved in the marketing and distribution of goods and services. Retailing is one of the intermediary functions between the manufacturer and the intermediary functions between the manufacturingnd the ultimate consumer and its nature is such that it can deliver the place, times, form and possession utilities to the consumers.

The major functions carried out by the retailers include selecting the store location, sourcing and buying and sales promotion activities. Consumers seeks variety, convenience and quality while shopping be it for grocery, clothes, food, music or even books. To match the consumer needs and demands, the retailers have come out with various store or retail outlet formats such as – convenience stores, chain stores, franchise, departmental store, speciality store, supermarket and so on.

CHAPTER QUESTIONS FOR DISCUSSION

1. What do you understand by the term 'Retail' and 'Retailing'?
2. Briefly give the reasons behind the growth of the retail industry.
3. What are the functions to be carried out by the retailers?
4. How do retailers and wholesalers differ in terms of carrying out their functions?
5. Write a short note on the different type of retailers.

ACTIVITY

Visit a big retail outlet near your college. Interact with the manager(s) and try to find out:

1. The reasons behind setting up the outlet in that area.
2. The category of customers visiting the outlet.
3. What marketing emphasis the retailer has been asked to focus upon?

❑❑❑

2 CUSTOMER BUYING BEHAVIOUR

LEARNING OBJECTIVES

After going through the chapter, you should be able to understand:

- About the retail consumers and understand their consumption behaviour
- Appreciate the stages in the buying process and the factors which influence customers buying decisions
- Analyse the decision-making processes involved in buying
- Learn about the consumer decision rules and situational variables influencing shoppers.

STRUCTURE:

- Introduction
- The Retail Consumer
- Stages in the Buying Process
- Factors Influencing Consumer's Buying Decisions
- Types of Decision-making Processes in Buying
- Consumer Decision Rules
- Situational Variables Influencing Shoppers
- Summary
- Chapter Questions for Discussion
- Activity

INTRODUCTION

Today, retailers exist in a market which is large, the competition is stiff and customer is treated as a king. The retailer is required to offer goods and services which will appeal to all classes and various market segments.

Since the retailing revolution is moving along the lines of the economic evolution of the society, the retailer is required to operate retail formats which will identify with different lifestyles of the various market segments. Hence, retailers are left trying to workout retail strategies to satisfy their customers better than competitors. For this, it will be very necessary to understand the customer's needs and buying behaviour.

In this chapter, an attempt has been made to learn about the retail consumers, their buying stages processes and factors influencing their purchase decision. We have also discussed about the types of decision-making processes in buying, consumer decision rules and the situational variables influencing shoppers.

THE RETAIL CONSUMER

In the recent past, CNBC TV had described the *consumer* as someone who has evolved from being a passive participant to an *active co-creator of value* today. This means retailers cannot understand consumer's needs and wants based on lucky guesses but have to be actively involved in gauging their mind and collect a database on them. While these moves are essential for understanding customers, it will need more than CRM (Customer Relationship Management) – systems and loyalty programmes, communication techniques, innovative pricing strategies, and attractive store design and layout which have to be innovatively applied to successfully penetrate the consumer's mind.

Retail marketing is looking into all aspects of the customer's purchase decision – influence of 'promotional campaign', assessment of the 'store and merchandise' displayed, willingness to pay the 'price' and 'how' easily it can be bought.

Understanding Consumer Behaviour

The constant changes in the demographic and psychographic profile of Indian consumers is giving the retailers a blurring picture. The consumer is no longer willing to accept anything less than she deserves. While the retailer is not able to read her mind and decide whether to categorise the housewife as not fully educated or a person with no awareness. Nor is the retailer able to classify a working woman as a non-spender who contributes all her earnings to the family kitty only. This is the reason why retailers go about studying their (consumer's) behaviour.

Consumers generally go through various stages in buying process while selecting a retailer and buying merchandise. These stages in the buying process are shown in Figure 2.1. But it must be recognised that customers may not always go through the stages as shown in the Figure 2.1. For instance, a person may be influenced by an advertisement seen in the newspaper and decides to purchase a *Kodak* digital camera. He may then identify a specific retailer say GK Vale and Sons, as the suitable outlet at the same time. So, the customer in this instance has decided on the product he wants to purchase and also the specific retailer, thus skipping some of the stages in the buying process. Moreover, the customer may be engaged in different behaviours depending upon whether it is a *habitual decision-making* (purchasing familiar merchandise bought in the past), *Limited Problem-solving* (moderate effort and time involved and customers have some prior experience with the product/service and the risk involved is moderate) or *Extended Problem-solving* (customers spend considerable time and effort to analyse alternatives and the decisions involve a lot of risk and uncertainty).

Retailers try to influence customers engaged in extended problem-solving by providing brochures describing the merchandise, its specifications, have informational displays and knowledgeable salespersons to guide the customer when he enquires about the merchandise.

In case of limited problem-solving, the customers may go for impulse buying (buying on the spot after seeing the merchandise) influenced by the merchandise displayed at the retail outlet. At *Food World* outlets displays such as *'Fresh vegetables at very low prices'* sign is placed at the entrance of the outlet. Thus, depending upon the type of decision-making process the customer is engaged in, *i.e.*, he or she may go through different stages in the buying process.

STAGES IN THE BUYING PROCESS

Need Recognition: The buying process starts with the '*Need recognition*' stage, when customers recognise and experience an unsatisfied need. Retailers use a variety of ways to stimulate problem recognition and motivate customers to visit their outlets and purchase merchandise. These could be in the form of direct mailers, publicity, special discounted prices, within the store – displays, frontage, visual merchandising and so on. Such activities from the retailer's side can trigger need recognition within the individual customer. The needs which induce and motivate customers to go for shopping and purchase merchandise can be classified as functional or psychological. Functional needs are directly related to the functional performance of the product: For example, a lady may purchase a make-up kit based on the expectation that this make-up kit will help her to look better. *Psychological needs* are associated with the personal gratification that customers can feel after shopping or purchasing or owning a product. Many products satisfy both functional and psychological needs. For instance, a customer may purchase a *Park Avenue* shirt not only to enhance his self-image but the shirt also satisfies the functional need for clothing.

Retailers try to satisfy these needs through innovative shopping purchasing merchandise experience. They attempt to *stimulate customers* with exciting graphics and photography on their websites and catalogues. Malls such as *Central (*Future groups mall*)* have proved to be a place where *social interactions* take place because of the food court, where people prefer to sit, talk and eat. Some customers shop to satisfy their *need for status*. Some customers like to purchase jewellery from *Tanishq* showrooms, because of the aristocratic gentility conveyed in the store's ambience. At times, customers purchase merchandise to *reward themselves* (say purchase personal grooming products such as perfumes), retailers try to treat such customers with 'personalised' services.

Information Search**:** After recognising the need, customers will now seek information about retailers or merchandise which will help them to satisfy the felt need. Generally, the amount of information being sought will depend upon: the nature and utility of the product being purchased, characteristics of the buyer and typical aspects of the market (competitors, time factor, etc.), and the buying situations under which, the purchase is being made.

The role of the retailer at this stage is to use the various marketing mixes so that the customer's search ends at the particular retailer's website or outlet. That is, the retailer must use visual appeal, attractive store design, broad assortment of competing brands, colours, sizes, attractive promotional offers, reasonable prices, etc., such that the customer gets confident on obtaning all information required to make a purchase decision from this outlet only.

Take the example of *Café Coffee Day*, India's largest chain of cafes, which had celebrated its achievement of 150 cafes in 37 cities across the country with the opening of a unique 'Book Cafe' at Vasant Kunj in New Delhi. This was a part of *Café Coffee Day's* new strategy to enable customers to enhance the coffee experience so that their search for excellent coffee ends at the outlet. The 'Book Cafe' concept was attended by customers and young authors, who were allowed to leisurely browse through an interesting section of books while enjoying their coffee.

***Evaluation of Alternatives*:** The multi-attribute model provides the framework for developing a retailing strategy and understand how customers use information to evaluate the alternatives and select the one which best satisfies their needs.

The multi-attribute attitude model works on the notion that customers view a product or retailer as a collection of attributes or characteristics. The design of the model is such that one can predict a customer's evaluation of a product or retailer on the basis of:

- Its performance on relevant attributes.
- The importance of those attributes to the customer.

Coupons such as above, can motivate customers to shop at *Westside*

- The retailer can, with the help of the model try to develop programmes for attracting customers to shop at their store. They can conduct market research to obtain information on:

(*a*) The other stores which the customer may consider.

(*b*) Those benefits or features considered by customers while evaluating and selecting a retailer.

(*c*) The customers' ratings on each store's performance based on the features selected.

(*d*) The weightage (important weights) that customers attach to the characteristics.

On the basis of the above information, the retailer must develop programmes which increases the likelihood of customers remembering the particular retail outlet. After identifying the benefits being sought by customers, efforts must be made to match the store's performance on those counts.

Purchasing the Merchandise: In this stage when customers are planning to purchase the merchandise, retailers could adopt certain steps which will increase the likelihood of the customers converting their positive evaluations into actual purchases. These could take form of:

- Keep a complete stock of popular merchandise in the right assortment and sizes available.
- Offer a liberal policy regarding merchandise returns and refunds, if the same merchandise is easily available at competitors outlets.
- Offer credit facilities, less time gap between perceived and actual waiting time and convenient (and more) checkout terminals.

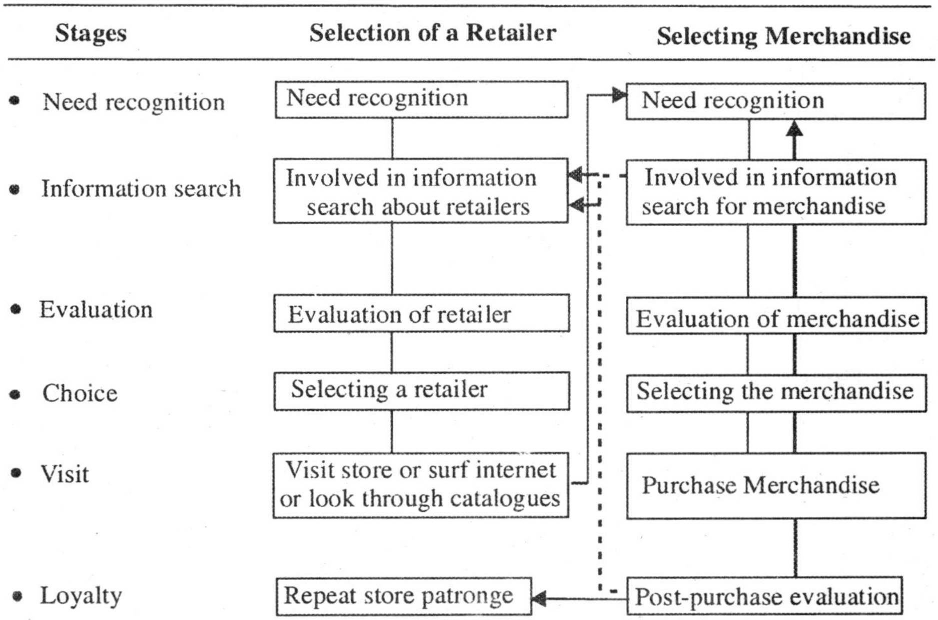

(*Source*: Levy. Micheal, Weitz. A. Barton, *Retailing Management*, 5th edn., Tata McGraw-Hill Publishing Company Ltd., New Delhi, 2003,.pp. 111).

Figurte 2.1: Stages involved in the buying process

Post-purchase Evaluation: The buying process doesn't end with the customer making a purchase. But it will be the post-consumption evaluation of the product or service which will indicate whether the customer is happy after purchase and usage of the product. This becomes a part of the customer's internal information and is very likely to affect in future, the store or retailer's merchandise product decisions. If the customer is *satisfied* post-consumption, he or she will be motivated to purchase at that store or outlet. But post-purchase *dissatisfaction* or experience occurs it may result in complaining to the retailer and probably patronising other stores.

FACTORS INFLUENCING CONSUMER'S BUYING DECISIONS

Customers buying decisions are affected by their social environment comprising of the customers' family, reference groups and culture apart from his/her personal characteristics, *i.e.,* beliefs (about retailer and product's performance), values (in terms of importance of weights) and attitudes (evaluations of retailers and merchandise).

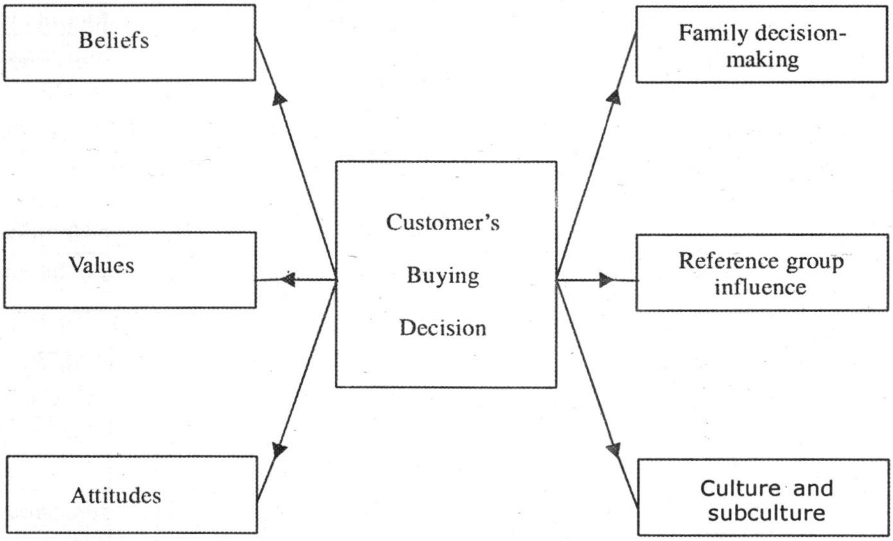

Figure 2.2: Factors influencing customer's buying decisions

Family

Family decision-making takes place when purchases are made for the entire family. Hence, retailers must try to understand the role of the family members in the decision-making process and try to influence them. They should workout packages or programmes so as to attract all family members and satisfy all their needs also. *McDonalds* has a range of packages to make the experience of eating at McDonalds outlets very satisfying for the children and other family members. For instance, in case of the '*Happy Meal Offer*' the toys displayed and 'Nemo' birthday parties are an attraction for the children. Finally, McDonalds are rated highly by customers especially on parameters such as-ambience, food taste, prompt service, cleanliness and hygiene, value for money and overall a very satisfying experience.

Reference Group

Reference group may consist of either family members, friends, coworkers, *etc.,* from whom the customer seeks information and uses it as a basis for the comparison for beliefs, feelings and behaviours.

These reference groups can affect the customers' buying decision by:

- Providing information
- Providing rewards for specific purchasing behaviours
- Enhancing the consumers self-image

For instance, among youngsters or college-goers, the reference group can greatly influence their purchase decisions. Specifically this group can affect their shopping trends and act as opinion leaders. These youngsters may have a teen broad member whom many of the students would like to emulate and identify themselves with. So, the retailer must try to identify the reference groups of various categories of customers and workout programmes to communicate through advertisement and other promotional activities and influence their purchase decisions.

Culture and Subculture

Culture is everything a person learns and shares with members of a society, including ideas, norms, morals, values, knowledge, skills, technology, tools, material objects and behaviour.

In India, we have our own share of beliefs, values, customs, etc., which distinguishes us from the other countries. Some of the uniqueness having relevance for marketing include, the caste system (with subcastes – rituals, eating habits, dressing style, etc.), the living pattern (or style), celebrating festivals, marriages and so on. We also follow certain mores or reasonably strong norms such as — respect for elders, patriotism, drinking is a taboo and condemned by society.

We also have subcultures, which are sets of learned beliefs, values, attitudes, habits and forms of behaviour that are shared by subsets of society and are transmitted from generation-to-generation within each subset. For instance, the subcultural category of religion will be Hindus, Christians, Muslims, Jains, etc. Subcultures can be based on geography region, religion/caste, age, occupation, social class, etc. For example, traditional Indian wedding functions and ceremonies last for two-three days and apart from the rituals followed by each community (or caste) typical gift giving culture is followed. Most of the close relatives are to be given gifts in the form of clothes by the bride's parents. To take care of this need attractive packaging and wrapping can be offered by retailers. Even store design and visual merchandise can be presented in an attractive manner apart from advertising and having tie-ups with professional agencies (who take complete contract of the marriage arrangements), etc. Such efforts on the part of the retailer can go a long way in influencing customers' buying decisions. Retailers in India are using their own strategy to understand consumer behaviour and adopt market segmentation strategies accordingly.

The Customers Care Associate and Director, (Operations) *Shoppers' Stop* Sanjay Badha says that before establishing the location for any store, they (Shoppers' Stop) study consumer behaviour to understand the potential of the market and also the buying pattern of the consumers. A study is also done to know how the consumer moves within the store. This information helps them in planning the layout, creating association between different categories and on how best the store design can help the consumer in the buying process. They also conduct interviews, use observation and have even tried online data capture through information kiosks at the store. Changes are then made to the elements of product mix and service elements. For example, based on the above methods, it was realised that there was a need for internal service guarantee on alteration especially for quick delivery. Accordingly, the quality of alteration was also improved by introducing lock machines and steam irons at Shoppers' Stop.

Although collecting data about customers is essential, Shoppers' Stop also has been using a unique CRM (customer relationship management) systems and loyalty programme. They analyse the purchases made by their First Citizens (members of their loyalty programme) and create relevant schemes and offers, which act as inputs in creating the right product mix. Apart from the above they also regularly measure and monitor the customer satisfaction index.

In Box 2.1, based on the KSA Technopak Consumer Outlook 2004, study, categorising customers has been proposed and presented accordingly.

Box 2.1 Viva Youth Power: KSA Technopak Consumer Outlook 2004

Indicating the changing demographics in favour of the young, the KSA Technopak Consumer Outlook 2004 study reveals that India has the lowest medium age of 24 and about 50 per cent or roughly 500 million people are below the age of 20. In 2003, corporate salaries in India grew at over 10 per cent, faster than most of the developed economics (*Economic Times*, January 2004) and the KSA study indicates that discretionary spending has risen by 15 per cent in the last financial year.

The KSA Technology study proposes three evolving customer categories:

- ***Technologies' Babies*** (8-19 years) are the technology savvy, gadget-wielding young consumers, who splurge on music, books, mobile phones, eating out, footwear and apparel. The 22 million urban middle-class teens in India spent an estimated $ billion in 2001.

  (***Source:*** Euro RSCG-Star view report).
- ***Aggressive, independent, indulgent and career-driven, The Impatient Aspirers*** (20-25 years) can be called the Generation C; the 'just-be-myself' variety for whom creativity and customisation are of prime importance. World-class education is the biggest status symbol for this age group.
- ***Balance Seekers*** (26-50 years) are the sober, sophisticated consumers who spend with caution and seek convenience. For them disposable minutes are at premium and the line between work and play often tends to blur. This status conscious class has a fondness for gadgets. The KSA study reveals that 350 plasma TVs are sold annually in India and the number is growing at 30-40 per cent, clearly indicating this status conscious segment's fondness for high-end gadgets.

  (***Source: Retail Biz,*** July 2004).

TYPES OF DECISION-MAKING PROCESSES IN BUYING

The success of *'Indica'* car and its variants is because Tata Motors was able to understand the importance of the decision-making process undertaken by compact car buyers who were looking out for quality at reasonable prices. But consumer decision-making is not a single process. Deciding to purchase a car will be different from deciding to buy a bathing soap. The consumer decision-making processes can be examined at two levels:

- By examining the extent of decision-making
- By understanding the consumer's degree of involvement in the purchase.

	High Involvement	***Low Involvement***
Decision-making Behaviour (Information search evaluation alternatives)	*COMPLEX DECISION-MAKING* (products such as automobiles, digital camera, ipod, TV, computers, etc.)	*LIMITED DECISION-MAKING* (breakfast items, cold drinks, snacks, seeing movies, etc.)
Habit (Little or no Information search, considers only one brand)	*BRAND LOYALTY* (Groceries, sports shoes, etc.)	*INERTIA* (tissue napkins, vegetables)

Figure 2.3: Types of consumer-decision making

(***Source:*** *Consumer Behavior*, Henry Assael, 6th Edn., 2001).

A look at Figure 2.2 will indicate that while examining the extent of decision-making, it can be said that consumer's take their decisions after undergoing a cognitive (thought) process of information search and evaluating the brand alternatives. However, little or no decision-making may take place if the consumer is satisfied with a particular brand which is purchased consistently (say the same brand of toothpaste or Talcum powder is purchased everytime). Here consumer decision-making can be seen in the form of a continuum *from decision-making to Habit.*

The second angle of examining consumer decision-making is by looking at the degree of involvement. The level of involvement can be in the form of all continuum from high-to-low involvement purchases. *High involvement purchases* are very important for the consumer. This means it can be closely connected to his or her ego and self-image and probably involving some financial, social or personal risk. For instance, the consumer is planning to purchase a new mobile phone, say. In this case now the consumer will channalise his time and energy to weigh the product alternatives before settling on a particular model which will suit his ego and self-image. Further, he will make the purchase from an outlet where all this is met.

When the consumer has to undergo *low involvement purchases,* the financial, social and psychological risks may not be very high. So, the consumer may not feel it is worth-spending considerable time and effort in searching for information, about the various brands or range of alternatives.

Decision-making versus Habit and Low versus High Involvement

If one were to *consider decision-making* versus *habit* and *low* versus *high involvement,* there can be four types of consumer purchase processes.

(a) The *complex decision-making* takes place when involvement is high. Say the consumer has decided to purchase an *LCD* TV. Since this purchase is important to the consumer he will be

engaged in taking time to search for information and process it in more detail. He will evaluate various brands by using specific criteria such as-brandname, look, specific functions, price, etc., before taking a final decision to purchase the LCD TV from a particular retail outlet.

(b) When the consumer makes decision through low involvement, it is said to be a *limited decision-making process.* Sometimes, the consumer goes through a decision-making process, even if he is not highly involved probably because he does not have much experience with the product. *For example,* a consumer may on seeing a new line of snacks that can be prepared in the microwave oven, will read the package and purchase a smaller pack of the same on a trial basis. Since the consumer was not involved or aware of the product category, she may purchase a small pack to compare it with the regular snacks. In this case, the information search processing is limited and only a few brands are evaluated.

At times, limited decision-making may take place when low involvement is there and the consumer is also seeking variety, out of being bored using the same brand. *For example,* the consumer may decide to purchase *Sunfeast Cashew Biscuits* as she is bored with the continuous consumption of "Britannia's *GoodDay* Cashew biscuits. Such decisions may not be preplanned and could easily be taken inside the shop.

(c) Limited decision-making or even complex decision-making *may not take* place *everytime* the consumer purchases a brand. When the consumer makes the same choice repeatedly, he or she learns from past experience and with little or no decision-making may purchase the brand which is most satisfactory. Take for instance, the purchase of *Reebok* jogger shoes or *Complan.* In both the cases, the purchase was important to the consumer (*Reebok* are comfortable jogging shoes because he is health-conscious; and he has *Complan* because of its nutritional value).

In the above instances of the decision-making processes, it is seen that they (decision-making) are all consumer- oriented. That is, the *degree* of involvement and decision-making is more dependent on the consumer's attitude towards the product than on the product's characteristics. For instance, one particular consumer may be involved in the purchase of Complan because of its nutritional value while another consumer may find all brands *(Bornvita, Boost, Horlicks, etc.),* to be the same and he may switch brands in search of variety.

(d) The fourth choice in Figure 2.2 is referred to as *inertia* or the stage where there is low involvement with the product and no decision-making. Here the consumer is only looking to the convenience factor. He is purchasing the same brand not because he is brand-loyal but because he feels it is not worth the time and trouble taken to search for an alternative. Examples could be the purchase of vegetables or tissue paper. These may be purchased on a regular basis from a convenience shop, by the consumer.

Thus, the various decision-making processes which may be of interest to the marketer and retailer can be categorised into three namely:

- Limited problem-solving or dissonance reducing buying behaviour.
- Complex buying behaviour or extensive problem-solving.
- Habitual buying behaviour or routinised response behaviour.

CONSUMER DECISION RULES

It has been observed by retailers, that consumers adopt certain decision rules which facilitates identifying stores to shop or selecting brands. Broadly, consumer decision rules can be classified into:

1. Compensatory rules, and
2. Non-compensatory rules

Compensatory Division Rule

According to the compensatory decision rule, the consumer evaluates store or brand options in terms of each relevant attribute and computes a weighted or summated score for each option. The computed score will indicate the store's (or brand's) merit as a potential retail or purchase choice. It is assumed that the consumer will select the store or brand, that scores highest among the alternatives evaluated. Another unique feature related to the compensatory decision rule is that it allows a positive evaluation of one attribute to balance out a negative evaluation on some other attribute. To quote a hypothetical example: Say a customer has to make a choice from shopping at Food World, More or Reliancefresh (assume). As seen from Table 2.1, while required to make a choice from the three retail outlets, the prospective shopper is most likely to select the 'Food World'.

Table. 2.1: Compensatory decision rule to evaluate stores

Attributes/Features	Food World	More	Reliancefresh
Range of merchandise available	8	7	6
Services	6	5	6
Price	7	7	9
Distance	8	7	7
Atmospherics	5	5	5
Total	**34**	**31**	**33**

Noncompensatory Decision Rules

Unlike compensatory decision rule, noncompensatory decision rules would not allow a positive evaluation of a store or brand on a single attribute to compensate for a negative evaluation on some other attribute. There are three types of noncompensatory rules.

Conjunctive decision rule: As per this rule the consumer will identify a specific minimal acceptable level as a cut-off point for each dimension. This will enable the prospective customers to consider other acceptable options from multiple alternatives, which can further be evaluated (using other decision rules) to finally select the store or brand of his choice.

Disjunctive decision rule: As per this rule, the prospective customer will decide on a specific minimal acceptable level for each attribute/dimension considered. So, he will select a store or brand only if it meets or surpasses the limit established for any one dimension.

Lexicographic decision rule: Under this rule, the shopper tends to rank the dimensions in terms of their perceived salient features or importance. Then he will make a comparison of the various brand alternatives in terms of a single attribute which is considered to be most important. If a particular store or brand scores reasonaly high on this top ranked dimension (irrespective of the scores on any of the other attributes), it is selected and the process ends there. For the remaining store (or brand) alternatives, the process is repeated with the second highest ranked dimension and in this way, the procedure is repeated till one of the store's or brand is finally selected, since it outscores the others on a particular dimension.

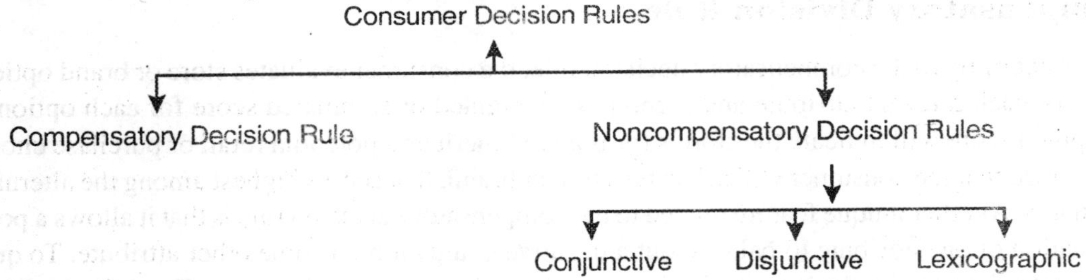

Figure 2.4: Types of consumer decision rules

A knowledge about the different types of consumer decision rules will enable the retailers and marketers to develop suitable marketing strategies as well as the desirable communication strategy. They could try to gain an understanding of the type of decision rules being used by the shopper in his attempt at selecting the right store or brand.

In a survey, certain consumer segments were identified based on specific shopping rules being followed by them (Chetan Bajaj, R. Tuji, N.V. Srivastava, Retail Management, 2005). They can be classified as:

- **Practical loyalists:** Loyal shoppers who look out for ways to save on the products and brands purchased by them.
- **Bottom line price shoppers:** These are shoppers who purchase only the lowest priced products and dont have brand loyalty.
- **Opportunistic Shoppers:** These are regular shoppers who prefer to use coupons or sales to purchase products and brands which fall in their evoked set.
- **Deal Hunters:** As the term indicates, these are customers who look out for 'deals' or 'bargain purchases' and are not necessarily loyal.

SITUATIONAL VARIABLES INFLUENCING SHOPPERS

Shopping situation can also influence the customers buying behaviour. Situational variables will include all the factors present particular to a place and time and may not be in occurrence to a (prior) knowledge of the personal (in relation to the individual) and stimulus attributes. These attributes could include the store location, time of the day, atmospherics, staff's behaviour and so on. Broadly, the situational variables can be classified into four dimensions:

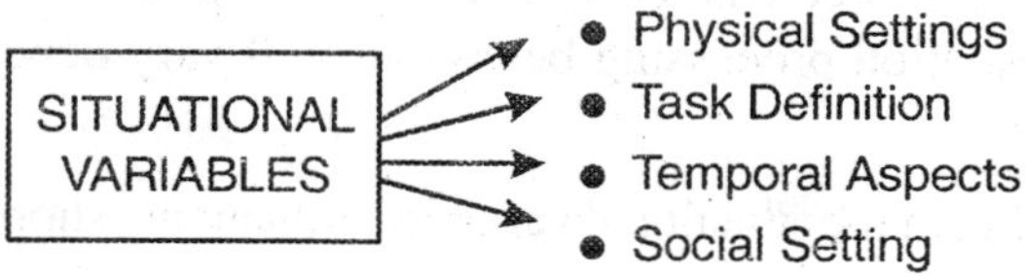

Figure 2.5: Dimensions of situational variables

Physical Setting

The physical setting refers to apart from the location of the store, even the environment within the shop, the atmospherics, visual merchandising, etc. For instance, today we see an expanding food retailing sector. Food retailers and food courts in any mall, irrespective of their size, are ideally located and drawing in more customers. For, the mall culture has become a new wave of family entertainment destination. The large spaces with a large variety of branded stores, selling consumer durables, non-durables, and entertainment has been attracting many customers. Consumer pull is probably a very important influencing factor in food retailing. So, to take care of this, food retailers are trying to improvise on the physical setting of the outlets by offering value-added services like drop boxes for cheques and credit cards, proximity, good ambience, fresh and certified products and so on. For instance, *Haiko Supermarket* (Mumbai) offers their customers a care-lobby near the entrance of the store and other services like wheel chairs for handicapped customers, which enables them to shop and so on.

Social Setting

The social setting of the store indicates everything – the courteous attitude of the security staff, helping kindness and due consideration displayed by the sales staff, roles of those accompanying the shoppers and even the display of the merchandise facilitating proximity of the other customers and so on. In short the entire layout of the store should be consumer-friendly. For example, at *Haiko Supermarket,* products are arranged such that when a consumer walks down the aisle, she can start with breakfast products, then snacks, lunch items and so on. The outlet has also got pictorial signage put across the store indicating the different sections. Thus, by providing consumers the locational benefit along with the right value proposition and social setting, retailers can become successful.

Temporal Aspects

There are certain temporal aspects like time constraints (time at which the store remains open), availability of seasonal products, etc., which have to be made conducive and consumer-friendly.

So, retailers have to keep their shop open according to the time suitable to the target segment. Similarly, they should also ensure that seasonal variations in the available product range is made in accordance to the target customers' requirements.

Task Definition

Task definition is more specific to the individual shopper and encompasses all the cognitive and motivational indications of the shopping situation which will include the various information search, evaluation stages, etc., involved in the consumer decision-making process. As we have already seen earlier in the chapter, the information processing behaviour will vary depending upon the type of product, purpose of buying, etc.

Thus, a clearer understanding of the situational variables influencing shoppers will enable retailers to plan their marketing mix properly.

SUMMARY

The consumer of today is someone who has evolved from being a passive participant to an active co-creator of value. So, retailers go for retail marketing which looks into all aspects of the consumer's purchase decision – influence of, promotional compaign, assessment of the store and merchandise displayed, willingness to pay the 'price' and 'how' easily it can be bought. The retail consumer goes through various stages while selecting a retailer and merchandise. These include 'Need recognition', information search, evaluation, choice, visit and loyalty.

Customers buying decision gets greatly influenced by beliefs, values, attitudes, family decision-making, reference group influence and culture and subculture. The consumer decision-maing processes can be examined at two levels. Namely, by examining the extent of decision-making and understanding the consumer's degree of involvement in the purchase. Consumers in their pursuit of selecting stores and choosing brands are guided by certain decision rules, namely – compensatory and noncompensatory (conjunctive, disjunctive and lexicographic). There are even situational variables which can influence shopping behaviour. These can be classified into: physical setting, social setting, temporal perspective and task definition.

CHAPTER QUESTIONS FOR DISCUSSION

1. Who is a retail consumer and why is it necessary for a retailer to understand the buying behaviour of his target market?
2. Briefly explain the stages of consumer decision-making using an example.
3. Which are the factors influencing customers buying decisions? Explain giving suitable examples.
4. Explain the various types of decision-making processes involved in buying.
5. What are the consumer decision rules and what are the situational variables influencing the shopping behaviour?

ACTIVITY

Make a list of variables you think can influence consumers while shopping at a supermarket and a neighbourhood kirana shop. Interact with a kirana shopkeeper and a supermarket retailer in your area and collect inputs about the shopping behaviour of customers at their outlets. Compare this with the list you had prepared. To what extent do both match?

❑❑❑

3 RETAILING STRATEGY

LEARNING OBJECTIVES

After going through the chapter, you should be able to understand:

- The definition of retail market strategy, retailing concept and retail market.
- The approaches which can help the retailer to gain competitive advantage.
- Retailer's growth strategies.
- The strategic retail planning process.

STRUCTURE:

- Introduction
- Definition of Retail Market Strategy, Retailing Concept and Retail Formats
- Approaches to Gain Competitive Advantage
- Growth Strategies in Retailing
- The Strategic Retail Planning Process
- Summary
- Chapter Questions for Discussion
- Activity

INTRODUCTION

When a retailer starts growing and expanding his business operations, he will have to give a lot of thought to 'retail planning and strategy'. This is because there is intense competition in the retail environment combined with the emergence of new formats, changing technology, rising expectations of consumers and the risk of failure due to shifting economies. This has made retailers realise the importance of planning the retailing strategy to deal effectively with their environment, customer segments and competitors.

In this chapter, we examine the meaning of retail strategy, how to select a target market and retail format and build-up sustainable competitive advantage. We also discuss the types of growth opportunities that retailers may pursue and the steps involved in the strategic retail planning process.

DEFINITION OF RETAIL MARKET STRATEGY, RETAILING CONCEPT AND RETAIL FORMATS

A retail strategy is a statement clearly defining the retailer's target market, the (retail) format planned to be followed to satisfy the customer's needs and the bases upon which they plan to build-up sustainable advantage. The *target market* refer to all the market segments identified by the retailer. *Retail format* will be the retailer mix used depending upon the mixture of merchandise (and service), offered, location, store design and layout, pricing policy, marketing and advertising policy. *Sustainable competitive advantage* means that the retailer tries to build-up an advantage over competitors which will last for a long period of time. Thus, the *retail strategy is a definite plan outlined by the retailer to tap the market and build-up a sustainable relationship with their target consumers.*

The retail strategy will define the organisation's purpose, and help the retailer to foresee the challenges and workout tactical plans to face them.

Usually, the retail strategy will involve:

(i) *Selecting* the suitable *target market segment* and *retail format*

(ii) Work on approaches that will help the retailer to gain competitive advantage

Retailing concept is management-oriented and enables the retailers to focus on the needs of its target customers and work at satisfying these needs more effectively than competitors. Identification of the target market by the retailer is important. By selecting a target market, the retailer is able to focus on a group of consumers, whose needs they have to attempt to satisfy. *Retail format* refers to the retail mix which will be used by the retailer to satisfy the needs of his target market.

Unlike market which is a place where buyers and sellers meet, *retail market* refers to a group of consumers with similar needs (a market segment) and a group of retailers using a similar retail format to satisfy those consumer needs. The target consumer segments can be defined in terms of their geographic location, demographis, lifestyle, benefit sought and so on.

APPROACHES TO GAIN COMPETITIVE ADVANTAGE

It is already mentioned earlier in the chapter that a very important element of the retail strategy is to gain sustainable competitive advantage. The purpose of the retail strategy is for the retailer to meet the target customers needs on the basis of sustained competitive advantage. That means, the retailer has to go beyond offering the usual – reduction in prices of products and services or offering deeper (or broader) merchandise assortments to target consumers. Such offers can easily be replicated by competitors and retailers may not be able to sustain their advantage.

Some approaches which can be used by retailers to gain sustainable competitive advantages are given hereunder:

(a) **Have a loyal customer base:** The retailer must work towards attracting and maintaining a loyal customer base. For instance, by having committed and dedicated employees, unique merchandise and superior customer-service will go a long way in attracting many loyal customers. So, in the long-term the retailer could develop clear and precise positioning strategies, workout attractive loyalty programmes and so on in order to build-up a loyal customer base.

The retailer will build customer loyalty by making a different and distinctive retail offerings and services consistently and thus reinforcing and maintaining this image.

(b) **Positioning:** Positioning is the designing and implementation of a retail mix so as to create a positive image of the retailer when compared to their competitors. Thus, the retailer needs to keep a track of the customer's perception about them and strive to create a positive image which is in consistence to what the target market wants. Generally, a perceptual map is used to understand the customer's image and preference for retailers.

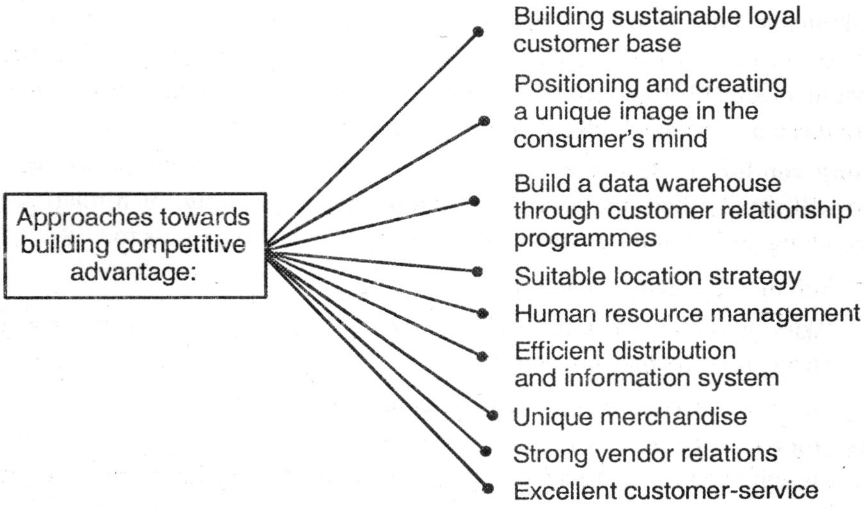

Figure 3.1: Approaches towards building competitive advantage

(c) **Develop customer loyalty programmes:** The retailer must workout customer relationship management programmes through storing the purchase information in a huge data warehouse. The data warehouse will help the retailer to analyse the type of merchandise and service certain group of customers are buying. This information can be used to tailor make their retail offerings to better meet the needs of their loyal customers.

(d) **Location:** Retailer's must identify store locations which will encourage greater footfalls keeping in mind the place and time suitability of their target market. They should create a market presence which is difficult for competitors to match. Many well known retailers go for multiple store locations which apart from ensuring competitive edge also facilitate scale of economies permitting frequent deliveries which also ensures fresh merchandise availability.

(e) **Human resource management:** Retailing involves a lot of labour intensive operations. So, employees play a major role in interacting with customers and providing a long-term relationship with them. Thus, retailers need to motivate employees, provide them with sufficient intensives and a very conducive working environment. Such efforts will instil in the employees a strong positive organisational culture of being committed to their job.

(f) **Efficient distribution and information systems:** Retailers always strive for efficiency in operations. This can be achieved if they are able to offer the right assortment of merchandise, at the right place, right time and at prices lower than that of competitors. Retailers will be able to achieve efficiencies by investing in sophisticated distribution and information systems.

(g) **Unique merchandise:** Generally, retailers stock and sell popular brands which is most likely to be available at competitors outlets also. However, nowadays there are many well known retailers (*Shoppers' Stop, Globus, Westside*, etc.), who are offering consumers their own inhouse brands or labels. Through such unique (inhouse brands) merchandise retailers are able to offer customers variety, quality and at affordable prices too. Private labels enable retailers to have a control over their consumers' needs, purchase of merchandise and so on, i.e., basically efficiency in supply-chain management. Simultaneously, the consumers are able to afford trendy quality products because the retailer is able to provide them these products, which are competitively priced also.

(h) **Strong vendor relations:** Retailers need to workout strong relationships with vendors, who will supply them the necessary merchandise. Generally, such relationships develop over a long period of time, when the retailer gets exclusive rights to:

- Sell merchandise in a region
- Workout special working terms of purchase which other competitors who do not have strong relation may not enjoy
- Get access to the merchandise, in case of short supply

(i) **Customer-service:** Retailers have to work towards providing excellent customer-service. If this is achieved it will be a valuable strategic asset in the hands of the retailers. In order to achieve consistency in offering good customer-service, retailers need to invest in committed employees who believe in offering superior services. It takes a long time to build-up the reputation as a retailer who provides excellent customer-service. This can definitely help in gaining substantial edge over competitors.

GROWTH STRATEGIES IN RETAILING

There are four types of growth opportunities which can be followed by retailers:

(a) Market Penetration

(b) Market Expansion

(c) Retail Format Development

(d) Diversification

However, market penetration and market expansion are two opportunities which can be used by retailers in the existing retailing formats.

(a) Market Penetration

Is a growth strategy directed towards existing customers. Here the retailer attempts to attract customers who though fall in the current target market do not shop at their outlets or they can device ways to induce current customers to visit a shop more than once and purchase more merchandise on every visit.

Some of the **approaches** for increasing **market penetration** include:

- Opening more stores in the target market
- Modify the store timings to suit the target customers needs.
- Attractive display of merchandise to induce impulse purchases.
- Train salespeople to cross-sell merchandise.

Cross-selling means salespersons in one department (say trendy dress section) will try to sell complementary merchandise from other departments (say fashion accessories) to their customers.

(b) Market Expansion

Is a growth strategy because it enables the retailer to use the existing retail format in new market segments. Tata's hypermarket **'Star Bazzar'** had opened its first store in Mumbai (Dahisar) and then they launched their second store also in Mumbai with the aim of offering the best value to customers across a wide array of products. The aim is to meet the basic as well as the premium needs of the target market.

(c) Retail Format Development

The retail format development provides an opportunity to offer a new retail format with a different retail mix to the same target market. **Videocon Industries Next Retail Brand** had planned to enter into small format stores under two brands **Next Express** and **Next Digital.** Next Express was to offer only select product categories, while Next Digital only IT-related products. Both these retail formats were to be operated via company owned and franchise operations. In this way they wanted to expand their network to class B and C towns. Further, Next Retail had also planned to experiment with the Shop-in format by taking in some of the Planet M stores in Standalone Next formats. **Plant M** was supposed to incorporate new sections such as — gaming, mobiles and music products: (Retail Biz, September 2008).

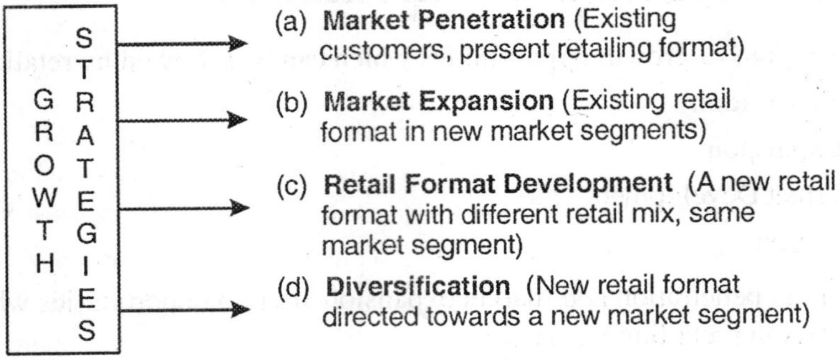

Figure 3.2: Growth strategies of retailers

Diversification: Diversification takes place when a retailer introduces a new format to serve a totally new market segment. Diversification strategy is said to be a related opportunity when the existing target market or retail format shares something in common with the new opportunity. This could be in the form of purchasing from the same vendor, using the same channel of distribution or management information system or communication media, etc., whereas in case of unrelated diversification, there will not be any common sharing between the new business opportunity on the existing format.

THE STRATEGIC RETAIL PLANNING PROCESS

The strategic retail planning process involves a set of steps the retailer goes through while developing a strategic retail plan. It explains how retailers select target market segments, determine the appropriate retail format and then build-up sustainable competitive advantages in the form of steps. These steps are as follows:

Step 1: Define the Business Mission

The first step in the strategic retail planning process is to define the business mission. The mission statement is usually a broad description of a retailer's objectives and the scope of activities it plans to undertake. It will indicate the general nature of the target segment and the retailer formats which the company will consider.

Step 2: Conduct a Situation Audit

Once the mission statement and objectives are set, the next step in the strategic planning process is to have a situation audit. Situation audit means do an analysis of the opportunities and threats in the retail environment as well as the strengths and weaknesses of the retail business relative to its competitors.

While trying to analyse the opportunities and threats in the retail environment, the retailers may have to consider the market forces, competitive forces and the environmental forces. The *market forces* which could affect the consumers and their buying pattern include – market size and growth, sales cyclicality and seasonality. Market size (large, growing, mature markets, etc.), will be an indicator of whether the retailer will be able to generate revenues to cover his investments. The *competitive factors* affecting retail markets include: barriers to entry (due to scale of economies, customer loyalty and availability of locations), bargaining power of vendors and level of competitive rivalry. The *environmental factors* affecting the retail market includes the technological, economic, regulatory and social changes which can affect the market's attractiveness.

While performing the situation audit, the retailer will have to do a self-analysis in terms of – management capability, financial resources, operative strengths, merchandise capabilities, store management capabilities, locational strengths, loyal customers, etc., in order to determine the potential areas for developing competitive advantage.

Step 3: Identify Strategic Opportunities

After doing the situation audit, the retailer will have to identify strategic opportunities for increasing retail sales. These could include growth strategies for the retailer such as – market penetration, market expansion, diversification strategy, etc.

Step 4: Evaluate Strategic Opportunities

Once the situation audit is done, the next step involves making an evaluation of the opportunities in order to determine the retailers' potential to build-up a sustainable competitive advantage and reap long-term benefits. Typically, evaluating strategic opportunities calls for looking into market attractiveness and the strengths and weaknesses of the retailer. Such an evaluation will enable the retailer to make proper investments looking to the market opportunities and then build-up a strong competitive position.

Step 5: Establish Specific Objectives and Allocate Resources

The retailer's overall objective is included in the mission statement. The specific objectives are goals against which progress towards achieving the overall objective can be measured. The specific objectives include three components:

- The performance sought in terms of a numerical index against which progress can be measured.
- The time period within which goal is to be achieved.
- The level of investment required to achieve the objective.

The performance will be measured by looking into the return on investment, sales or profits.

Step 6: Develop a Retail Mix to Implement Strategy

The sixth step in the strategic retail process involves developing a retail mix for the strategic opportunity in which investment will be made and to control and evaluate the performance. The retail mix will include planning merchandise assortments, buying systems and merchandise, planning the retail communication mix and customer-service, store management, visual design and merchandising, etc.

Step 7: Evaluate Performance and Make Adjustments

The final step in the planning process relates to evaluating the results of the strategy and implementation programme. Evaluating the strategy and implementation programme will reveal whether the retailer is meeting or not the objectives set. If the objectives are being met, changes are not required. But if the retailer fails to meet the objectives, a reanalysis is done to review the implementation programmes and if necessary a new situation audit is worked out.

Thus, the strategic planning process will help the retailer to evaluate alternatives using financial theory and market attractiveness (or competitive position matrix).

1. Define the business mission
2. Conduct a situation audit
3. Identify strategic opportunities
4. Evaluate strategic opportunities
5. Establish specific objectives and allocate resources
6. Develop a retail mix to implement strategy
7. Evaluate performance and make adjustments

Figure 3.3: The steps in strategic retail planning process

SUMMARY

A retail strategy is a statement clearly defining the retailer's target market, the retail format planned to be followed to satisfy the consumers needs and the bases upon which they plan to build-up sustainable advantage. Typically, the retail strategy will involve selecting the suitable target market segment, the retail format and work on approaches which will help to gain competitive advantage.

Some of the approaches which can help the retailer to gain competitive advantage are: Have a loyal customer base, positioning and creating a unique image in the consumer's mind, build a data warehouse, location strategy, human resource management, distribution and information system, unique merchandise, vendor relations and customer-service.

There are four types of growth opportunities which can be followed by retailers: Market Penetration, Market Expression, Retail Format Development and Diversification. The strategic retail planning process involving a set of seven steps which a retailer goes through while developing a strategic retail plan was discussed.

CHAPTER QUESTIONS FOR DISCUSSION

1. What are the meanings of the term 'Retail Market Strategy', 'Retailing Concept' and 'Retail Formats'.
2. Briefly explain the approaches used by retailers to gain competitive advantage.
3. Give examples of retailers who have used a market penetration, a market expansion, a retail format development and diversification growth strategies. Justify your answer.

ACTIVITY

Assume you are thinking of opening a fast food outlet in Hyderabad. What are the steps in the retail strategic planning process which you will have to carryout for this? Make a list of your findings giving special emphasis to:

- Doing situational analysis of the local fast food market
- Identifying and evaluating alternatives
- Selecting the target market
- The retail mix elements to be used for the fast food outlet.

❑❑❑

4 ADMINISTRATIVE STRATEGY AND HUMAN RESOURCE MANAGEMENT

LEARNING OBJECTIVES

After going through the chapter, you should be able to understand:

- The role of human resource management in retailing
- The retail organisational designs and structures
- How do retailers develop employees' skills, commitment and motivate them.

STRUCTURE:

- Introduction
- Importance of Human Resource Management (HRM) in Retailing
- Competitive Advantage through Effective HRM
- Retail Organisational Designs and Structures
- Developing Employees' Skills, Commitment and Motivating Them
- Summary
- Chapter Questions for Discussion
- Activity

INTRODUCTION

It is said that the relationship an organisation has with its employees and the culture practised by them will go a long way in building sustainable competitive advantage. Retailing is a part of the labour intensive industry with the employees involved in performing all the major retailing functions. The critical retailing activities performed by employees include buying, assorting and displaying merchandise as well as providing customer-services. Thus, human resource management is a very important issue in the performance of retailing firms.

The chapter begins with defining HRM, and on how to build-up competitive advantage through effective HRM. We also have a look at retail organisational designs and structures and the ways to develop employees skills, commitment and motivate them.

IMPORTANCE OF HUMAN RESOURCE MANAGEMENT (HRM) IN RETAILING

Meaning of HRM

Human resource management is a function mainly concerned with people at work and with their relationship within the organisation. Leon C. Megginson has described the term *Human resources as "the total knowledge, skills, creative abilities, talents and aptitudes of an organisation's workforce, as well as the value, attitudes and beliefs of the individuals involved"*. This means that human resources can be treated like any other natural resource which can be used for the development of the organisation. *Human Resource Management (HRM) can be defined as the planning, organising, directing and controlling functions for the purpose of employing, developing and compensating human resources leading to the creation and development of human relations within the organisation with the intention to contribute proportionately (due to them) to the individual, organisational and social goods.*

From the above definition of HRM it can be said that the main feature of HRM is being concerned with managing human resources at work, development of their people's knowledge, skills, capability, potentialities and thus help them to attain and achieve individual goals along with the organisational and societal goals using an integrated approach. Retailing firms will be able to achieve their financial objectives provided they manage their five critical assets effectively. These are namely the location site, merchandise inventory and warehouse, stores, employees and customers. When we talk of human resources the focus will be on the organising and management of employees.

Specific HR Conditions Relevant to Retailing

The functioning of the retailing industry is such that it has certain specific HR conditions especially because of: (a) the requirement of using part-time employees (b) the need to exercise control on expenses (c) the changing demographics of the workforce, and (d) issues relevant to global retailers.

Most of the retail outlets are required to function seven days in a week. They also remain open for long hours in order to cater to the needs of working people and family shoppers. Additionally, during holidays and weekends, the peak business hours occur during lunch time, late evening onwards and during sales. To take care of the additional working time, retailers are forced to employee part-time workers. Such workers are not committed fully to their jobs or the retailer and are more likely to change the job when better opportunities come their way.

Control Expenses

Often, retailers operate with thin margins and hence try to control expenses. So, they become cautious while paying wages to employees who perform low skill jobs on hourly basis. They may hire persons with little or no experience as sales associates in order to cut costs. The outcome of this could be high turnover, absenteeism and poor performance. Since such employees are required to directly interact with customers, it not only creates a bad impression but may also have a negative effect on sales and customer loyalty.

Changing Employee Demographics

The changing demographic patterns often results in a shortage of qualified personnel at the workplace. Some of the changing demographics are: increase in life span, extending the retirement age, start earning at a younger age, increase in women at workplace, change in attitudes at the workplace where young workforce along with the older generation and so on. Amidst all this diversity the young have to work with the old in order to achieve the retailer's goal. Managing this growing diversity and change in retail workforce is really a challenge for the human resource department.

Issue Related to Global Retailers

The world is a global village and there are retailers operating in more than one international market. So, for the international marketer it becomes very challenging to handle differences in economic systems, work ethics and labour laws — all of which may vary from one country to another. Depending upon the political-legal system prevailing in that country, the retailer will have to employ a suitable workforce and motivate them to work towards his (retailer's) goals.

COMPETITIVE ADVANTAGE THROUGH EFFECTIVE HRM

Unlike manufacturing firms where capital equipment is fast replacing the work performed by employees previously, in retailing the jobs are labour intensive. Retailers are dependent upon their employees to carryout retailing activities such as buying, displaying merchandise and providing service to customers. If retailers are able to manage their employees efficiently, it can even result in gaining a sustainable competitive advantage. This is because:

- Effective management of employees can help the retailer to gain cost advantage, for labour costs make-up a significant percentage of a retailer's total expenses.
- Since employees are actively involved in – selecting merchandise, providing information and assistance to customers arrange shelves and stock display, they (employees) can give that added touch which will differentiate the retailer's offerings from that of their competitors.
- Since employees' behaviour while interacting with customers is 'unique' and 'intangible' this gives the retailer potential advantages which will be difficult for competitors to duplicate.

We have already said earlier that the strategic objective of HRM is to match the capabilities and behaviours of employees with the goals (both short-term and long-term) of the retailing firm. The human resource management performance can be measured in terms of employee productivity and employee turnover.

Employee productivity can be measured as:

$$\frac{\text{Retailer's sales or profit}}{\text{Total number of employees}}$$

Employee productivity can be improved either by increasing the sales generated or by reducing (or lowering) the number of employees or both. It is to be noted that on the one hand employee's productivity is directly related to the retailer's short-term profits. While, on the other hand, employees attitudes expressed in terms of job satisfaction and commitment to job will directly affect customer satisfaction and thereby have implications on the long-term performance of the retailer.

Employee turnover can be expressed as the rate of change in the number of employees of a retailing firm during a definite period. This takes into consideration the extent to which old employees leave and new employees join the retailing firm. Retailing firms have to be very careful while taking short-term decisions such as reducing labour costs when sales and profits decrease due to increased competition. For, although by employing part-timers the retailer may temporarily reduce costs and increase short- term productivity and profits, it could result in adversely affecting the long-term profit through low employee morale and decrease in customer satisfaction (or service).

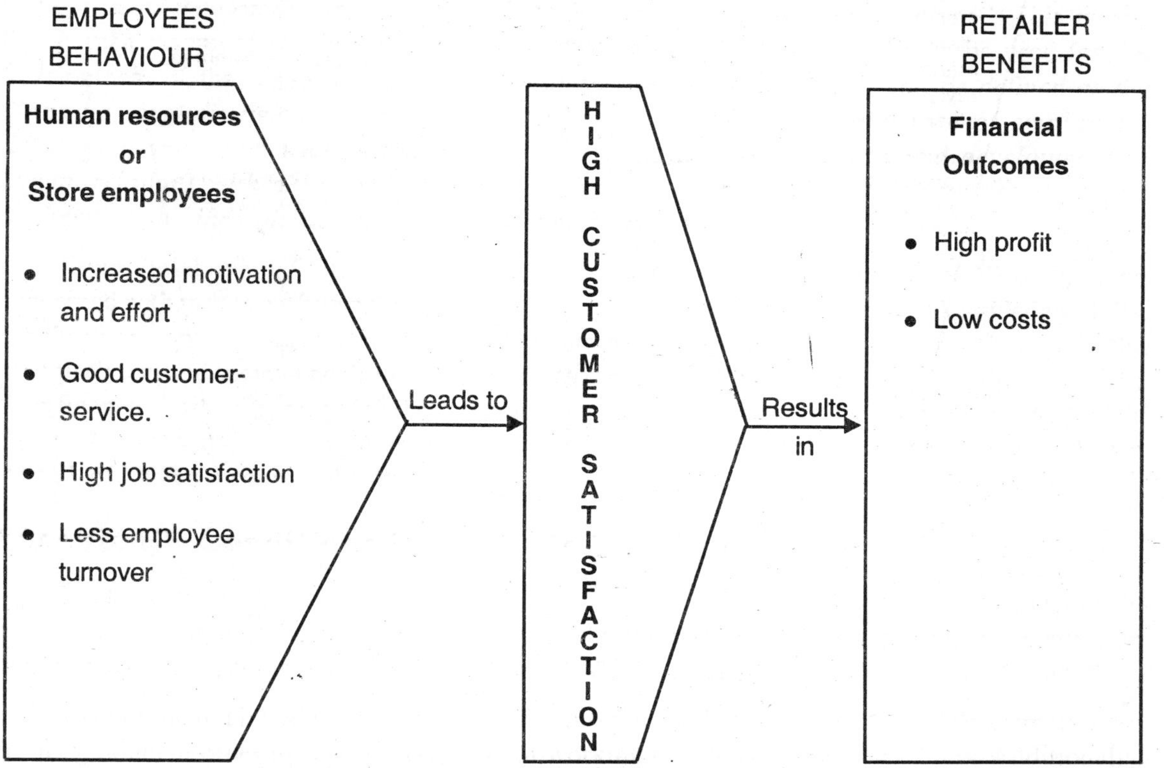

Figure 4.1: Relationship between employees' behaviour and the retailer's benefits

The importance of human resources in retailing can be seen from the fact that the product or service which a customer takes back home from a retail outlet is a combination of *merchandise* and *the service* delivered to him/her through the human interaction between the outlet's staff or employee and the customer. Customers who are satisfied with the service provided at the outlet are more likely to patronise the store in future.

Figure 4.1 shows how positive store employees behaviour can lead to high customer satisfaction which will benefit the retailing firm in terms of high profit and low costs. Figure 4.2 gives an overview of the management tasks to be carried out by senior employees of the retailing firm.

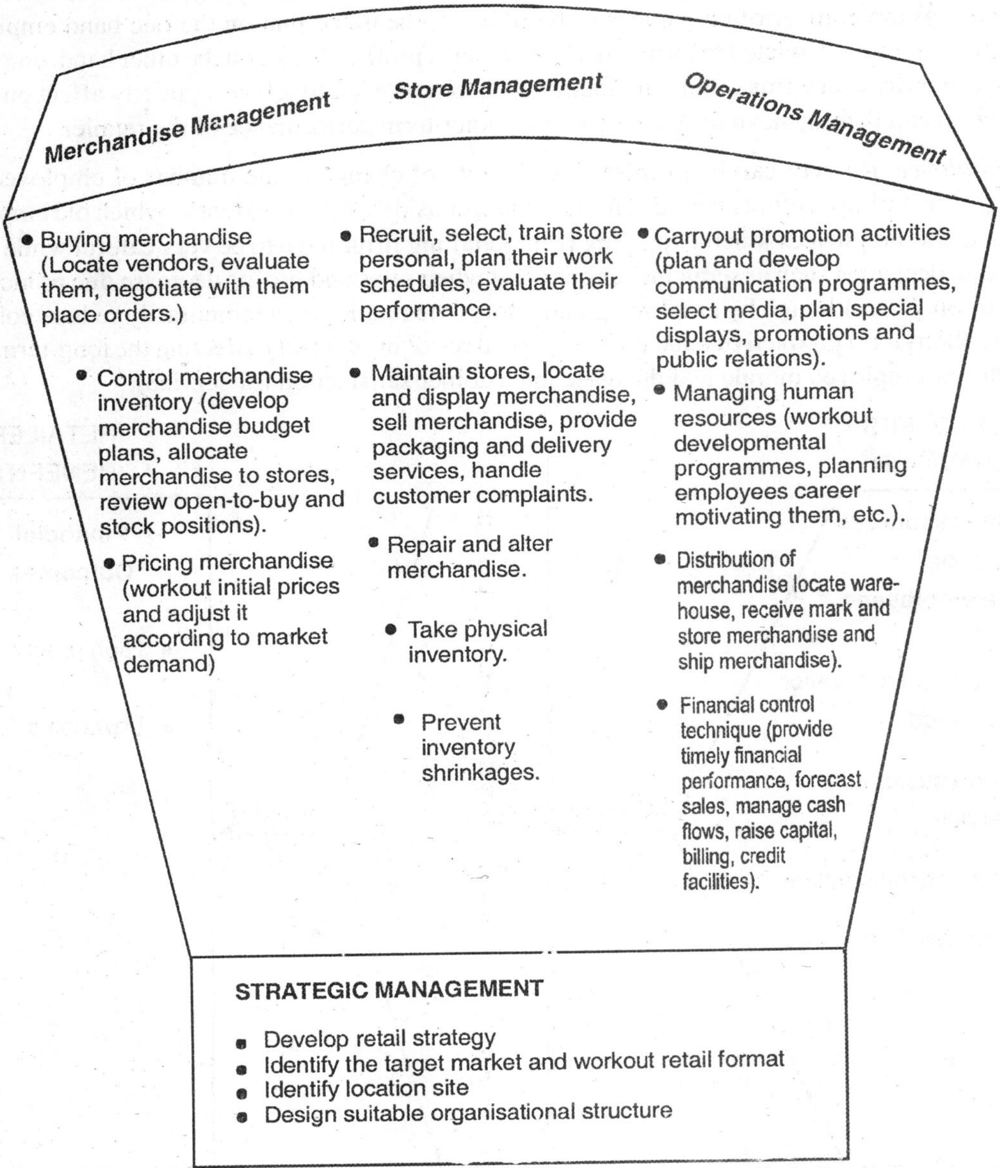

Figure 4.2: Managemer . tasks performed in retail firms

Location of the retail outlets- *Lifestyle Store* Gurgaon (above) and *Shoppers' Stop* (Malad, Mumbai) and spaciousness makes shopping for the customers a pleasant experience.

Studies have indicated that there is a close relationship between employee satisfaction and customer satisfaction. This implies that the human resources managers at retailing firms have to adopt policies and programmes which will emphasise on high employee motivation and performance. Moreover, human resource management in retailing is quite challenging because it *employs part-time employees* (apart from regular employees) to work during peak periods and for longer hours. These part-time employees (who may be required to work at odd hours) may not be very much committed to their jobs and the retailing firm and are more likely to quit the job than full-time employees. Another issue is the need for retailers to operate on thin margins and thus control expenses. They (retailers) are *hesitant to pay high salary* or wages to hourly employees who perform low skill jobs. To control costs, inexperienced or low wage employees are employed often leading to high turnover, absenteeism, poor performance and low motivation. Added to this, it is such employees who will be directly interacting with customers. And retail employees poor appearances, manners, and attitudes can have a negative effect on sales and customer loyalty. Thus, while playing a vital role in supporting a retailing strategy, HRM calls for developing policies and programmes to develop an enthusiastic and committed workforce.

RETAIL ORGANISATIONAL DESIGNS AND STRUCTURES

The organisational structure is a formal system, wherein the various activities to be performed by specific employees are identified and delegated, clearly indicating their lines of authority and responsibility. This system of delegation is designed so as to support the accomplishment of goals and make decisions to implement strategies.

The first step while working out the organisational structure is to determine the tasks to be performed by the retailing firm. Broadly these activities can be categorised into four tasks, namely: strategic management, merchandise management, store management and operations (administrative) management.

Those involved in strategic management carryout the strategic marketing and finance decisions. Administrative tasks are performed by those having specialised skills in human resource management, finance, accounting, real estate and management information system. They are required to develop plans, procedures, and provide information to assist operating managers to implement the retailer's strategy. In retailing firms, generally, the merchandise management tasks are carried out by the line or operating managers. These managers take day-to-day decisions which directly affects the retailer's performance.

Working on the Retail Organisational Design

While developing the organisational sdesign, certain aspects have to be taken into consideration (shown in Figure 4.3). Based on the individual *employee's expertise and specialisation,* a relevant limited set of activities are assigned to him/her. For instance, an employee who is an expert at identifying and selecting a good retail site will be required to concentrate and focus on this area.

Thus, through specialisation the employee will concentrate on certain tasks for which they have the unique skills and training and with expertise they can increase the productivity. When employees are given the necessary authority and responsibility they are able to effectively undertake the responsibilities assigned to them and this can lead to productivity increase. For instance, the store managers must have the authority and be responsible for selecting salespersons and training them according to the store's requirement. If this task is performed effectively it will lead to an increase in productivity. Of course, at times there could be conflicts when benefits of matching responsibility and authority come in the way of matching that with the 'specialisation'. Take the example of the store manager who may recruit, select and train salespersonnel, he will have all the authority and responsibility over how the merchandise will be sold. But the store manager will not have the authority to purchase the various categories of the merchandise. For, it will be the merchandise manager who will be exclusively responsible for the profitability of the merchandise category.

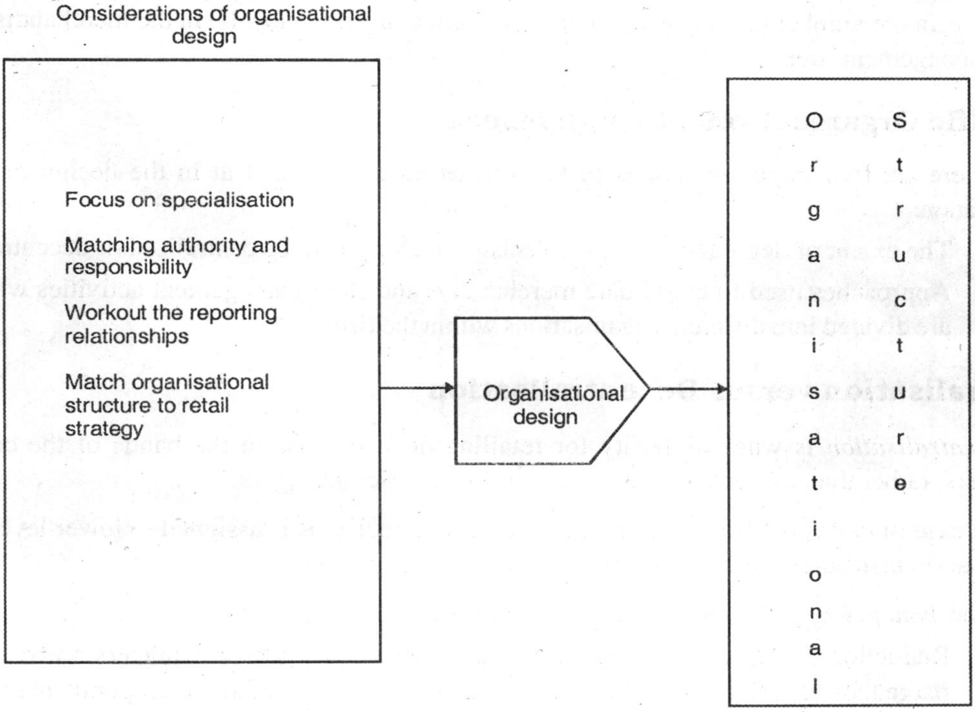

Figure 4.3: Considerations for working out a suitable retail organisational structure

Working Out the Reporting Relationship

While designing the organisational structure, care should be taken to decide on the reporting pattern and relationships. The retailer should ensure that the superior has the correct number of employees (subordinates) reporting to him, *i.e.,* neither too less (when costs can go up due to increase in the number of managers supervising too less employees) nor too much (effectiveness of managers may go down when too many employees report to them).

So, depending upon the nature of the job (or tasks), skills required and location, the retailing firm has to decide on the appropriate number of subordinates required under the supervisor/manager. Ultimately it is to be borne in mind that the design of the organisational structure should match the firm's retailing strategy. The retail organisational structure will differ according to the type of retailer and size of the store. For example, owner-managers of a *single store* may simply assign tasks to each employee and monitor to see that all activities are carried out properly. In case of *chain of stores,* managers are required to supervise outlets which are geographically distant from each other. In such retailing chains, the buying and store management tasks are separated. The stores and store employees could be located throughout the geographic region. Whereas, merchandise (buyers) planning, marketing, finance, visual merchandising, human resource managers and employees are placed at the corporate head office. The activities and management functions are divided into strategic management, store management, merchandise management (or management levels) in the merchandising and store management and administrative management areas.

The main difference between the organisational structure of a department store and other retail formats is in the number of people and managers (or management levels) in the merchandising and store management areas.

Specific Organisational Design Issues

There are two important issues to be considered and worked at in the design of a retail organisation:

- The extent or degree to which the decision-making is to be centralised or decentralised.
- Approaches used to coordinate merchandise and store management activities when they are divided into different organisations within the firm.

Centralisation versus Decentralisation

Centralisation is when authority for retailing decisions are in the hands of the corporate managers, rather than dispersed to store, regional or district managers.

In case of *decentralisation* the authority for retail decisions is assigned to lower levels in the organisation instead of the corporate managers.

The *benefits of centralised decision-making* are:

- Reduction in costs especially overhead costs because lesser managers are required to make the various decisions since everything is taken care of at the corporate management level.
- By coordinating buying across geographically dispersed stores, the company achieves lower prices from suppliers.
- Centralisation provides an opportunity to have the best people to make decisions (in their area of expertise) for the entire firm.
- Centralisation helps to improve efficiency with standard policies and guidelines being used across stores.

The *limitations of centralised decision-making* are that it makes it difficult for the retailer to adopt to local market conditions, respond to local competition and labour markets. In order to overcome these limitations, usually large retailers rely more on their information system to make merchandise and operation decisions at the corporate head office. (Read Box 4.1 on the decision-making style followed at *Pantaloons*).

Coordination of Stores and Merchandise Management

It is not very difficult for small independent retailers to coordinate their store's buying and selling activities. Being in close touch with the customers, the owner-management are able to buy the merchandise and ensure that their salespersons sell it.

But in large retail firms the buying and selling functions are organised into separate divisions. Typically buyers will specialise in buying merchandise and are dependent upon the store managers and staff to sell it. Thus, the former are dependent upon the latter to understand customers' demands and needs. Retailers make use of four approaches to coordinate the buying and selling activities.

(a) Retailers use methods to increase buyers' contact with customers and improve informal communication between buyers and store personnel, and also selling the merchandise bought by the firm.

(b) Increase customer contact and communication by having buyers visit the stores and interact with the department personnel they buy from.

(c) Involve employees to be responsible and assign them the job of coordinating buying and selling activities.

(d) Improve coordination between buying and selling activities by involving store employees in the buying process.

Thus, it is the responsibility of the human resources management department to develop a suitable organisational structure depending upon the size of the retailing firm and the type of merchandise bought and sold by it.

Box 4.1. Kishore Biyani's – Pantaloon Retail

A few years ago Biyani took colossal risks – which scared off most financers who were used to dealing with more conventional businessmen. He was fond of saying, "Most Indian retailers tend to copy blindly from Western models". I am looking for a Pan Indian model of retailing. Further, he was known for running a one-man show. But today, having been successful in four retail formats: The *Big Bazaar hypermarket, Food Bazaar*, *Pantaloons* apparel stores and *Central Mall*, investors have begun to notice him. And, Biyani has also begun to pay more attention to what the investors have told him that he needed to delegate in order to grow.

Heeding to the investors' advice, he (Biyani) went on a hiring spree. He selected Ved Prakash Arya, to handle operations, Jaydeep Shetty from Inox to create new brands, Sanjeev Agrawal to handle marketing, Kush Medhora from Westside to handle new store rollouts, Ambrish Chheda to look after Food Bazaar and handle business development, Bina Mirchandani to look after the merchandising and V. Muralidharan from Lifestyle to head Central Mall.

It was when Biyani told the above professionals that he wanted to abdicate everything except strategic planning and the selection of new locations. This inspired many like Kush Medhora to join Pantaloons. His job, opening new stores keeps him very busy throughout the year. According to him this expansion is fun and the retailing firm will easily be worth. ₹ 5,000 crore by 2007. He is also busy recruiting and interviewing aspiring Big Bazaar store managers. But managing Big Bazaar is tough because the margins are slimmer and the business runs on faster stock turn arounds. So, Pantaloons are looking out for people with an eye for number – a very different way of thinking from the other stores.

(***Source:*** *Business World*, June 14, 2004.)

DEVELOPING EMPLOYEES' SKILLS, COMMITMENT AND MOTIVATING THEM

A very crucial issue to be handled by the HRM department is to keep the employees highly motivated through identifying and developing their skills and commitment to their jobs. Motivation is derived from the word *motive, which means an inner state within the mind which energises, activates or moves and directs or channels behaviour towards the goals.*

"Motivation can be defined as an unsatisfied need which creates a state of tension or disequilibrium, causing the individual to move in a goal directed pattern towards restoring a state of equilibrium by satisfying the need."

As per the above definition the unsatisfied need within each individual may cause a state of tension, urging him or her to behave or act so as to satisfy this unfilled need. Thus, the challenge for retailing firm's HRM department is to work towards motivating their employees to work and contribute in achieving their firm's goal and retailing strategy.

Usually, firms have their own organisational culture, written policies and supervision and incentive packages which are used to motivate employees.

Organisational Culture

The retailing firm can develop an *organisational culture* – a set of values, traditions and customs in the form of unwritten guidelines which are passed on by older employees to newer ones. For instance, at *Godrej*, corporate culture is driven by values such as – quality, customer-orientation, commitment, discipline, integrity, learning, transparency, respect, teamwork and trust. Says *Adi Godrej* Chairman Godrej group: "This value framework is an unwritten constitution". According to *Nandan M. Nilekani, (Infosys Technologies).* "The most important aspect of HR management is that leaders should walk the talk. Walking the talk helps win your people's confidence and makes them committed. Commitment is buying into the vision of the organisation and having the energy to support it. Thus, in terms of ethical business conduct, of social commitment and of adherence to a strong value system, it will motivate employees when the senior management lead by example". Read Box 4.2, where Nandan Nilekani talks of investing in Human Capital.

Box 4.2. Investing in Human Capital

The 21st century will be shaped by intellectual capital. In this 'knowledge age', human capital drives progress. In this context, people are of any organisation's most valuable assets. More so, since success depends on the ability to recognise, learn and assimilate changes quickly, and on bringing business value to the customers by leveraging the assimilated knowledge. At *Infosys*, we have realised that *'learn ability'* is critical for success. Learn ability is defined as the ability to extract generic inferences from specific instances and to use them in new, structured situations. Thus, an organisation's ability to continually identify, recruit, develop and motivate its most precious resource, in an increasingly competitive and global marketplace, is a critical success factor.

Today, thanks to globalisation, our customers, investors and vendor-partners come from across the globe. The demands of a global stakeholder base will require the creation of a new workforce. Consequently, a rising percentage of the workforce is made up of people across geographies. Hence, an important aspect of HR management today is to manage cultural diversity.

Organisations have to devise ways to utilise a wide range of experiences, perspectives, preferences and styles in order to deliver value to its clients. A very important aspect of this is for the organisation to have a strong value system – a protocol for behaviour that enhances the trust, confidence, commitment, and enthusiasm of employees across locations and cultures. This builds the character of the organisation and ensures sustained growth. Further, this helps attract, retain and motivate the best talent. Employees are drawn to work for such an organisation. Further, it will enthuse the employees to make bigger sacrifices and thus improve the bottom line.

(***Source:*** Nandan M. Nilekani, *Collector's Edition,* Vol. IV, *Business Today,* 2003.)

What Nandan Nilekani mentioned in Box 4.2 also holds good for any retailing firm. *McDonalds* are famous for the first class service provided to all its customers. This is a part of their organisational culture. It is through such strong organisational cultures that retailing firms convey to employees a feeling of what they ought to do on their jobs and how to behave with customers to be consistent with the firm's strategy. Values in the organisational culture are explained to new employees and then re-inforced through stories.

Culture is transmitted to employees by organisations in a number of ways such as-stories, rituals, material symbols and language. For instance, we quote here examples of *Henry Ford II* and *Nordstrom.*

- It is said that during the days when *Henry Ford II* was Chairman of the Ford Motors Co. one would have been hard pressed to find a manager who had not heard the story about Mr. Ford reminding his executives when they were acting too arrogant: "It's my name that's on the building". The message was clear: Henry Ford II ran the company!
- *Nordstrom* employees are fed the following story which communicates about the company's policy towards customer returns: When this retail chain was in its infancy stage, a customer came in and wanted to return a set of automobile tyres. The sales clerk was unsure of how to handle the situation. As the customer and the sales clerk spoke, Mr. Nordstrom happened to walk-by and overheard the conversation. He immediately intervened and asked the customer how much he had paid for the tyres. Mr. Nordstrom also asked the clerk to take the tyres back and provide a full cash refund. After the customer received the refund and left, the perplexed clerk looked at the boss and said: "But, Mr. Nordstorm we don't sell tyres!" "I know", replied the boss, "but we do whatever we need to do, to make a customer happy. I mean it when I say it we have a no-question-ask-return policy". Nordstorm then picked up the telephone and called a friend in the auto parts business to see how much he could get for the tyres.

Firm's Policies and Supervision

A very fundamental method of coordination could be to have written policies clearly indicating what employees have to do and also have supervisors enforce these policies. For instance, most of the retailers have a written policy clearly specifying that goods once sold cannot be returned or exchanged and circumstances when such goods could be taken back by the retailer. Thus, employees can use these written guidelines for performing their jobs and whenever clarification is sought on any issue, it could be taken up.

Box 4.3. Work Hard, Gift Awaits you at Shop

Salary is no more that boring bank cheque. It now includes a gift cheque at Shoppers' Stop or Lifestyle, or a dining coupon at a restaurant. The incentive component of BPO employees is bringing in new pay order in the industry.

The employees spend considerable time deciding on what incentives they want. Like Pratima, who is making plans for her next month's salary. She is wondering whether she should tell her team leader to give her incentives in the form of a garment shop gift voucher or settle for a pizza store coupon.

Reason: For the BPO professionals, the gift vouchers come on their terms. "We as a team decide on the gift vouchers. Invariably we settle for big departmental stores or superstores because the product range is wide", says Pratima.

That's the new pay order in the BPO industry where incentives form a good chunk of pay packets. While monthly and quarterly cash incentives are doled out by almost every BPO company, the focus is now on making it more attractive. "There is an incentive even for the first sales call you make. On many occasions, the company that hires the call centre pays the incentive but in dollars and pounds", says Mahesh, a BPO employee. Many of his colleagues, however, still prefer to get their incentives in gift coupons simply because cash incentives push up tax liability.

The retail sector too seems to be enjoying this new change in salary structure. Shoppers' Stop CEO B.S. Nagesh says his company churned out a revenue of ₹. 20 crore from its institutional sales last year though its target was ₹. 15 crore. He says a variety of industries like IT and BPO, are using gift cheques, besides the traditional users like credit card companies, hotels and airlines. The latter, however, use it to reward customers and agents for their loyalty.

The retail industry believes that the future can only get better as the young professionals in the BPO sector would prefer to shop without paying, rather than take home taxable incentives. Lifestyle International managing director Kumar S. says, his company's clients for gift cheques are primarily IT and BPO companies in BPO hubs like Bangalore, Gurgaon and Malad in Mumbai. Now he is looking at offering it to banks and insurance companies. If you find the malls and departmental stores too crowded in the next few years, don't be surprised with the supervisor who will do the needful.

(***Source:*** *The Times of India*, Bangalore, 20th September, 2004.)

***Incentives*:** Another way of motivating and coordinating with employees can be done by using incentives. These incentives can vary from commission gift cheques, bonuses, to nonfinancial incentives (recognition and praise). Commission could be compensation based on a fixed percentage of merchandise sold by them. Whereas, bonus is an additional compensation awarded periodically on the basis of evaluation of the employee's performance. Box 4.3 makes interesting reading on how BPO employees are provided incentives in the form of coupons/gift cheque to shop at various retail outlets.

The retail managers also receive additional income on a profit-sharing basis in the form of cash bonus or stock options. Although incentives are very effective in motivating employees to perform the activities on which the incentives are based, care should be taken to see that these incentives may not cause employees to ignore other activities.

Developing Employee Skill and Commitment

A term which cannot be avoided by retailing firms is employee turnover. However, employee turnover can be reduced if they are able to build-up an environment of mutual trust and commitment. When a firm practises and demonstrates commitment, employees will respond by working very hard and being loyal to the organisation they work for. Employee commitment can be increased when the retailing firm:

Develops Employee Skill Through Selection and Training: When retailing firms invest in their human resources by making significant contribution towards training programmes, where they are given opportunities to learn more in their area of operation, it is an indication that the firm cares for its employees. Training is a very vital aspect in retailing because it is the employees who are in touch with the customers and hence responsible for satisfying their shopping needs and solving shopping problems, if any.

Shopper's Stop, one of India's largest organised retailer has used globally trained manpower with globally competitive technology and financial resources – with the vision of becoming India's number 1 global retailer. The specific sophisticated planning tool in Human Resource Management System used by Shoppers' Stop has enabled it to gain competency in managing manpower and salary planning. For more details read Box 4.4.

Empowering Employees: Empowerment can be referred to as the process when managers share power and decision-making authority with employees. With empowerment employees become more responsible and accountable for the store's performance. They are more confident in their abilities to provide very good service to customers and thus are more committed to the firm's success.

Developing Partnering Relationships with Employees: HRM departments also try to increase commitment of the employees towards their jobs by creating partnering relationships with them. Retailers try to create such relationships by doing away with status differences among employees, adopt a policy where hiring of employees is done from within the organisation and by introducing programmes such as *flexitime, job sharing, child care* facilities and so on. Such measures taken by the retailers will go a long way in ensuring employee commitment and motivating them to perform their jobs well.

Box 4.4. Shoppers' Stop use of Oracle Financials and HRMS

HRMS manages in-house training needs and transits training from a calendar-driven role to a more strategic one. It also helps to cover the training process from definition of the training environment and planning, to the conducting of training programmes and updates of employee skill profiles. HRMS is a complete end-to-end, hire-to-retire solution for HR processes used by *Shoppers' Stop*. HRMS is delivered through five individual applications:

- ***Personnel*** (This application has been implemented at Shoppers' Stop).

Applicant tracking and recruitment – resume database maintenance, selection process, reference checks and pre-employment tests, define organisational structures that can be built around functions, positions and reporting structures.

- ***Payroll*** (Already implemented)

Generic business rule based system designed to handle complex enterprise payroll rules, organisation specific rules for compensation and statutory elements such as tax and insurance, used to effectively administer total employee compensation.

- **Benefits** (Already implemented)

Simple and easily understood management of complex benefit programmes, plans grouping for focused benefit plan administration, employee and employer specific rules.

- ***Training*** (Application in progress)

Manages in-house training needs and transits training from a calendar-driven role to a more strategic one.

- ***HR analyst***

Executive information system for analysis of HR history across distributed locations.

The above are initiatives undertaken by Shoppers' Stop to streamline the HR process.

(***Source***: *Retail Biz*, May 2004)

Emerging Trends in Retail HRM

The challenges before the HRM functionary is the managing of a diverse workforce, having to do with part-time workers, balance the challenges of the firm and become more profitable and satisfying to both the employees and the employer and use of technology to increase employee productivity.

While, the basic principle of managing diversity is the recognition that employees have different needs and it means accepting and valuing differences and charting programmes accordingly.

HR professionals try to manage diversity by offering diversity in training programmes to develop cultural awareness and improve interpersonal skills, show respect to others and treat people as equals. They also involve support groups (like higher level managers to help lower level managers) who are assigned the job of mentors to guide junior employees and help them to solve problems arising on the job. The HR also works out career development programmes for the employees, who after hardwork can look forward to suitable promotions.

Technology can help HR (Human Resource) professionals to use intranets to automate and streamline human resource operations. Thus, HRM can shift most of the routine, time-consuming procedures to technology. Then, they need to concentrate on personnel retention and development. HR professionals need to be coaches, mentors and succession planners. In the long-run, HRM must be viewed as a strategic consulting partner providing innovative solutions and influencing key decisions and policies.

Rajesh Kaushik and Anurag Chandra (of *Cedar Consulting*) are of the view that HR department is rarely involved in the company's strategic planning exercises or marketing or strategic decisions. Very often, it is perceived as a drain on the company's profits. But if a retail chain is to succeed, a transformation of this perception is required. It is necessary for a more proactive and strategic role from the HR department in supporting the corporate strategy. The HR function should balance the challenges of the company and thus become satisfying and profitable to both the employees and the employer.

Building the HR Score Board

In order to facilitate a more dynamic role for the HR function in retail, Kaushik and Chandra have suggested usage of HR score cards as a solution to monitor performance. The HR score card building involves the following steps:

Step 1 – Clearly Articulate the Business Strategy: The retailing firm must have a strategy, clearly described and easily communicable which is a prerequisite for a successful strategy implementation.

Step 2 – Build the Strategy Map: This step is an essential part of managing HR as a strategic function, providing the organisational logic transforming HR from a transaction and operation-oriented function into an organisational asset with strategic impact.

Step 3 – Link HR Strategy Map to the Overall Corporate Strategy: This is an important step. It will indicate how the organisation chooses to define HR deliverables and the roles to be played by both line managers and HR professionals in managing people as strategic asset.

We can take the example of the retail industry, where in order to fulfil the desired business outcome of creating an excellent shopping experience, the HR process, delivery, systems and skills need to be adequately articulated. HR score card will point out the measures of the management's strategic performance. *Step 2* will determine the drivers of future sales growth with improved customer satisfaction, which will be driven by the quality of the shopping experiences. *Step 3* identifies the HR deliverables required to improve the quality of the buying experience. In retail, it will be the frontline staff who are knowledgeable, helpful and courteous who drive the buying experience. Thus, HR deliverable and the focus of HR management's strategic performance in this case is the extent to which it delivers a sales staff who is knowledgeable, helpful and courteous.

HR score card has proved to be an effective tool to translate corporate strategy and assist the firm in implementation of the strategy. HR professionals create HR initiatives and systems which ultimately deliver the employee performance required to execute the organisation's strategy.

SUMMARY

Retailing forms a part of the labour intensive industry with the employees involved in performing all the major functions. Thus, human resource management is a major function to be deal with. Leon C. Megginson has defined Human Resource as "the total knowledge, skills, creative abilities, talents and aptitudes of an organisation's workforce, as well as the value, attitudes and beliefs of the individuals involved. The specific HR conditions relevant to retailing are: part-time employees, changing demographics of the workforce and specific issues related to global retailing.

The strategic objective of Human Resource Management (HRM) is to match the capabilities and behaviour of employees with the goals of the retailing firm. HRM performance can be measured in terms of employee productivity and employee turnover.

The organisational structure of retailing firms is designed taking into consideration the tasks such as – strategic management, merchandise management.Store Managment and operations Management.Generally, retailing firms try to motivate their employees by having clear-cut policies and supervision, incentives and developing their skills and commitment through exposing them to proper training programmes, empowering them and creating partnership relations with them.

CHAPTER QUESTIONS FOR DISCUSSION

1. Why is human resource management given a lot of importance by retailing firms when compared to manufacturing industries?
2. Briefly explain why retailing firms have to exercise a lot of care while working out the organisational design and structure?
3. Suppose a well-known retailer, already owning a chain of departmental stores in a city (say Hyderabad) is planning to open a similar store in rural Andhra Pradesh. As a college student you have been asked to workout a suitable organisational design and structure. How would you go about doing this?
4. Suppose a family owned, long established store has started facing problems due to high employee turnover, with the coming up of a chain of stores in your city. What type of employees incentives would you suggest to this retailer and why?

ACTIVITY

Meet a salesperson of a 'Discount Store' and talk to him and find out how committed he is to his job, what are the incentives being given to him and what are the changes, if any, being sought in the organisational structures by him?

Meet another salesman of a speciality store and carryout a similar exercise as above. What differences and similarities do you find in the two stores 'Human Resource Management' Functions?

❑❑❑

UNIT II

MERCHANDISING AND PRICING STRATEGIES

5 MERCHANDISE MANAGEMENT

LEARNING OBJECTIVES

After going through the chapter, you should be able to understand:

- The meaning of merchandise management and how to categorise the buying process
- The importance of setting objectives for merchandising plan
- The role of sales forcasting and the assortment planning process in retailing
- How buying system can help retailers and buyers

STRUCTURE:

- Introduction
- Meaning of Merchandise Management
- Categorising the Buying Process
- Setting Objectives for Merchandise Plan
- Sales forecasting for Retailing
- Determining the Assortment Planning Process
- Buying System
- Open-to-buy (OTB) System
- Summary
- Chapter Questions for Discussion
- Activity

INTRODUCTION

The strategic aim and primary objective of every retailer will be to sell merchandise and services. This necessitates the development and implementation of a merchandise plan by the buyer, with the objective of ensuring the sale of their merchandise. This means that the merchandise buyer has to decide what to buy and how much to buy. Today, the market is filled with both small and large retailers who are required to take vital merchandise related decisions of many individual items from hundreds of vendors. So, the successful retailer will be the one who can take competent decisions on:

- What merchandise items are to be bought?
- What quantities of items have to be bought?
- When (or at what time) these items are to be bought?

Thus, the buying process must be well organised, in a systematic and orderly manner to clearly communicate to the ultimate consumers – 'the best quality products and the organisation' whose merchandise are being purchased. The buyer will have to adopt a merchandise management process by which they (retailers) can offer the right quality of the merchandise at the stores, clearly reflecting and meeting the various market segment needs and wants. A lot depends upon the ability of the merchandiser to select and display (or present) merchandise in a unique manner, allowing one store to differentiate itself from another store.

This chapter examines the strategic and planning management issues involved in merchandise management. The chapter commences with describing the meaning of merchandise management and how category management process works as the basic unit of analysis for making merchandising decisions. There have also been discussions on the importance of setting objectives in merchandise management and the significance of sales forecasting as an integral component of any merchandising plan and deciding the merchandise category in order to determine how much of the merchandise is to be bought. We have tried to understand the role of merchandise assortment planning process and buying systems which will help the merchandise planner to determine how much of the items are to be bought. The chapter concludes with discussions on the open-to-buy system which will help the buyers to project and control the buying decisions.

MEANING OF MERCHANDISE MANAGEMENT

Simply stated merchandise management is concerned with the planning and controlling of the retailer's inventories. This implies that *Merchandise Management involves a process by which a retailer attempts to offer the right quantity of the right merchandise in the right place at the right time along with meeting the financial goals of the company.* As per this definition the person(s) involved in merchandise management has to balance the financial requirements of the organisation based on a strategy of merchandise planning and purchasing. David Gilbert has suggested a more complex role of merchandise management. According to him *Merchandise Management is the planning and implementation of the acquisition, handling and monitoring of merchandise categories for an identified retail organisation.*

This definition emphasises on certain key aspects:

- Merchandise is being acquired for meeting demand in future, so forward planning is necessary in relation to changing consumption tastes and demand.
- The merchandise required, is to be acquired from either the wholesalers or manufacturers and is to be handled appropriately to ensure that it will be sold in perfect conditions.
- Since the financial aspects of buying merchandise is considered to be an investment decision, it is necessary to monitor all the aspects of the process to ensure that adequate returns are achieved.

Thus, merchandise management requires systematic as well as adherence to the concept of marketing.

CATEGORISING THE BUYING PROCESS

Category is the basic unit of analysis for making merchandising decisions. It would be impossible to work on the buying process without grouping merchandise into various categories. Moreover, the complexity of the organised retail operations makes it mandatory for grouping the buying process into individual categories. This is done so as to ensure that the buyer is able to understand the different market segments.

Meaning of Category

In general, *a category is an assortment of items which the consumer may perceive as substitutes for each other.* If one were to take the example of the apparel industry, it can be categorised into ladies apparel, gents apparel and kids apparel. Each of these categories have some typical (or similar) characteristics. For instance, childrens' uniform are purchased from vendors who are similar to each other. This merchandise is priced and promoted to appeal to a similar target market. And the price promotions are timed for the same period during the year, i.e., school reopening time in June.

Of course, retailers and their vendors may have their own definitions of category. Say, the vendors may assign personal haircare product shampoo with conditioner into different categories based on the significant differences in product attributes. But this product when displayed in a kirana shop might be put under a single category of personal care products based on the buying behaviour of the consumers visiting the store. 'Disinfectants' could be assigned to a 'Disinfectants' category or combined with detergent, soap, broom, moping cloth, etc., in 'Home care products' category.

At retail outlets or departmental stores, merchandise may be categorised in terms of brands such as *Harpic toilet cleaner* or *Sanifresh* or *Food World's liquid disinfectant.* Thus, based on the customers' liking, he/she will purchase the product usually patronised by them. Further, it facilitates the buyer to purchase merchandise when there is coordination in the planning, distribution and promotion of merchandise displayed. Irrespective of how the category is defined, there must be acceptance among supply-chain members on the 'category' definition and it must be based on what is logical to the consumer.

Category Management

Category management is the process by which a retail business is managed with the objective of maximising the sales and profits of a category. This means that retailers will organise their merchandising activities around brands or vendors so as to maximise gain in the form of increased sales and profits. *The category management approach involves having a category manager or buyer to oversee every aspect of the merchandise management.* Thus, the onus of responsibility for managing that one category lies in the hands of the category manager. And the success or failure of a category will ultimately be the responsibility of the category manager. Another benefit of having a category manager will be that the stores assortment of merchandise is represented by the ideal combination of sizes and vendors, which will earn the maximum possible profit from the allocated space.

Retailers are dependent on their vendors for furnishing or sharing with them information about the areas (and customers) serviced by them. Such information and sales data will help the buyers to manage inventories in a better way. At times, the retailer may have a favoured vendor, known as the *category captain,* who forms an alliance with the retailer to gain consumer insight, satisfy consumer needs and improve the performance and profit potential across the entire category.

Morever, the retailer may be having his own system of categorising merchandise. So, it is necessary that we familiarise ourselves with certain terms, which will help to understand in the buying organisation the category fits.

Merchandise Group: There could be a merchandise group comprising of senior managers, who will be responsible for several departments.

Departments: There could be departments managed by divisional merchandise managers, who will be responsible for a department. These divisional merchandise managers will be responsible for a number of buyers or category managers.

Classification: Each buyer purchases a group of items or SKU (Stock Keeping Unit) for the same type of merchandise supplied by different vendors. In some retail organisations, responsibility for buying merchandise is divided between a buyer (or category manager) and a merchandise planner. The planner will be responsible for buying the right quantities of each item, allocating the items to stores, monitoring sales and suggesting markdowns and effectively, they implement the assortment plan developed by the buyer. Thus, both the buyer and planner will be the merchandising team.

A stock keeping unit (SKU) is the smallest unit available for managing the inventory.

SETTING OBJECTIVES FOR MERCHANDISE PLAN

Retailers will have to work on the financial implications of their merchandising activities. Financial plans start at the top of the retail organisation and then are divided into various categories. Whereas, buyers and merchandise planners develop their own plans and negotiate with the organisation. The overall merchandising strategy is worked out by the top management. Table 5.1 gives a comparison between the steps worked out by the top management in deciding the merchandising strategy and how the buyers and merchandise planners work on the merchandising categories.

Table 5.1: Comparison between top management's merchandising strategy and buyers' and merchandise planners' merchandising approach

Top Management's Merchandising Strategy	Buyer's and Merchandise Planners' Merchandising Approach
• Defining the target market.	• Study their categories past performance.
• Establishing performance goals.	• Look at trends in the market.
• Based on general market trends decide which merchandise classifications need more or less emphasis.	• Based on market trends, try to project the assortments for merchandise categories for the coming seasons.

The merchandising plan will be a financial buying blueprint for each category, which takes into consideration the firm's financial objectives along with sales projections and merchandise flows. Once the merchandise plan is ready, the buyers and planners develop the assortment plan.

Phases in Merchandise Planning

In all marketing-led approaches, ultimately it will be the consumer who will dictate the strategy options. This aspect is illustrated in Table 5.2 which talks of the merchandise plan considerations (or steps or phases). The customer is concerned about the assortment profile especially with regards to width and depth, sizes, quality, exclusiveness, availability and cost. Based on the understanding of the expectations, *i.e.,* type of customer base expectations, a particular structure for the buying organisation is worked out. For instance, if exclusivity is required, a selective *sourcing* approach is adopted, for 'quality emphasis', quality control is exercised. Thus, after extensive research on all the alternatives the buyers will be expected to source the plan. The next step involves giving due financial considerations before meeting the company's profit and market consideration prior to acquiring the merchandise stock (Refer to Table 5.2).

Nevertheless, there are two aspects which will impact the merchandise stock.

- ***Availability:*** Availability will be dependent on the need to ensure that the 'right' level of stock is available to meet the demand of the consumer.
- ***Inventory Turnover:*** The inventory turnover requires working out on how long inventory is to be held before it gets sold out. This is because, the store will have to work out on stocking the optimal level of inventory, *i.e.,* neither there should be high turnover nor low turnover of goods.

Table 5.2: The considerations for merchandise plans

Marketing consideration	Store-image, trading format, environment, retail proposition, trends in fashion, potential buyers base.
Merchandise strategy options	Availability of stock based on assortment profile, quality, specific choice, seasonal requirement, estimated cost, promotional agreement.
Type of customer base	Items, range of purchase, time period (season) average transaction value for various products, frequency of visits and purchases.
Financial plans	Projections of profitability and sales, stock taking (investment and return), terms of contract and payment, corporate objectives and pricing strategies.
Merchandise assortment search	Merchandise must meet the following criteria: desired range, cost, price offer, brand policy, be available, delivery, stockholding needs and financial returns

Evaluating Merchandise Plan using GMROI Measure

At the corporate level, return on assets is used to evaluate performance of overall retail operations, using the following formula:

$$\text{Return on Assets} = \frac{\text{Net Profit}}{\text{Net Sales}} \times \frac{\text{Net Sales}}{\text{Total Assets}}$$

$$= \frac{\text{Net Profit}}{\text{Total Assets}}$$

But merchandise managers have control only over the merchandise they buy and manage and buyers have control only over gross margin. And there could be expenses involved with the operation of the stores and the management of the retailer's human resources, locations and systems. Hence, for getting to know the financial ratio which is useful for planning and measuring merchandising performance, the return on investment resource or Gross Margin Return on Inventory Investment or GMROI is considered. GMROI measures how much gross margin rupees are earned on every rupee of inventory investment. GMROI uses gross margin percentage and the sales-to-stock ratio (similar to inventory turnover).

$$\text{GMROI} = \text{Gross Margin percentage} \times \text{Sales-to-stock ratio}$$

$$= \frac{\text{Gross Margin}}{\text{Net Sales}} \times \frac{\text{Net Sales}}{\text{Average Inventory}}$$

$$= \frac{\text{Gross Margin}}{\text{Average Inventory}}$$

The average inventory in GMROI is taken as a cost, because a retailer's investment in inventory will be the cost of the inventory and not its retail value. GMROI combines the effects of both profits and turnover, enabling the retailer to measure, compare and evaluate departments (with different margin/turnover profiles) merchandise classifications, vendor lines and items. Further, because GMROI can be related to the retailer's overall return on investment, it can also be used to evaluate buyers' performance.

Inventory turnover is used to evaluate how effectively managers utilise their investment in inventory.

$$\text{Inventory turnover} = \frac{\text{Net sales}}{\text{Average inventory at retail}}$$

or

$$\text{Inventory turnover} = \frac{\text{Cost of goods sold}}{\text{Average inventory at cost}}$$

Usually retailers express inventory turnover rates on an annual basis rather than for different parts of a year. There are many advantages of a high inventory turnover for the retailer. But too high inventory turnover may put retailers at a disadvantage. Refer to Table 5.3, Which given an overview of the advantages and disadvantages of High Inventory Turoves

Table 5.3: Advantages of 'high' inventory turnover and disadvantages of 'too high' inventory turnover

Advantages of High Inventory Turnover	Disadvantages of too High Inventory Turnover
• A rapid inventory turnover results in fresh merchandise stock being made available for customers, which can lead to increased sales volume.	• Too high inventory turnover may limit the merchandise categories or the number of SKUs within a category. So, if a customer does not find the merchandise sought by them, it could lead to lower sales volume.
• When inventory sells quickly, there is less risk of merchandise becoming obsolete, thus, resulting in lower markdowns and increase in gross margins.	• To achieve rapid turnover buyers may buy smaller quantities of merchandise more often but cannot take advantage of quantity discounts and economies of scale.
• Rapid inventory turnover and fresh merchandise stocks will do a lot to boost the sales staff's morale.	• In spite of having too high inventory, the buyer spends the same time for printing invoices, receive merchandise and pay invoices, thus resulting in increased operating expenses.
• When inventory turnover is high, the money locked up previously in inventory can be used for buying more merchandise.	
• Increase in turnover would result in decreased operating expenses due to lower inventory carrying cost.	

• Inventory being a current asset, if assets decrease and sales remain the same or increases, the asset turnover increases, directly affecting the return on assets, the key performance indicator for top management.	

Thus, the retailer has to take care of the inventory turnover and ensure that it is maintained at an optimal level. Although, rapid inventory turnover is preferrable to a slow turnover, the retailer should exercise care and see that the turnover may not be pushed to the point of diminishing returns.

SALES FORECASTING FOR RETAILING

Sales forecasting is a very important aspect of the merchandising plan and the retailer has to forecast sales in order to decide on how much to buy.

Forecasting Merchandising Based on Category

While developing a sales forecast, the retailer must be able to predict how well product categories will sell over a period of time. Although the product category typically goes through a set pattern of start off (low) increase, plateau and finally decline stages, the pattern shape may vary from category-to- category. While discussing about category life cycles, it will be necessary to note some commonly found variations on it. These are:

Fad: A *fad* is a merchandise category which generates a lot of sales for a short time span, at times even less than a season. Examples are *Pokeman cards, fancy hair clips, certain computer games* or *video games,* etc. Fads are illogical and unpredictable and the retailer must recognise a 'fad' during its early stage, store sufficient stock before competitors replicate and also recognise the 'peak period', and see that the merchandise is sold out before the 'fad' fades out.

Fashion: *Fashion* as a category of merchandise can last for several seasons, with sales varying from one season to another. The life span of fashion depends upon the category type and target market. For instance, wearing of *denim jeans* is a fashion because these are comfortable and can be worn on many occasions (college/office, casual outings, parties, etc.). Today's fashion-conscious youth (females) have a preference for lighter and trendier ornaments which can be used for a variety of occasions.

Staple merchandise (also referred to as basic merchandise)**:** The staple merchandise category are those which have continuous demand over an extended period of time. These are merchandise sold at grocery shops, hosiery wear, men and women's intimate (or inner wear) apparel, etc., which over a period of time can go into decline.

Seasonal merchandise: These are merchandise whose sales fluctuate from season -to- season. For instance, cotton wear (saree and dress materials) sells more in summer, whereas woollen sweaters will sell more in winter. So, retailers will have to plan their merchandise purchases based on seasonal the demand.

The forecasting and inventory management system used for fads, fashion merchandise and staples will be different. Ultimately, it will be the buyer's skill, experience and creativity which will enable the buyer to select quantities for specific SKUs.

Develop a Sales Forecast

The most convenient way of developing a sales forecast will be to adjust the past sales to make projections for the future, especially for fashion merchandise, at the category level. While, for staple merchandise, sales forecasting is done at the SKU level.

The retailer or buyer will have to identify and select various sources of information for forecasting sales at the category level. These include examining the past sales volume (seasonal changes, etc,). make modifications while forecasting based on economic trends or published data (in journals and magazines like *NCAER, AC Nielson India* Shopping Trends, etc.), obtaining market information directly from customers or holding interviews directly with the customers (depth interviews and focus groups), observe trends at competitor's stores or seek information from consultants or organisations which offer several services associated with the procurement of merchandise such as – *Seacom Solutions, Creative Arts, Polaris Retail Infotech Limited (PRIL),* etc.

Forecasting at the Store SKU (Stock Keeping Unit) Level

It is more difficult to forecast and predict sales at SKU levels. This is because while forecasting for SKUs at more aggregate levels, the store level variability gets averaged or summed out of the data. Of course, today Information Technology had enabled the usage of sophisticated systems for store level forecasting which can furnish weekly sales at the store and SKU level. It is also feasible to implement sales forecasting solutions which require massive computational power and are commercially available to retailers.

Collaborative Planning, Forecasting and Replenishment (CPFR) is a software which uses data to construct a computer generated replenishment forecast which is shared by the retailer and vendor before it is executed. CPFR will indicate if there are unusual sales patterns, then with the approval of the retailer and vendor, the computer automatically makes modifications in the merchandise stock to be sent to the stores or distribution centre based on the changes drafted in the forecasting plan.

The CPFR system is framed so as to facilitate easy accessibility by multiple buyers and vendors within the retail chain. With CPFR, it is possible to get a higher GMROI because usage of the sophisticated forecasting and inventory management software can lead to an increase in sales and gross margin and reduction in in-store inventory levels. Further, with a more accurate forecast, the in-store merchandise availability increases, resulting in fewer out-of-stock situations. Since CPFR is internet based, the data is more economical and easily accessible by both big and large retailers.

DETERMINING THE ASSORTMENT PLANNING PROCESS

A very fundamental strategic question faced by each retailer is deciding on what merchandise assortment is to be carried out so as to achieve competitive advantage. It will be the trade-off between *variety, assortment* and *product availability* which will help to determine the merchandising strategy. But first we will try to understand the meaning of these key terms.

- ***Variety:*** Variety refers to the number of different categories of merchandise within a store or department.
- ***Assortment:*** Assortment refers to the number of SKUs within a category.
- ***Product Availability:*** Product availability refers to the percentage of demand for a particular SKU which is satisfied.

The retailer works out on the trade-off between variety, assortment and product availability depending upon the particular marketing strategy. Usually the retailer will workout a retail strategy keeping in mind the following aspects:

(*a*) The particular target market towards which they are commiting their resources.

(*b*) The type of retail offering which the retailer plans to use in order to meet the target market's needs.

(*c*) The bases upon which the retailer will attempt to build-up competitive advantage.

While working out the variety, assortment and product availability, certain factors have to be considered.

Table 5.4: Factors affecting variety, assortment and product availability

Factors Affecting Variety and Assortment	Factors Affecting Product Availability
1. Work at profitable mix of products. 2. Corporate strategy towards assortment. 3. Physical characteristics and layout of the store and internet site. 4. Workout a balance between too much versus too little assortment. 5. Assortment based on complementary merchandise.	1. Workout for a trade-off between inventory investment and product availability. 2. Plan sufficient back-up of stock to meet each SKU's stock demand. This will depend upon: • Product availability the retailer wishes to provide. • The fluctuations in demand. • Lead time from the vendor. • Fluctuations in lead time. • The vendor's product availability also affects the retailer's back-up stock.

Table 5.4 gives a brief view on the factors affecting the retail strategy decision. The retailer will have to focus on those factors which affect the variety, assortment and product availability in assortment planning process. While trying to determine the variety and assortment for various category

of merchandise, the buyer will try to identify the profitability of the merchandise mix and invest in products and space accordingly. The corporate stand and strategy will enable the buyer to determine on how to store the portfolio and category of merchandise stock. The retailer will have to consider the amount of space which will be required to properly display and store the merchandise, design attractive websites so that customers can navigate through them, stock and display merchandise which are complementary to each other and work a balance between too much and too little assortment. Similarly, while working at the product availability, the retailer must plan the inventory such that he is able to meet the demand in time with sufficient base stock and buffer stock and also keeping in mind the likely fluctuations in lead time.

Once the planning of GMROI, inventory turnover, sales forecast and assortment planning is done with, the assortment plan giving a general outline of what is to be carried in a particular merchandise category is to be worked out by the retailer.

'Weekender' displays a large variety of complementary merchandise at their outlets

Box 5.1. JDA Systems for Effective Merchandise Management

There are certain systems used by retailers worldwide to streamline various processes, which are briefly touched upon hereunder:

- **Merchandise Management System:** Over 350 retailers worldwide have licensed Merchandise Management System (MMS). The retail host system for the IBM i Series environment. This system gathers, integrates and distributes data throughout the organisation to support the core inventory control, cost and price management, purchase order management, automated replenishment and allocation of products.
- **Arthur Merchandise Planning System:** This system work on end-to-end merchandising cycle from planning and purchasing to delivering to front end, by providing accurate visibility into the warehouse.

- **Warehouse Replenishment (Auto Purchase Order):** This enables merchandisers/buyers to forecast demand and order projections in the standard order pattern.
- **Store Replenishment (Auto Transfer):** This system centralises store level replenishment with Advanced Store Replenishment by JDA-MMS (Store Replenishment) to provide a versatile forecasting method at a SKU/store by SKU/store basis and thus manage SKU/store combinations.

(***Source***: *Retail Biz*, May 2004, pp. 18-19.)

Range Planning

A retailer's stock range is described in terms of its *width* and *depth*, sometimes referred to as assortment whose range is determined by the company policy. The 'width' is with reference to the number of categories found in the merchandise line and different generic classes of product or merchandise carried. The 'depth' refers to the sizes, colours and prices within a particular generic class of product. Every retailer will seek to offer a respective range of stock, which will be an integral part of their strategy. Specialist stores, say the *HMT* watches showroom will offer a lot of depth but with a narrow product range. At the supermarket, profitability will come from offering an extensive range of product-lines, some with a comparatively slow rates of stock turn, but with a healthy profit margin. In case of departmental stores, the customer will be offered more product-lines and more variety than at a *Bata's* shop selling quality footwear. The customers' perception of added value will be guided by the extent of the range offered by the store. Profitability will be achieved by having a high rate of stock turn as well as keeping costs at a minimum. Take for instance in case of hard discounters like *'Big Bazaar'*, the offer is extremely competitively priced – which is a key concern of the target customer. Further, the product-line proliferation is that what the customers expect of this discount strategy and this would also have its impact on stock turn and costs.

In case of toys and apparel, the merchandiser has to, on the one hand meet customers' expectations and at the same time maintain stocks against an anticipated rise in demand, without wasting resources. This is a challenging job for the merchandiser, i.e., to do range planning because in case of products such as toys and apparel, the annual turnover is concentrated in a few weeks of the year. This will have implications for supply-chain management with limitations on distribution networks capacity. Because during 'peak' periods, there will be excess physical demand to carryout the warehousing, transportation and staff (personnel) functions to facilitate merchandise handling functions.

Another trend which is visible is the type of range planning to be carried out by multiple chain retailers such as the *Food world,* is to become *'Category retailers'*, *i.e.,* to meet all of the customers needs within a particular category merchandise. Such large 'category' stores concentrate on one category, thus making it possible to display a broad assortment and good selection of merchandise, offered at lower prices with moderate service.

While at developing the range planning and allocation of merchandise, the retailer(s) have to undertake the following:

- Develop a keen understanding of the selection process undertaken by the consumers.
- Take decisions on the core and seasonal merchandise to be stocked.

'UPS' promises to provide efficient supply-chain benefits to its customers' needs.

- Agree on the range planning, *i.e.,* style, size and colour mix – depth and width.
- After considering the sales to stock level targets, use one of the stock inventory planning methods to arrive at the optimum level of stock.
- Relating the range plans to individual stores and workout the possible promotional plans.
- Informing the buyer(s) on agreed source.

Ultimately, the retailer must understand that range planning needs are customer driven. They can start with identifying the product attributes most important to the customer and then workout the depth and width assortment profiles, keeping in mind the estimated sales and profit performance. Range planning is also referred to as merchandise assortment planning and as mentioned earlier can also be worked out at each category level up to the SKU level. This means that it will be possible to identify problems in sales or inventory holding at any level and modify or rectify the actions accordingly.

Planogram

A graphical range assortment plan is called the planogram. Planogram facilitates display of the range in a visual way with digitally stored images manipulated into collage-type storyboards. These are space planning software packages (AC Nielsen Support) which help in graphic base stock mapping, resulting in easy replenishment planning and effective store utilisation.

Table 5.5: Loopholes and benefits of proper Assortment Planning

Existing Loopholes in Current Assortment Planning	Benefits of Proper Assortment Planning
• Retailers use different kinds of range planning systems – partly range planning and partly financial planning for the entire planning activity. • Existing assortment planning tools are helpful at the macrolevel,but micro levely merchandising is still carried out using user intelligence, thus making companies highly vulnerable. • Due to high volume and all consuming business requirements, proper planning is often ignored.	• Better assortment width helps in positioning the store giving consumers the chance to identify themselves with 'their' store and leverage the benefit of loyalty. • Timely assortment planning helps in streamlining the process of ordering and distribution planning and also to manage lead time. • Better assortment planning results in specific products to cater to the needs of specific customers, resulting in lesser dead stocks and better return on stocks. This serves to reduce the requirement of markdowns to push up the merchandise. • Properly planned assortment will result in lower development costs and better consistency in brand range.

Although most retailers use assortment planning methodology which vary on many aspects there are certain general parameters which act as loopholes in the approach. At the same time assortment planning is a key differentiator in today's progressive retail organisations, having many benefits. Both these aspects have been shown in Table 5.5.

Mayank Jain, Retail Domain Business Analyst, Infosys Technologies, gives his view on assortment planning strategies for the retail industry in Box 5.2.

Box 5.2 Assorted Solutions

Changing consumer attitudes and buying behaviour have forced retailers in the apparel industry to rethink the manner in which business is done. The highly demanding consumer has compelled retailers to have a large product range, which, in turn, leads to a rise in inventory holdings. High lead times, seasonality, evolving consumer tastes and size are some issues that create stiff competition in the marketplace, making discounting an inevitable option. In such a scenario, it becomes tough for retailers to thrive profitably. To add to the complexity, a seamless supply-chain is a long way off, leading to a very high concept to shelf-time. With these levels of complexity, proper planning and execution of the available assortment becomes inevitable for better capital productivity.

Market Modifications

Consumer attitudes in India are changing and the shopper base for core products such as apparel for men and women is shrinking. In contrast, the consumer base for products that fall under smaller categories, such as youth clothing and tennis footwear, is expanding. Consumers are certainly positively predisposed towards apparel, clothing and footwear, but an absence of the desired product mix encourages them to shift loyalties.

A major culprit here is the lack of synchronisation between product availability and the consumer's buying cycle. Shoppers are usually pressed for time and desire value from their purchases. As a consequence, most shoppers know exactly what they want when they walk into a store and impulsive purchases are declining. In such a scenario, it becomes increasingly important to arrive at the proper product mix by seamlessly integrating assortment planning, buying, production and design. A closer look reveals that assortment planning is the solution to the problem.

Planned Success

Assortment planning in the fashion industry includes decisions on the kind of products, their quantity, colours and sizes, and their target audience. Though this directly affects product selection, price, timing and micro merchandising, it has traditionally been de-emphasised due to hectic retail schedules and lack of best practices. Managing delivery and meeting marketing and financial obligations consumes valuable time. This forces organisations to take the easy way out: repeating assortment breadth and depth from previous seasons, creating store assortments based on store volume, and ranking items primarily by sales volume.

Decisions and Considerations

Key decisions	Key considerations				
What	Consumer profile	Store image	Past sales	Sales trend	Fashion forecast
How much	Sales trend	Budgets/ targets	Open to buy quantity	Economic order	Projected sales
From where	Flexibility	Vendor capacity	Quality	Lead time	Economic order quantity
When	Lead time	Projected sales	Fashion change	Cost advantage	Inventory holdings

The above list is merely indicative but it underlines the complexity of assortment planning. Retailers who are able to channelise merchandise appropriately can reduce their inventory-carrying costs and also improve margins. Customers who are pressed for time are unlikely to look any further if the assortment offered fulfils their needs. Such an assortment aids retailers in reducing the impact of price-driven buying and also in maintaining sound customer relations.

To attract consumers in today's increasingly competitive market, assortment planning must focus on creating appropriate product dimensions based on the consumer's desires and shopping patterns. In the case of apparel, the business becomes more complex as appropriate assortment planning must take into account not just lifestyles, climates and trends, but also the change in lifestyles and shopping habits. Furthermore, assortment planning must present a compelling mix of products to illustrate the company's strategic vision.

Source: *Retail Biz*, June 2004, pp. 34-37.

BUYING SYSTEMS

Assortment planning helps the retailer to workout a general outline on what types of merchandise should be carried. Whereas, buying systems will help the buyers and merchandise planners to decide on how much to buy. Generally, retailers use two distinct types of buying systems:

(a) A staple merchandise buying systems for basics.

(b) A merchandise budget for fashion merchandise.

Staple merchandise buying systems are used for merchandise which follow a typical (or predictable) order-receipt-order-cycle. This buying system uses past history for each staple SKU to forecast demand and sales at the category level. Most of the merchandise found in food and discount stores in addition to some categories in speciality and departmental stores like underwear, socks, etc., fits this criterion.

The retailer must use the 'Inventory Management Report' containing information on sales velocity, inventory availability, amount of order, inventory turnover, sales forecast and the quantity to order for each SKU to carryout buying functions. This is because staple merchandise buying systems comprise of a number of computer program modules to help the buyer and merchandiser to determine how much to order and when. Mainly, these systems enable buyers to carryout three functions:

- At the SKU level, monitor and measure the average current demand.
- Forecast the future SKU demand with making adjustments for seasonal fluctuations and changes in trend.
- Workout ordering decision rules for optimum restocking.

Merchandise Budget Plan for Fashion Merchandise

The merchandise budget plan helps to workout the inventory investment in a category over a period of time. It cannot be referred to as a complete buying plan because it does not indicate the quantities or the specific assortment to buy. The plan merely specifies how much money is to be spent each month to achieve sales and turnover and also the GMROI objectives.

The merchandise plan helps to coordinate the supply and demand for merchandise as well as to ensure that the financial goals are achieved. Further, the plan coordinates the activities of buyers of merchandise for different categories, so as to ensure that there is a balance and avoid situations where there is too much merchandise in some categories and not enough in others. Of course, the actual sales may differ from the sales forecasted in the merchandise budget plan. For working out the merchandise budget plan, the buyer will have to examine the monthly sales expected as a percentage of the total sales, the factors which could reduce the inventory level (due to markdown, shrinkages, discount to employees, etc.), the stock-to-sales ratio at the BoM (Beginning of Month) and the GMROI. Thus, for the buyer, the GMROI, inventory turnover and the sales forecast can be used for planning and control. Based on the above inputs, the buyer will plan to purchase the merchandise for the various category levels. As discussed earlier in the chapter, fashion products can have seasonal fluctuations in demand. So, after the selling season, the buyer can understand how the category actually performed when compared to the plan for control purposes.

OPEN-TO-BUY (OTB) SYSTEM

Open-to-buy (OTB) helps retailers to project and control future buying so that the flow of merchandise in the store synchronises with the expected or anticipated sales at a desirable stock turn rate, which will ensure a positive cash flow. Organised retailers prefer to follow the OTB planning so as to eliminate over buying or under stocking, reduce confusion and help the organisation to make more profits.

OTB system provides the buyer with a plan for purchasing merchandise after using the merchandise budget plan or staple merchandise system. That is, it keeps track of merchandise flows, as they are occurring. This system keeps a record of how much is spent each month and thus how much is left to spend. Specifically put, OTB is a planning tool to assist in setting budgets for sales and merchandise inventory levels and monitor the existing (or current) status of the OTB amount. This will workout to be the amount remaining to be ordered to meet the budget.

There is a tendency among retailers to overstock when sales increase and understock when they are low. But with the help of an OTB system, the retailer can workout the ideal amount of stock to be kept on hand at the beginning of any given month and the amount of new merchandise to be received during the month.

An efficient OTB plan must contain the following elements: Sales Forecast, Advance (or Forward) stock cover, the stock requirement, Opening Stock, Actual intake requirement; (difference between required opening stock), stocks on order, stock open to receive (deducting stock on order from the intake requirement), and closing stock. Benefits of OTB are given in Figure 5.1.

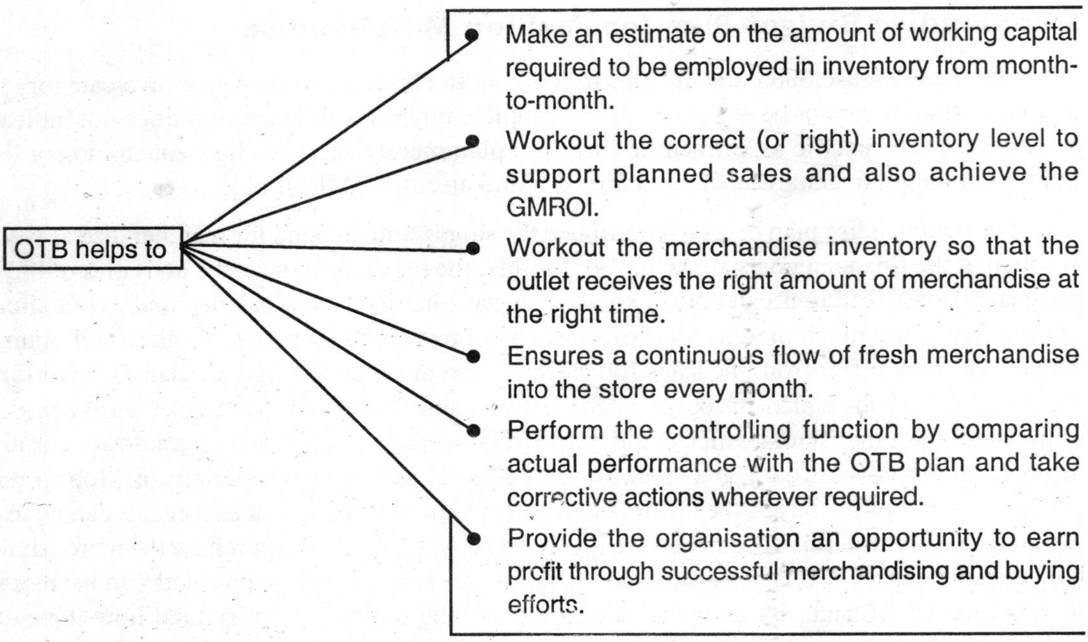

Figure 5.1: Benefits of an efficient OTB plan

After the merchandise is purchased, the merchandise buyers of multiple chain of stores have to look into the differences in the sales potential of various stores as well as the characteristics of the customer base and then allocate merchandise to various stores.

Handling Out of Merchandise Situations and Evaluating Merchandise Performance

At times lack of proper merchandise planning could result in out-of-stock situations. This could be because the distribution channels are multilayered and unorganised and by the time the product reaches the hands of the customers, it must have passed through as many as 3-4 intermediaries. Further, the supply-chain aggregates the inefficiencies of poor demand forecasting techniques, lack of proper communication between intermediaries and certain specific issues intrinsic to the concerned sectors as shown in Table 5.6.

Table 5.6: Specific issues affecting supply-chain inefficiencies and inventory levels.

Sectors		
Manufacturers	**Distributors and Superstockists**	**Retailers**
• Dependent on remote manufacturing locations. • Emptying the merchandise stock in the pipeline much before all mega promotions and launches. • Providing only limited stocks to the other intermediaries. • Poor or bad demand forecasting methods used. • Infrequent production runs for limited time periods.	• Delay in delivering stock to retail distribution point by the vendor. • Inadequate working capital forcing distributors to maintain lesser than demand stocks. • Stocking errors resulting in stockout situations. • Under pressure from manufacturer's sales staff to carry more of unproductive stocks.	• Usage of improper or poor demand forecasting methods. • Bad relationships with vendors leading to poor service from them. • Logistic errors at the distribution centres of chain stores. • Tendency of retailers to push higher margin brands and understock lower margin brands. • Poor assortment planning process at stores level.

Retailers have a tendency to keep a higher safety stock to avoid supply inefficiencies which could lead to higher working capital requirements. To avoid all such problems retailers are integrating the entire supply-chain. In India also many large retailers have moved in the direction of direct supply-chains to end retailers thereby eliminating a lot of channel and middlemen inefficiencies. For instance, the setting up of organised wholesale cash and carry formats like *Metro Cash and Carry* enables retailers to directly source their requirements from a single source. This not only eases logistical compulsions but also streamlines the entire supply-chain process.

As a part of merchandise planning process, retailers use various procedures for analysing merchandise performance. These procedures could be *ABC Analysis* which can be done at any level of merchandise classification (from SKU to department) to determine which items should never be out of stock, those items which could be occasionally allowed to be out of stock and those items which should be deleted from stock selection. Thus, merchandise is rank-ordered from highest to lowest and the buyer uses this information to workout a inventory management policy.

The *Sell through Analysis* is a comparison between actual and planned sales to decide whether early markdowns are required or if more merchandise is required to satisfy demand. Thus, this method is more useful for examining the performance of individual SKUs. The *Multi-attribute Method* evaluates vendors using a weighted average score, worked out on the basis of the importance of various issues and the vendor's performance on those issues.

SUMMARY

Merchandise management is the planning and implementation of the acquisition, handling and monitoring of merchandise categories for an identified retail organisation. Category is an assortment of merchandise items which the consumer may perceive as substitutes for each other and use it for categorising merchandise. Category management involves having a category manager or buyer to oversee every aspect of the merchandise management. While setting objectives for merchandising – certain marketing considerations such as – merchandise strategy options, type of customer base, financial plans and merchandise assortment search have to be looked into. Merchandise plan can be evaluated by using GMROI (Gross Margin Return on Inventory) which measures how much gross margin rupees are earned on every rupee of inventory investment. Retailers have to do sales forecasting of the merchandise to be bought depending on which category the item falls into, *i.e.*, fad, fashion, staple merchandise or seasonal merchandise and also at the store keeping unit (SKU) level. Collaborative planning, forecasting and replenishment (CPFR) is a computer software generated replenishment forecast to be shared by the retailer and vendor before it is executed.

Merchandise assortment planning process is to be carried out by each retailer to earn competitive advantage. This requires to determine a trade-off between variety, assortment and product availability. Apart from range planning, *i.e.*, merchandise assortment planning, planogram a graphical range plan using software packages is being used to facilitate easy replenishment planning and effective store space utilisation. Buying system (both staple merchandise and fashion merchandise) helps the merchandise planner to determine how much of the merchandise items is to be bought. The OTB (Open-to-buy) system helps retailers to project and control future buying so that the flow of merchandise in the store matches the anticipated sales at a desirable stockturn rate along with a positive cash flow.

CHAPTER QUESTIONS FOR DISCUSSION

1. Suppose you have joined a newly opened retail outlet dealing in 'Fashion' and 'Fad' items. What type of merchandising plan would you workout to manage the above merchandise?
2. Define Merchandise Management. What is the role of category management while taking merchandising decisions?
3. Write a short note on the strategic decisions involved in the 'Assortment Planning Process'.
4. Briefly explain the role of 'Buying Systems' in merchandise planning.

ACTIVITY

Meet the store manager of an outlet selling Western apparel for women in Hyderabad (say Allen Solly) and find out how do they plan merchandise for their target customers young, contemporary and fashionable women).

❑❑❑

6 RETAIL PRICING

LEARNING OBJECTIVES

After going through the chapter, you should be able to understand:

- The role of pricing in retail market
- Factors affecting retail pricing
- Pricing strategies and approaches
- How consumers respond to prices

STRUCTURE:

- Introduction
- Meaning of Price and Its Role in the Retail Market
- Factors Affecting Retail Pricing
- Pricing Strategies and Approaches
- How Consumers Respond to Prices
- Summary
- Chapter Questions for Discussion
- Activity

INTRODUCTION

Pricing is a very important issue in retailing. Pricing decision by retailers is a very sensitive as well as a hard one to make. This is because prices for retail products and services have to be determined taking into consideration the seasonality of demand and the likely perishability of the product due to a change in fashion or due to the expiry date. Setting of the right price by the retailer can influence the quantity of goods or services purchased by the consumers, which is turn will be reflected in the total revenue and profit earned by the retail store. Moreover, for the retailer, without adequate margins, his business will not survive for long. He is able to maintain his market position only by ensuring the right cash flow, profitability and growth. So, the retailer has to follow the right strategy by offering quality, selection and availability of products and services at competitive prices. Whereas, for the consumer the right price will be 'that' which she is willing to pay for the products and services purchased. So, the retailer has to take sound pricing decisions since it is a very sensitive issue.

In this chapter, we will have a look at the factors influencing retail pricing and try to understand the various approaches and (pricing) strategies. While working out the retail prices, it will be necessary to look into the likely impact of the various prices on the customers' purchase behaviour. The chapter concludes with discussions on consumers response to prices.

MEANING OF PRICE AND ITS ROLE IN THE RETAIL MARKET

A simple definition of price says *"Price is the monetary value assigned by the seller to something purchased, sold or offered for sale, and on transaction by buyer's, as their willingness to pay for the benefits the product and channel service delivers"*.

The definition indicates how the retailer considers pricing – as a cash flow or income generating function from the view of the customer who views price more than 'money'. For the customer, the 'price value' is a complex set of perceptions. Moreover, the purchase will include the complex, emotional and functional benefits derived from the product and the brand. Consumers have convinced retailers to adopt pricing policies which offer greater value for money. Thus, retailers are forced to price their products and channel services taking into account the complexity created by the seasonality of demand, the inherent perishability of the product due to factors such as – fashion, beyond the sell by date, etc., the firm's overall objectives and reputation of the business.

Retailers have realised the growing importance of pricing decisions today, with customers looking for *good value* (the relationship of what the customer receives against what he/she has to pay for it), when they purchase goods and services. To some customers, a good value means getting merchandise at a low price. While there are others who don't mind paying extra or more as long as they feel they are getting their money's worth in terms of product quality or service.

Retailers have responded suitably, keeping in mind the role of pricing in the growth and expansion of the business. The long-term pricing objectives may include the number of sales periods, the range of prices and total number of products to be made available and the positioning of the store and merchandise in relation to price. Such pricing goals will *convey an image of the retail outlet* to the consumer, which will be indicative of its approach to pricing. Further, pricing has to be integrated with the other aspects of marketing mix after taking into account the target market. For instance, Pantaloon Retail (India) announced about the launch of the country's biggest *Food Bazaar* outlet in Mumbai, spread over an area of 20,000 square feet, air-conditioned store to provide consumers with new levels of standard in convenience and comfort, quality and quantity and store service levels. Thus, consumers at Food Bazaar were to experience new offerings like fresh food, ready-to-cook and take-away food, *i.e.,* all the cooking needs of today's housewife were being made available under a single roof. For the consumer, since household items are available at wholesale prices at this outlet along with saving time, it also helped the busy housemaker to shop in a clear and comfortable environment at value-for-money prices.

Trent, which owns and operates the Westside chain of departmental stores had announced the launch of its hypermarket chain, 'Star India Bazar', in Ahmedabad. The company was looking forward to presenting its budget conscious household customers a wide variety of products and great saving opportunities through the Star India Bazar hypermarket. The large assortment of products included staple foods, beverages, health and beauty products, vegetables, fruits, dairy products, household items, garments and consumer electronics all being made available under a single roof.

Pantaloon Retail India's *Big Bazaar* invites the budget conscious customers to shop at their outlet.

FACTORS AFFECTING RETAIL PRICING

There are several factors which can influence retail pricing, and they are listed below:

- ***Perception of Substitutes Effect:*** Buyers have the tendency to compare the product with its substitute, especially in case of high priced products. They may select a substitute or even forgo purchasing the product if they believe the overall value is unacceptable.

- ***The Unique Value Effect:*** Buyers will be less sensitive to the product's price, the more they consider its value to be unique and differentiating from competing products. For instance, customers are loyal to *Hindustan Lever's* (HLL) or *Procter & Gamble's* (P&G) products because they are perceived to be offering better and superior products with the unique value effect.

- ***Difficult to Compare Alternatives:*** Consumers show less sensitivity to the price of the product when they find it more difficult to compare alternatives. This can even lead to an increase in demand of more established brands, greater store loyalty so as to reduce the perception of risk.

- ***The Price Quality Effect:*** A higher price may indicate that the product is of a superior quality. One of the consequences of this may be that customers may be less sensitive to prices. For instance, increase in price of *Reebok* sports footwear may signal improved quality but not many customers would accept increase in price of *Speed* (petrol) to indicate a quality advantage over other competing 'petrol brands'.

Effect on Expenditure: Customers are more price sensitive (especially in budget conscious households), when the expenditure is quite huge in absolute terms or forms a big percentage of their household income. In such cases, the household expenditure is carefully controlled.

Perceived Fairness Effect: Buyers are more price sensitive if they perceive the price of products to be beyond what is considered to be 'reasonable and fair'. In case of household products such as disinfectants, bedspreads, toothpaste, soap, etc., it will be relatively easier for the customer to compare the offers among alternative brands and switchover to cheaper alternatives. Since price is associated with both the 'quality and status' aspects by customers, retailers will have to understand the way in which perceived price changes can affect the customer's demand pattern.

- ***Other Factors Influencing Retail Pricing:*** There are several other factors which can affect the retailer's pricing policy. These aspects include:
  - The perishable or durable nature of the product (say fashionable products or some 'sell by date' items).
  - The level of competition in the industry can influence the retailer's pricing decisions.
  - *Volatility of the Market:* At times forward planning may be required when there are short run fluctuations in international costs, the need to stock salable items, to take care of shortages in supply or shrinkage rates and so on.

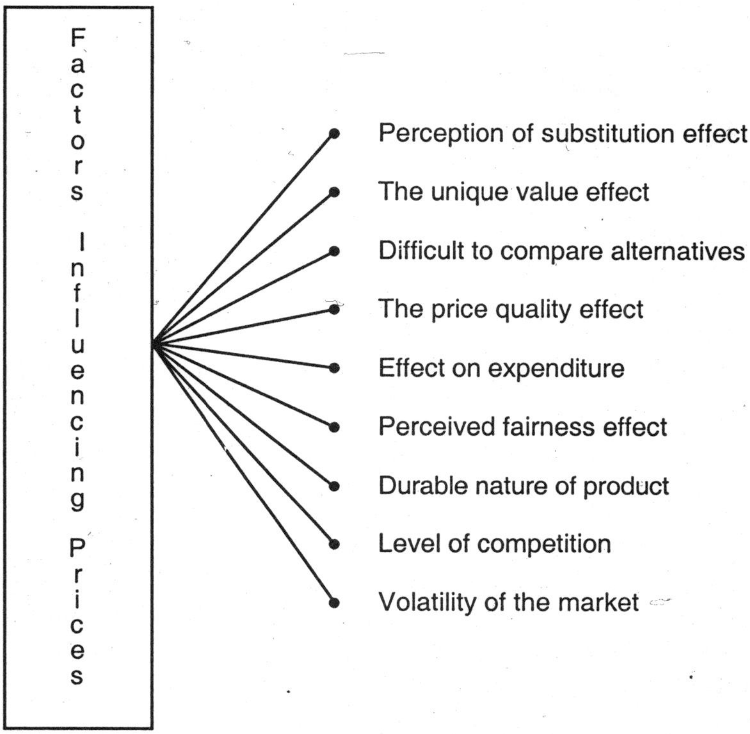

Figure 6.1: Factors affecting retailer's pricing decisions

The customers' choice of products based on retailer's pricing decisions is quite a complex issue because many issues can affect the consumers' choice process. This is probably because on the one hand price may be an indicator of quality but on the other hand a whole lot of issues such as — company reputation for branded products, after-sales service guarantees (especially for higher priced products), number of competing brands, urgentness of the situation, etc., can all influence the consumers' choice of the brand or product and store to shop.

PRICING STRATEGIES AND APPROACHES

The retailer has to workout the pricing policy after considering the potential influences and factors which affect the market. Since the ultimate aim of the retailer is to earn long-term profit, he gives due consideration to the following:

- *Cost*
- *Demand*
- *Competitors moves*

In this section, only two approaches have been discussed for working out the pricing policy-decisions. They are *cost-oriented* and *demand-oriented* approaches to pricing.

Cost-oriented Pricing Approach

Cost-oriented pricing refers to setting prices based on the costs incurred by the retailer while purchasing a product or service for sale to its customers. This could take the form of:

- ***Cost-plus-pricing:*** Cost-plus-pricing method will be in relation to either marginal costs or total costs including overheads. This approach can be used for selecting the target market, ascertaining the costs of the goods in the store (storage costs, overheads, selling costs, estimate of shrinkages, etc.), determining the maximum ceiling price when compared to competitors and determining the initial mark-up from maintained mark-up and gross margin.

Where,

Initial mark-up is the difference between the retail selling price initially placed on the merchandise and the cost of goods sold.

Maintained mark-up is the difference between the amount obtained from actual sales of the merchandise and the cost of goods sold.

Gross Margin is net sales minus cost of goods sold.

The *benefit* of cost based pricing is that the retailer (or marketer) is able to know the net effect of any tactical price reduction once he has information on the cost break down of the product and the operating cost of each retail outlet.

The *weakness* of the cost based pricing method is that it does not give due consideration to:

- The demand for the product.
- The prices the marketplace will bear.
- The price levels offered by the competitors.
- Not appropriate for retail products which have to survive in a highly competitive environment.

- ***Rate of Return Pricing*:** The rate of return pricing method is also a cost-oriented method which provides the organisation with an agreed rate of return on its investment. This method, unlike the cost-plus method which focuses on the costs associated with running the business, concentrates on the profits generated in relation to the money (or capital) invested.

The drawbacks of the rate of return method are:

- This method does not consider the link between pricing policy to produce a sales volume which will cover overheads or make certain that the demand remains consistent or steady over a period of time.
- This method may not be suitable for retailers whose products have to survive in a highly competitive marketplace.

Demand-oriented Pricing Approaches

Demand-oriented pricing tries to work at determining prices which maximises profit. This method considers the factors of demand which could have an effect on the price changes as well as the sales of the products, when setting prices. *Long back Air Deccan* (now Kingfisher Red) had used demand based pricing method.

Discrimination Pricing

Discrimination pricing is also referred to as *variable* or *flexible pricing* and is used when products or services are sold at more than one price. Students and senior citizens are offered railway fares and airfares at lower prices when compared to other customers. Or say a customer known to a retailer may be given a special or personal discount on a flexible pricing approach basis due to the personal relationship the retailer may have with the individual. Discrimination pricing is often time related, for instant discount on house-hold products and clothes are offered to happy customers during festivals such as – Diwali, Christmas, New Year and so on. In order to ensure that price discrimination succeeds, it is necessary for organisations to identify those customer segments who in the absense of the price differentials would not buy the product. For example, the 'Post Office' scheme for 'Senior Citizens of India', offering 9% rate of interest has motivated many seniors to invest in this scheme. Discrimination may also be based on raising the price of products which have more demand. So, the retailer may offer different prices to different people depending upon the nature of the offering and competition.

Backward Pricing

This method of pricing is market-based and focuses on what the consumer is ready to pay. As the term suggests, the price is worked backwards, *i.e.,* to start with, an acceptable margin is agreed upon. Then costs are closely monitored so as to match with the price that is considered to be acceptable. If required adjustments can be made to the quality of the product or service offer in order to suit the cost led needs of this technique. Retailers who adopt this method of selling on a price led basis insist on their suppliers to meet certain specified costs, even if this may result in a compromise on the quality front.

Price lining can be associated with this approach. It simplifies the procedure for merchandise comparison for the customer by fixing a number of price lines within each classification. Retailers will then purchase goods which gets into each line. The retailer, in order to communicate a value difference to the consumer, should provide for a substantial monetary difference between the price lines. The price lines are selected based on the strength of consumer demand. The benefits of price lining include:

- Increase in sales volume by providing for large assortment at each price line.
- More clarity among salespersons who can offer and convince customers to go for various price offers.
- Improved buying process as buyers have to focus on the retail price point and 'buy backwards'.
- Improved – pricing – effectiveness with less markdowns and displays and promotional programmes.
- Facilitates control with more price coordination and lesser pricing variables.

Competitive pricing promotion adhered to by Indian Airlines (now Air India).

Skimming Pricing

Skimming pricing method is adhered to when there is a shortage of supply of the product or the product (or brand) is associated with exclusive value and hence the customer wouldn't mind paying a premium price for the same. For instance, a consumer buying a traditional piece of jewellery for a wedding, festivals or any other special occasion might want to indulge in an exclusive piece and may be willing to pay a premium price. Retailers selling high value lifestyle accessories, premium jewellery, watches, top fashion houses dealing in high fashion, cosmetic companies with strong brand names use the skimming approach of pricing.

Leader Pricing

At times retail products may be priced competitively such that it may result in loss on those products but may generate more overall demand for other items. The leader items are sold near to cost rather than at a loss. The retail outlets may sell 'sweets' or bulbs as loss leaders during the cristmas festival in order to achieve more sales of other related purchases. The reasons behind the use of leader prices is to increase retail store visits, more purchases and the perception of good value. The main reason for selecting leader pricing is to price the product low enough to attract numerous buyers.

This approach is very often used by supermarkets such as *Big Bazaar*, *Giant,* etc., which feature leader items on a regular basis. The limitations of this approach is that retailers have to monitor the usefulness of this price promotion because customers may be selective in what they purchase. This is because customers may restrict their purchases to items which offer lead prices. So, retailers have to workout lead prices after ascertaining whether it may compete with other items. Box 6.1 highlights what *Big Bazaar* and *Giant* had done to become discount retailers.

Competitives Pricing: This approach is employed to match the competitors pricing methods. While adopting a competitive pricing approach, the organisation as well as the retailer needs to have knowledge of actual costs as well as an understanding of the importance of the pricing policies of competition from the buyer's perspective too. Competitive pricing approach is more a reactive form of pricing rather than a proactive form.

Market Penetration Pricing

Market penetration pricing is adopted when the firm or brand wants to penetrate the market or establish itself quickly in a market. Under this approach, prices are set below competitors' prices so as to create a high initial acceptance of the organisation's or retailer's offer.

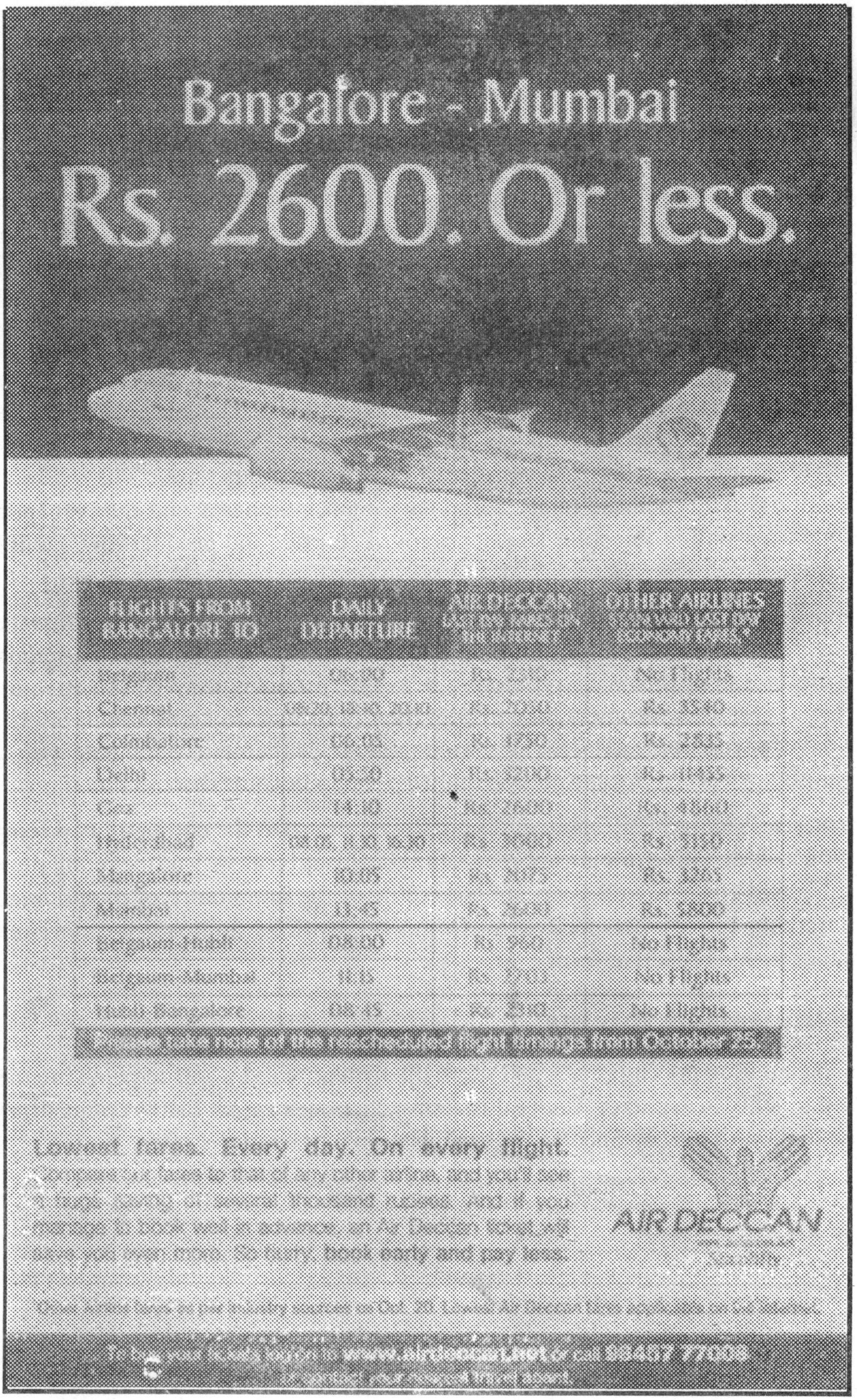

Long back Air Deccan (now Kingfisher Red) had adopted the market penetration pricing.

Box 6.1. Discount Retail

• The secret to the discount format is sourcing. While in most international discounting formats the merchandise categories are quite stable; it is the way in which the retailer sources these that make the difference. At *Big Bazaar* the promotors clearly realised that they did not have product expertise in all the merchandise categories that they offered. "We plan to offer an apparel store, a footwear store, a utensil store, a photo shop, a tailor, a pharmacy, a grocery – all under one roof, at discount prices," says Kishore Biyani, MD, *Pantaloon Retails.*

So, the company adopted a 'consolidator' concept. It has chosen partners who are major national players in these categories and thus have the capacity to buy in bulk. These players are given space in the store, with a clear understanding that they have to provide the best deal in town. In some cases the store has tied up with regional players like 'Shop-n-save' and 'Vitan' in Hyderabad and Bangalore to run the grocery section.

The terms tend to be favourable to both parties. There are no rentals, electricity and air-conditioning charges for the consolidator, leading to a faster break even. The margins are shared by *Big Bazaar* and the consolidator in a predetermined ratio. In categories like pharmacy and FMCG where discounting is not possible, its cross subsidised by other categories.

• ***Giant,*** the hypermarket opened by the RPG group operates differently. The store has a distinct focus: groceries. RPG operates a successful supermarket chain, *Food world*, which has developed a sourcing and merchandising model. *Giant* piggybacks on this back-end infrastructure and since it is able to provide much higher volumes to the manufacturers it is able to get better deals, which it passes on the customers.

The two chains have different pricing models. Giant works on step-up discounts: higher discounts on larger purchases. "Our aim is to make people buy more and have higher stock turns. So, we see to it that the kilo-to-kilo price of a 25 kg rice bag is lower than that of a 10 kg rice bag", says Raghu Pillai President and CEO, Retail sector, RPG Enterprises. In each category, the company has a killer SKU (Stock Keeping Unit), priced at a substantial discount but on the whole it maintains base prices lower than market price.

(***Source:*** *The Economic Times*, 12 December, 2004.)

• ***Psychological Pricing:*** This is an odd pricing policy. Retailers may price products below a round figure to communicate a perception of the price being low enough for the customer to buy the same. For instance, the retailer may offer OTG oven at ₹ 1,990 to woo customers who may perceive the price as less and are willing to purchase it. Nevertheless, there is no conclusive evidence to indicate that such pricing policies may make a significant impact on profits.

Everyday Low Pricing (EDLP)

Many retailers are using the everyday low pricing (EDLP) strategy, wherein the prices are continuously maintained at a level between the normal store price and the price of the discount offered by competitors, *i.e.,* the price of the products are 'low' enough to be competitive as well as remain stable. These retailers attempt at generating all year round demand by setting prices at the right level. This strategy is followed by Kishore Biyani for his Pantaloons' stores, *Big Bazaar, Food Bazaar* and RPG's *Food world.* EDLP as a pricing strategy is more suitable to big retailers who have significant economies of scale and buying power. EDLP policy has the following advantages:

A sample of psychological pricing

- This policy helps the retailer to *'establish a market position'* by ensuring customers that they are able to purchase quality merchandise at reasonable (or low) price.
- Since the policy is followed throughout the year, the retailer can workout image-building programmes and other promotional activities at customer relationship management.
- With the sales staff being exposed to training programmes, they can be trained to spend appropriate time with the customers and provide a higher level of service.
- When there is more demand for the products it would be easier for the retailer to manage the stock situation and take care so as to avoid stockout situations.
- If proper care is taken by the retailer, in spite of offering lower prices the overall effect can be visible in the form of increased turnover and hence profitability.

In spite of its many benefits, EDLP may not suit small retailers, because it would be difficult to maintain lower prices throughout due to lack of economies of scale in buying and also a competitive market. Even retailers selling fashionable accessories may not find EDLP to be a suitable pricing policy because of the nature of the business and the product demands that initially a high price setting may be good for the business.

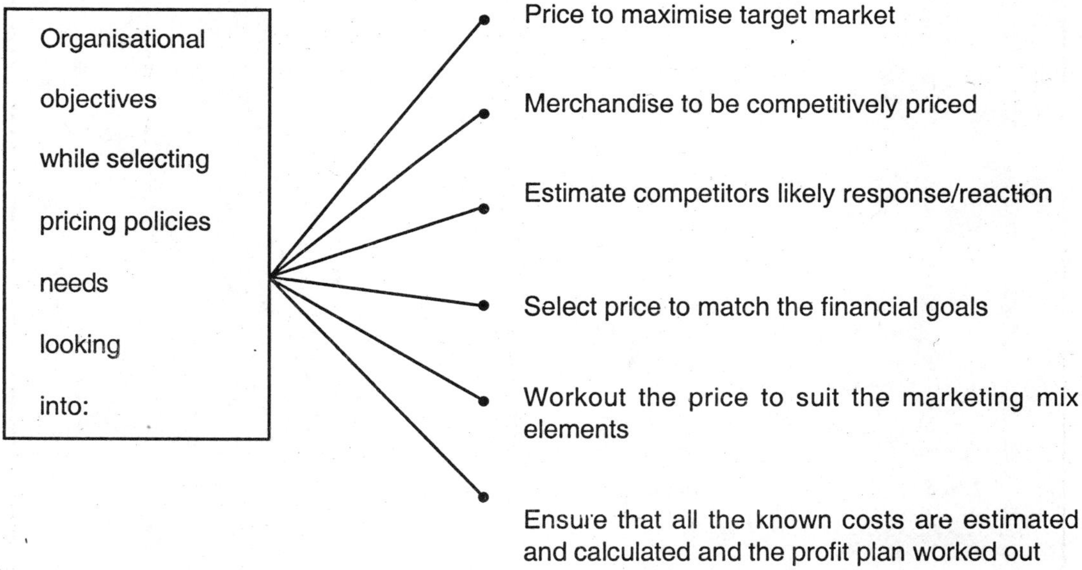

Figure 6.2: Organisation's pricing policy considerations

Ultimately, pricing is very important for the customer since it is all about 'offering' merchandise at a value and with benefits as a part of the exchange process. At the same time, pricing as a part of the marketing mix is to be set at the right level so as to generate enough profit for the retailer. Some of the important considerations by organisations while selecting prices are listed in figure 6.2.

Internet Pricing: Today the internet or online trading is becoming popular. Some firms encourage auction sales over the internet. *Air India* had lot of takers for its scheme wherein the airline ticket(s) for some of its domestic air routes, were sold via bidding over the net. Customers communicate the price they want to pay for an airline ticket from say, Bangalore to Mumbai. Air India then attempted to sell the seat to the lowest bidder.

State Bank of India encourages customers to enjoy internet banking services.

Another leading online auction site is *Baazee.com* which has been bought over by global online auction major *eBay*. Internet shopping is a great tool for comparison shoppers, who visit various sites looking for bargain shopping or find the lowest price for a specific product or item.

In the recent past many Indian portal sites have also moved towards e-commerce. The web communities built around these portal sites have been effectively targeted to sell and buy anything from books to CDs to home appliances to movie tickets online. A survey by *International Data Corporation* (the premier global market intelligence and advisory firm in the information technology and telecommunications industries) in 2002 on the Indian e-commerce transactions market had revealed that B2C (Business-to-Consumer) business carried out on an online format was expected to grow to ₹ 2,300 crore by the end of 2006. In this domain there are two types of players —

(*a*) Companies which have entered the retail market through the online route like *Rediff.com, Baazee.com, Indiatimes.com,* etc.

(*b*) The traditional brick and mortar companies like the *LG Electronics, Indian Railways, Jet Airways, Air India* and so on.

Benefits of Online Retailing

- For the consumers online retailing offers them the convenience and comfort of shopping from anywhere and anytime.
- Many e-retailers offer their customers customised products and services, which may be difficult for in case of a typical brick and mortar store.
- A few of the websites offer consumers products at a lower rate and also with an auction option, thus making it more cost beneficial and an easier option.
- Retailers can enhance their supply-chain efficiencies through online procurement and B2B (Business-to-Business) exchanges which facilitate integrated, near-real time reordering and replenishment from a finely pruned, well integrated vendor base. Such operational efficiency helps in saving considerable time and cost.
- Online trading helps retailers to acquire and put to use vast quantities of data about consumer buying behaviour and purchasing pattern.

A recent market study shows that people have lesser time to actually go shopping on a regular basis especially when this is related to their monthly shopping. And this is where online shopping scores higher over traditional offline shopping. Moreover, retailers are also adopting innovative ways to attract and retain new customer segments and provide for an enjoyable e-shopping experience.

HOW CONSUMERS RESPOND TO PRICES

While setting the retail prices, it will be necessary for retailers to workout the price elasticity and how it can affect the demand. In this context, two issues have to be remembered:

1. Price elasticity is a 'concept' related to the product price.
2. Price sensitivity is directly related to the consumer.

Price sensitivity, in turn affects price elasticity. While working out the 'price' for a retail product or service offering, price elasticity will indicate the extent to which consumers will respond to 'a change in price'. For instance, recently Maruti Suzuki had raised the price of its car models, except that of the Alto model. The Maruti dealers would be interested in knowing whether customers would purchase their brand of cars even when the price has been raised. Similarly, they would also be keen to know a significantly more number of customers who would purchase a car if the price is low.

If a product offering is price elastic, a change in price will result in more quantity being demanded. For instance, if a kirana shop is to lower the price of some of its grocery products (when compared to the general market price), more of his merchandise likely to be demanded by customers. Of course, this may not hold true for all category of products or all customers. For, there are some category of customers who perceive higher price of products and service offerings as an indication of better quality and luxury. Say, high-end customer's visiting a spa or the beauty saloon may not purchase those services if they were offered at cheaper rates (or prices).

The retailer needs to exercise great care while setting prices for price elastic products and services. Customer have the tendency to make a comparison with the competitors offerings, so if the retailer's offerings are priced higher, it should be justified with added features and benefits. Whereas, in case of price inelastic products or services offerings, a change in price will not affect the demand of the same. So, irrespective of the price charged, the demand will be relatively stable. Moreover, usually merchandise which are price inelastic are specific items, with no similarity or substitutes available. So, the retailer can change a higher price for such product service offerings.

Price Sensitivity

While determining retail prices, the retailer also needs to tackle the issue of price sensitivity. To take care of this, an understanding of how demand operates between price points is to be noted while working out the price policy. Even within the retail industry, there could be differences between market segments say the youngsters and upper middle income groups, whose tastes and preferences may vary from one period to another. Accordingly, the relative elasticities of demand for these segments will also be different. Thus, all the factors (discussed earlier in the chapter) can affect price sensitivity.

Elasticity is a key element in the consumer decision process. Elasticity measures the sensitivity in the quantity demanded to a change in the demand determinant. The mathematical formula of elasticity is as follows:

$$\text{Elasticity} = \frac{\text{Percentage change in quantity demanded}}{\begin{array}{c}\text{Percentage change in price or other marketing mix} \\ \text{elements or any other demand determinant}\end{array}}$$

For price elasticity, the denominator will change to a percentage change in price. Since the price and quantity are inversely related, the coefficient of price elasticity is nearly always negative. This means that when there is a fall in price, the quantity demanded will increase and when the price rises, the demand will tend to reduce. So, it can be said that if the retailer want to maximise profits, then he should fix the mark-up such that it will vary inversely with price elasticity.

SUMMARY

Price can be defined as the monetary value assigned by the seller to something purchased or sold or offered for sale and on transaction by a buyer, as their willingness to pay for the benefits the product and channel service delivers. The various factors affecting retail pricing such as – perception of Substitutes Effect, the unique value effect, difficult to compare alternatives, the price quality effect, effect on expenditure, perceived Fairness effect among others were discussed.

The retailer has to workout the pricing policy after considering the potential influences and factors which affect the market. Two approaches, namely **cost-oriented** pricing approach and **demand-oriented** pricing approches were discussed. In order to know how consumers respond to changes, while setting retail prices, retailers will have to consider the price elasticity issue and how it can affect the demand.

CHAPTER QUESTIONS FOR DISCUSSION

1. What is the meaning of the term 'Price' and bring out its role in the marketing mix?
2. Discuss about the various factors — influencing pricing decisions.
3. Briefly explain the various approaches to pricing.

ACTIVITY

Meet the manager of (a) kirana shop in your neighbourhood, (b) a departmental store, and (c) a leading independent retailer in Hyderabad. Find out the pricing approaches followed by each one of them. What differences do you find while comparing their pricing strategies?

❑❑❑

7 RETAIL PROMOTION AND COMMUNICATION

LEARNING OBJECTIVES

After going through the chapter, you should be able to understand:

- The meaning of promotion in retailing
- The importance of advertising as a promotional tool in retailing
- The other retail promotion and communicating techniques

STRUCTURE:

- Introduction
- Importance of Promotion in Retailing
- Methods of Communicating or Retail Promotion:

  Paid Form:
  - Advertising (Types)
  - Steps Involved in Retail Advertisement Campaigns
  - Sales Promotion
  - Store Atmosphere
  - Personal Selling

  Unpaid Form:
  - Publicity
  - Public Relations
- Factors Affecting Choice of Communication Methods
- Summary
- Chapter Questions for Discussion
- Activity

INTRODUCTION

Retail promotion involves a mix of the marketing elements of communication used to inform the target group of the retailer's store, its offerings, which will not only help to increase the demand but also help the retalier to earn profit. Promotion alone cannot work in isolation to achieve retailer's marketing objective. Usually, promotion is used along with the other constituents of the marketing mix, such as pricing markdowns, in order to stimulate demand for the retail store's offerings and encourage subsequent store visits. In fact, consistent retail promotion efforts to convey the store's offerings in conjunction with a good set of promotional campaigns will help to create a positive image of the outlet.

In this chapter, we begin with defining retail promotion, discuss about the importance of promotion in retailing and the methods of communicating with customers. We have also tried to analyse the role of advertising, the steps involved in preparing advertising campaign and the other forms of communication. An attempt has also been made to analyse the factors affecting consumer's choice of communicating methods.

IMPORTANCE OF PROMOTION IN RETAILING

Retail promotion involves a mix of communication activities carried out by retailers in order to make a positive influence on the customers' perception, attitude and behaviour which can lead to an increase in store loyalty, store visits and product purchases. While setting the promotional objectives, the retailer has to exercise care that these objectives will provide specific, measurable, actionable, realistic and timely outcomes (or results). For this, the retailer has to identify the specific market, the merchandise (product or service), goals (specifically set) and the period for which the promotional activities will be carried out. Simply put, the basic purpose of a communication programme is to inform customers about the retailer, build appealing brand images of their merchandise and the services offered as well as workout activities to develop customer loyalty and thus create strategic advantages.

Communication programmes can be worked out to realise the short-term objective of increasing sales during a particular period or to achieve the long-term objectives of earning profits for which they need to create or modify a retailer's brand image. All retailers strive to achieve the most effective response from the target market, *i.e.,* develop a continuous increase in demand for their products or services. It is for this purpose that all their promotional efforts are inclined – to build-up a brand and create products (or services) awareness. Through a promotional compaign, the retailer seeks to:

- provide *information* and *knowledge* about the products to the consumers.
- ensure that the consumer develops a *favourable attitude* towards the retailer and his products.
- sell the benefits of their (retailers') merchandise so that the potential customer *feels conviction* and is more likely to purchase the same.

Advertising and sales promotion are more popular forms of promotion to which most customers relate. Apart from these, the other promotional forms include public relations and personal selling. *Retail promotion can be defined as any form of communication which informs, influences and prompts the target market to act upon any aspect of the retail sponsor.*

METHODS OF COMMUNICATING OR RETAIL PROMOTION

Retail promotion methods of communicating with customer will include:

- Paid impersonal communications
- Paid personal communication
- Unpaid impersonal communications, and
- Unpaid personal communications

Paid Impersonal Communications Methods

Paid Impersonal Communications includes advertising, sales promotions, store atmosphere and websites.

Advertising refers to any paid form of non-personal communication through the media about a product, which has an identified sponsor. Advertising is used to communicate with a mass (or broad target market). Advertising is generally used for the purpose of changing attitudes of customers, building store image, communicating to customers the range of its (store's) product offers as well as achieving sales. Through the advertising communication process the retailer attempts to make credible offers to prospective customers such that they develop a favourable attitude towards the store and their products. Of course, ultimately it is presumed that this will finally lead to the act of purchase.

The *advantages* of advertising are:

- The retailer is able to communicate with a large number of people (or target market) through a single message.
- Advertising helps in the development of a two-way communication flow, *i.e.,* from media opinion leaders to opinion seekers (personal conversation between friends and colleagues about stores or its offers).

The various types of advertising include:

Product Advertising: Product advertising is used to promote merchandise which is new, exclusive and superior in certain specific aspects of quality, design and its benefits.

Markdown Event Advertising: This advertising is to create excitement about a particular period during which the products are being offered at lower prices by the retailer.

Institutional Advertising: This type of advertising is used to highlight about the benefits of the shopping centre or shopping mall as a pleasurable place to visit and shop.

This type of advertising try to highlight about the availability of the range of stores (or branded products), parking facilities available or other consumer benefits.

Cooperative Advertising: As the term indicates cooperative advertising involves sharing of the costs of an advertising campaign either between the manufacturer and retailer(s) or agree to provide joint branded window display material and point-of-sale material.

Steps involved in Retail Advertisement Campaigns

Working out an advertising campaign is a big task for the marketer and retailer. The advertising campaign can create a significant impact on the customer's mind and affect his (or her) future buying behaviour. For preparing the advertising campaign, various factors such as psychology of customers, market demand and supply conditions, level of competition, product's specific features, funds allocated for promotion and looking at the effectiveness of the advertising media have to be taken into consideration. There are six steps involved in preparing an advertising campaign.

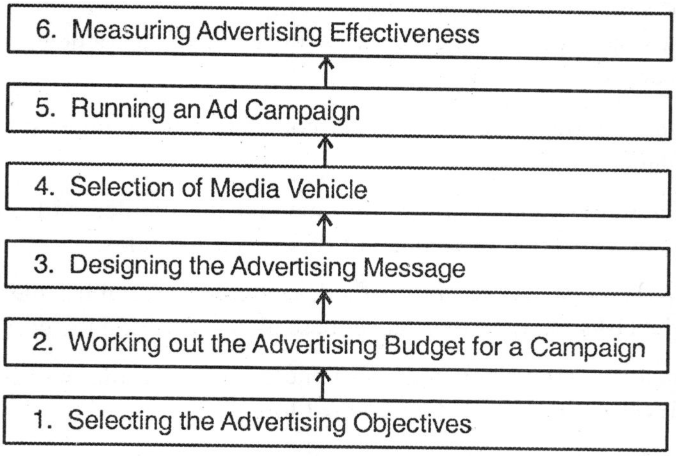

Figure. 7.1: Steps involved in an advertising campaign

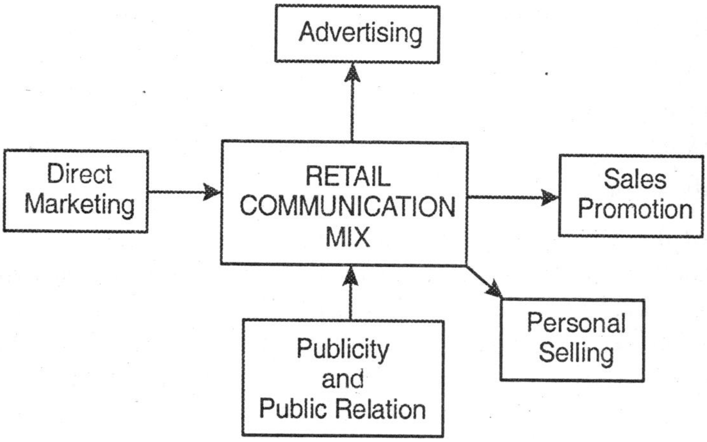

Figure 7.2: Tools of retail communication mix

- **Selecting the Advertising Objectives:** The advertising objectives must be in line to the retailer's objectives. Usually, the ad tends to focus more on certain aspects like: Time period, from when the store started operating, types of merchandise sold, location of the store, competition from other retailers, size of the market, vendors (or suppliers) support. The ultimate objective and goal of the retailer and hence the advertising (goal) will always be to increase the sales volume. Thus, for advertising objectives, it will be necessary to focus on the market, product (or merchandise), consumer and competition.

- **Working out an Advertising Budget for a Campaign:** A well designed retail advertising campaign needs to be supported by proper budgetary allocation. The advertising budget will be with direct reference to the objectives set. The four widely used methods for determining the expenditure on a retail campaign are:

Affordable method: Often, due to financial constraints the retailer will set the budget at a reasonable or 'affordable level'.

Percentage of a sales method: Under this method the retailer will budget his advertising expenditure in terms of a specific percentage of the forecasted sales.

Objective and task method: As per this method, a retailer will establish the advertising objectives and then works out the tasks required to achieve these after estimating the cost of performing them.

Competitive-parity method: Here, as the term indicates, the retailer will allocate the advertising budget at the same level as that set by their competitors.

- **Designing the Advertising Message:** The advertising messages are generally created and conveyed through the advertisement copy. This message must be created in such a way so as to get the customer audience's attention, create interest, arouse desire and induce a positive buying behaviour. The 'must factors' to be considered while designing the ad copy are:
  - Attention value,
  - Memorising recall value
  - Suggestion value
  - Conviction value
  - Educational value, and
  - Appeal to the instinct.

- **Selection of the Media Vehicle:** There are many media alternatives, before the retailer, to select from. Most of the popular media include the print (Newspapers, Magazines and direct mail) Television, FM Radio, E-mail, Outdoor media (billboards, posters and neosigns). In India it is common to see many local retailers using the local TV networks as the marquee which floats continuously on the TV screen. Retailers offering services such as beauty saloons, gym/health clubs, food outlets (popular food joints), spa, etc., use flyers to provide information on their launch, sales promotion or any other special benefits.

- **Running as Ad Campaign:** Running of an ad campaign will involve taking decisions on when to have a pretest run of the advertisement to check and verify before its wide commercial release. This will facilitate, if required modification to be made in the advertising copy before its wide release. Of course, the advertising programme will be executed in accordance to the advertising goals set and budget allocation. Typically, this task is entrusted either to a department or to an outside agency.

Measuring Advertising Effectiveness

As mentioned above, the advertising campaign is created so as to achieve the objectives set. Hence, the retailers will definitely be interested in knowing and measuring the advertising effectiveness. This is a complex job and includes two main components:

- Measuring communication effectiveness
- Measuring sales effectiveness

Measuring of advertising effectiveness will help to: (a) determine the success of the campaign with respect to the advertising objectives set, (b) to identify the layout or, illustration most popular, (c) identify the strength and weaknesses of the various media used.

Some of the pretests conducted to ascertain the potential effectiveness of the ad include: Readability studies, eye movement analysis, recall tests, concurrent tests, response tests and attitude change tests.

The sales effectiveness of advertising is usually measured by using the **Historical approach** and **Experimental approach.** The unorgansied retailers rely on their own experience to judge and evaluate the effectiveness. Even an increase in the inquires related to products and stores as well as footfalls are common indicators of the communication and ad effectiveness.

Media Selection: Advertisers prefer to use the most cost-effective media to deliver the desired number of exposures to the target customers. The effect of exposures on the target audience will depend upon *reach*, *frequency* and *impact.* So, the media planning manager will have to workout the most cost-effective combination of reach, frequency and impact, with him the budget money allocated. Generally, the media vehicle is planned by taking into consideration certain factors such as the target customers, media habits product profile, message compatibility and cost of the media.

A very popular method used by communication theorists to explain the way 'advertising' works is known as the 'DAGMAR' model (Defining Advertising Goals for Measured Advertising Results.) This model describes the sequence or stages through which the prospective customer has to move. (Figure 7.3)

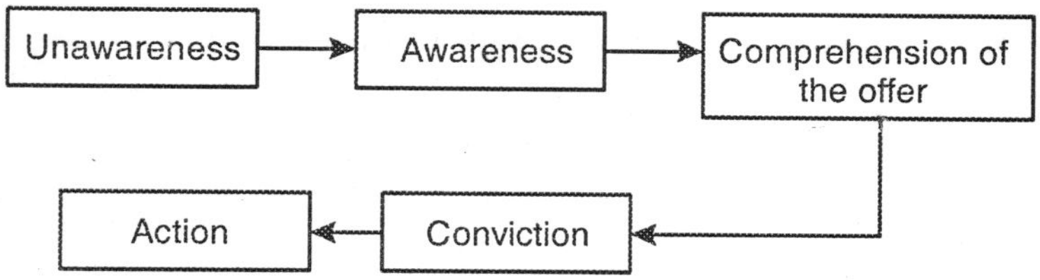

Figure 7.3: Stages through which the prospective customer has to move

The customer may be unaware of the various product and service offerings. Through advertising, the retailer tries to make the prospective customer aware of his store and the range of offers. Through the advertising communication process, information has to be clearly transmitted so that it can be decoded and comprehended properly by the customer. The message should be clear and help to create a favourable attitude towards the store and products/services offered. This should then be followed by the act of purchasing the same, by the customer.

Thus, advertising is a mass communication media used by retailers with a potential of inducing positive buying behaviour among customers.

Sales Promotion

Sales promotion encompasses paid communication activities other than advertising, public relations and personal selling, that stimulate consumer purchases and dealer effectives. Sales promotion is an important controllable variable used by retailers create psychological associations in the buyer's mind, with the power to change their purchasing pattern.

Promotion planning becomes a part of the marketing strategy planning. Promotions have the power to change purchasing pattern. The retailers on the one hand are worried over monthly losses and are increasingly forming alliances with branded manufacturers to reduce prices. But, on the other hand, most branded goods manufacturers are not keen to reduce prices since they feel they would not be able to increase the rates when the market sentiment improves. So, in order to survive and grow in such an environment retailers are focusing on price and efficiency along with in-store promotions, entertainment and fun.

During the recent recession retailers started using bargain sales, huge discounts at their outlets in order to stimulate sluggish demand and such efforts have also succeeded in pushing up the sales. Such sales promotion activities (or programmes) create excitement, increase footfalls and motivate people to enter and shop at a store.

Promotions can be of two types:

- ***Pull Promotion Strategy*** – where consumers are offered various incentives in the form of free samples, discount coupons, gift offers, etc.

- ***Push Promotion Strategy*** – where dealers are offered incentives such as target based incentives, display schemes for dealers and so on.

Sales promotion activities include displays, contests, prizes, samples, sweepstakes, frequent shopper programmes, etc.

'Cooperative advertising' involving manufacturer and more than one retailer advertising about the availability of 'Little Kangaroos' brand.

HOMESTORE is now
look
what I found this Diwali.
All the right reasons
to celebrate.
Celebrate this festive season in style. Pick the best Diwali gifts from a range of astounding products and amazing offers. Only at THS, the largest collection of the best in home ware.
Shop for Rs. 2500 and get a Gift Voucher of Rs. 500
The more you buy, the more you get!
Shop for Rs. 1000 and get a Tiffany Lamp for just Rs. 299
Aroma candles | Potpourris | Lamps | Ceramics | Linen | Furniture | Bathroom | Kitchen | And all things nice.
www.homestoreindia.com

(1) Home Store

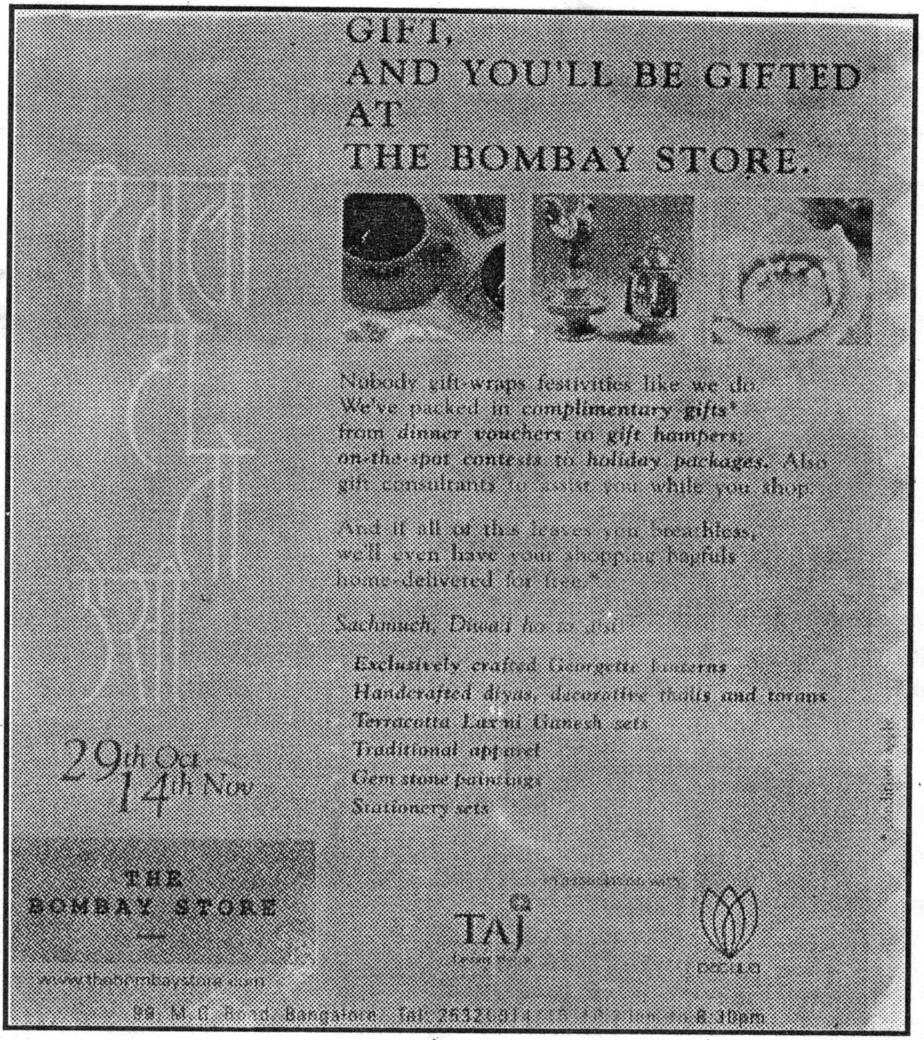

(2) The Bombay Store

(3) Silver Shoppe **(4) Airtel**

Various types of sales promotion activities worked out by different retailers.

Table 7.1: Various types of sales promotion techniques

Types of Sales Promotions	
Types	**Description**
Points to purchase	Window, floor and counter displays that allow a retailer to remind customers and stimulate impulse purchases. Sometimes, the displays are supplied by manufacturers.
Contests	Customers compete for prizes by completing a contest (game) such as a crossword puzzle, a slogan or a lottery. Winning is at least partially based on a correct answer (skill).
Sweepstakes	Similar to a contest, except that participants merely fill out application forms and the winner is picked at random (chance). No skill is involved. Direct-mail retailers use this tool quite often.
Coupons	Retailers advertise special discounts for customers who redeem advertised coupons. Customers clip coupons from print media or POP displays, and redeem them with the retailer.
Frequent shopper programmes	Customers are given points or discounts based on the value of their purchases. The points are accumulated to acquire goods or services.
Prizes	Similar to frequent shopper programmes, except that the retailer gives prizes immediately, such as glasses, silverware, etc,. to the winners. Usually, one piece of a set is obtained with each purchase.
Samples	Free tastes or smell.
Demonstrations	Products are shown: cleaning floors, mixing foods, and so on. Services are also demonstrated.
Referral gifts – matchbooks, pens, calendars, shopping bags	Presents or gifts are given to current customers when they bring in new customers. Items that contain the retailer's name are given to customers.
Special events	Include fashion shows, autograph sessions with book authors, art exhibits, and more.

In general the promotional objectives are to *Inform, Persuade* and *Remind* the target market about the availability of the retailer's products and promotional schemes. Specifically put, the basic objectives of sales promotion are:

(a) To bring about a favourable change in the demand curve by influencing customer attitudes.

(b) Specifically aimed at the particular target group(s).

(c) In advance define the objectives of a particular promotional effort as specifically as possible.

Once the sales promotion objectives are defined it will serve as a guide on the method of promotion to be used, message content, the choice of media, budget allocation required and so on.

The *benefits* of sales promotion include:

- have eye-catching appeal with distinctive themes and tools which help to increase short-term sales volume.
- helps to attract customers, maintain their loyalty and also encourage them to go for impulse purchases.
- use contests and demonstrations by using novel and complementary promotion tools wherein customers can also have fun.

Many of the sales promotions have only short-term effects, so they have to be used mostly as a supplement to other promotional tools. For example, point-of-purchase (POP) promotion consists of in-store displays designed to increase sales which are used by retail categories such as restaurants, apparel stores, audio/video stores, toy stores and sporting goods. The promotional perspective of POP will be to remind customers, stimulate impulse behaviour, facilitate self-service and reduce retail promotion costs if manufacturers provide displays. The long-term impact of POP has to be studied in-depth. Moreover, retailers also need to understand and agree on the function of the proposed point-of-sale (POS) areas. They need to have a good understanding of what their requirements will be with regards to the amount of space required at the POS. Well planned POS will help to communicate the organisation's mission, goals, services provided and other important information. Apart from this a clearly visible point of sale information also tells the customers that the retailer is providing a high level of sales of service with great concern to ensure care-free shopping, quick and efficient customer-service, home delivery, gift wrapping services and so on. All of this can translate into better store and brand loyalty.

Of course, the retailer should consider the following aspects while working out a sales promotion programme.

- The cost of the promotion in terms of employee time, the cost of the merchandise, free gifts items or promotional literature.
- Based on the campaign the increase in sales and profit or increase in awareness among customers.
- The secondary effects of the campaign in terms of switching demand from other retailer products.
- The likelihood of any additional sales other than the promotion with more customers being attracted to the store.

An assessment of the above issues will help the retailer to work at the different benefits of different types of promotion for, with increased competition success at the retail level will largely depend upon, innovative sales promotion strategies.

Store Atmosphere (Or Environment)

The in-store environment/aesthetics which can be translated into the store's physical characteristics, i.e., layout, signs, and displays, colours and lighting effects, pleasing music, visual merchandising, etc., together can have a positive influence in drawing customers to the store and creating the right appeal and image of the store in the customer's mind. The store's service, suitable pricing, display of its merchandise, etc., if taken care of, can lead to store loyalty.

Sales promotion offers from *Foodworld*.

Retailers Website: Most of the leading retailers have created their own websites to communicate with their customers. The websites are used by retailers to build their brand image, inform customers about their merchandise, location of the store, attractive pricing of their merchandise, special schemes and events and also sell their merchandise online (if desired by customers).

Paid Personal Communications

These paid personal communications include personal selling and e-mail.

Personal Selling is a form of communication process where the retail salespersons through a face-to-face interaction with customers try to convey about the store's offerings which will satisfy their needs. Today, with electronic media being used for communication, **e-mail** can be said to be another paid personal communication vehicle via which retailers can enter into communications with their customers. With the help of the internet database facilities retailers can obtain more information on their target customers and send personalised messages to each of them.

Unpaid Impersonal Communications

Publicity and *Public Relations* (PR) are two forms of unpaid impersonal communication.

Publicity is a form of communication involving unpaid presentations about the retailer in the form of a news story in the newspaper or mass media TV coverage. The benefit of PR is that such communications are aimed at potential customers and can be used to boost employees morale and investors' confidence in the financial capability of the retailers also.

Public Relations (PR) is also an unpaid impersonal communication vehicle which can be used to change opinion or achieve coverage in a mass media (such as space given for press release or favourable editorial view). Thus, a retailer with the help of good public relations can not only obtain editorial coverage but can even help to suppress potentially bad coverage. The *biggest advantage* of PR is that it can be used as a tool that to promote and enhance an organisation's image. It is also felt by the PR as a tool can promote and enhance an organisation's image. There is a tendency among people to consider PR as a highly credible form of communication and believe it to be less biased than the information provided by commercial advertisements. Thus, retailers can use PR in a planned manner and attempt to gain control by sending suitable press releases and photographs to the media and thereby creating a positive image of the retailer in the minds of its target market.

Unpaid Personal Communications

The *word-of-month communication* between the customers and the retailer is personalised and involves no additional cost for the latter. When satisfied customers become opinion leaders and convey a positive picture of the retailer and his merchandise to their friends and colleagues it will help to create a positive impression on the store's performance. At the same time, retailers also need to exercise care and provide good merchandise and serve their customers properly, or else unfavourable word-of-mouth can adversely affect the store's performance.

FACTORS AFFECTING CHOICE OF COMMUNICATION METHODS

While deciding on the use of the communication methods, the retailer will have to make a comparison in terms of control, flexibility, credibility and cost.

Control: Retailers will have more control when using paid against unpaid communication method. While using paid communications media such as advertising, sales promotion, store atmospherics, websites, e-mail, the retailers can have control over the time of its delivery. However, retailers cannot have control over the delivery of each salesperson's performance or even over the content and timing of publicity and word-of-mouth communications. Further, in case of unpaid communication media, since it is designed and delivered by persons not employed by the retailer, they can communicate either favourable or unfavourable information.

Flexibility: Personal selling, e-mails and websites can be personalised and used by the retailer depending upon the customer's specific needs and requirements. But the other methods such as advertising, sales promotion, etc., are mass communication methods and it will be difficult to personalise them.

Credibility: Customers will usually find publicity and word-of-mouth communication to be more creditable sources of information, since they are independent persons like friends and family who are personally known to them. Whereas, when salespersons and advertising are used by retailers, the customers may not fully believe the claims made by them because they realise that these are the methods used to promote the retailer's merchandise.

Cost: Publicity and word-of-mouth communication involve expenses to the extent that retailers have to incur costs to stimulate them. Advertising is reasonably economical because it addresses the mass audience at the same time. Whereas, personal selling involves more cost because money (or salary) has to be paid to the retail salespersons on a continuous basis because he or she is required to personally interact with the customer. E-mails can be sent to customers at low cost. However, it may be costly to design, update continuously and promote the site to attract visitors although maintaining a website may be relatively inexpensive.

Effectiveness of the Communication Methods

We have examined the communication methods in terms of cost, control, flexibility and credibility, we will now try to see how a few retailers have used various communication methods.

- FMCG *Kellogg's* had initiated a contest in partnership with *Mobile 2 Win*, a mobile marketing solutions company to induce brand awareness. The promotion had been aimed at providing a total interactive experience to children in the age group of 4-11 years by using its packaging/on pack visuals along with multiple touch points like websites and SMS for consumers to respond. The compaign involves children in the Kellogg's brand story and lures them to participate in a contest with clues provided on the back of the pack.
- *When Shoppers' Stop* had launched the designer store 'Buzz' at its new store in Malad (Mumbai) at *InOrbit Mall*, top models like Inder Sudan and Viveka Babaji and others

sashayed down the ramp to promote and display the pret creations of leading designers such as Raghuvendra Rathore, Rohit Bal, Sumeet Varma, etc. At this store customers were allowed to choose from over 350 brands, avail of excellent services and view the great ambience, all under a single roof. Shoppers' Stop is working towards making the shopping experience a more interactive one with fun and constant promotional activities planned with the aim of maintaining high customer excitement at the store.

- In 1999, *Frito Lays* reported a significant increase in sales when it started packing 'tazos' (disk-like structures) inside certain packs of chips. The tazo bait coupled with the catchy phrase *'Lelo Lays, Khelo Tazo'* was too good a temptation which children found it difficult to resist.
- *McDonald's India* has also observed a healthy sale of its Happy Meals offer especially when accompanied by a special offer. (Read *Box 7.1 on Freebie Promotions.*)
- *Kellogg's* plans to launch a limited edition pack of cereals shaped like a *spider's web*. The *Kellogg's Chocos Spiderman 2* promotion is a part of the global association between Kellogg's and the latest edition of Spiderman movies. The giveaways are specially designed 'Spidey Signals' with the limited edition pack, and 'Spidey Water Squirters' with every pack of Kellogg's chows, chows planets and stars and cornflakes.

Each pack also entitled consumers to a 20 per cent off on the movie, Spiderman DVDs/VCDs. The whole promotion also was supported by TV advertising.

The above examples reveal how retailers are trying out various communication techniques to woo customers. However, the retailer will have to plan the compaign after looking into the effectiveness aspect. Typically, advertising (mass media), websites, direct mailer, and print media are useful in building awareness and conveying information about the retailer and his offerings and prices. Direct or personal selling and sales promotion are effective when customers need to be persuaded to purchase products/services, encourage repeat purchase and build store loyalty.

Box 7.1. Freebie Promotions

Service with a difference works for most promotions and freebie campaigns are certainly not immune to this mantra. Offering a freebie just because the competition is doing so is likely to do nothing save for spurring on a price war between competitors. As Mr. Kapoor [Chairman and MD, Samsika Marketing Consultants] says, "If your competitor is offering a free lipstick, you can cash in by offering advice on how to apply lipstick".

Promotions don't always have to mean spending a lot of money; sometimes tapping the right market can work wonders for a brand. For example, very few retailers have thought of tapping the senior citizen' market, which is termed as the 'grey market' by Mr. Kapoor. This section of the population often possesses resources in the form of money (on account of savings) and time (as most of them have retired). Despite this, it is a section that is largely ignored by organised retail. "Since there is a lot of parity in the market any way, promotional campaigns should ideally serve to introduce disparity." Loyalty programmes offered by certain department stores demonstrate that even moneyed consumers can be targeted by freebie campaigns. Service is an important factor in this case although redeemable points serve as a good incentive. Members of loyalty programmes are usually regular customers so efforts need to be made to add a personal touch while delivering service to these customers.

It is important that the free gift reaches the consumers in the condition it was intended to. Often, the free gift never reaches consumers, and hence, in pack promotions are generally considered safer. Freebie campaigns should ideally be accompanied by advertisements. This will serve the dual purpose of increasing the visibility of the brand as well as informing consumers about the campaign. While utilising on-pack promotions, information about the freebie should be printed on the pack and not stuck on in the form of a label that can be torn off easily.

Freebie campaigns, though effective, need to be utilised with discretion. Run-of-the-mill freebie campaigns are unlikely to result in sustained sales and it is the only campaigns with a difference that will have long-term benefits. All in all, the purpose of freebie campaigns should go beyond just offering temporary gratification; such campaigns should serve to increase brand visibility and build brand image, which are the most important factors that contribute to increased long-term sales.

(***Source:*** 'Seductive promises', Harshini Shah, *Retail Biz*, August, 2004.).

SUMMARY

Retail promotion can be defined as any form of communication which informs, influences and prompts the target market about any aspect of the retail sponsor. Retail promotion involves a mix of communication activities carried out by retailers in order to make a positive influence on the customer's perception, attitude and behaviour which can lead to an increase in store loyalty, store visits and product purchases. Retail promotion communicating with customers include paid impersonal communications, paid personal communications, unpaid impersonal communications and unpaid personal communications. Paid impersonal communications include advertising, sales promotions, store atmosphere and websites.

The advertising campaign prepared by the retailer can help to create a significant impact on the customer's mind and affect his or her future buying behaviour. This compaign is carried out in the form of six steps. The other paid personal communication includes e-mail and personal selling via retail salespersons, unpaid impersonal communications include: publicity and public relations and unpaid personal communications are word-of-mouth from customers to others. While deciding on the use of the communication methods, the retailer will have to make a comparison of certain factors such as control, flexibility, creditability and cost.

CHAPTER QUESTIONS FOR DISCUSSION

1. Explain the significance of retail promotion communications in the entire retail marketing mix.
2. What are the various forms of communicating promotion mix elements?
3. Which are the various types of advertising and explain the various steps involved in the advertising campaign?
4. Briefly explain the various forms of paid personal communications, unpaid in personal communications and unpaid personal communications.

5. Assume you are organising a cultural festival in your college. Which and how can you use the various forms of paid and unpaid promotion techniques to workout an integrated communication programme?

ACTIVITY

Ask your friends who have vehicles about the specific retail store communication techniques which were used by the showroom from where they purchased their vehicle and make a list of this. Visit another vehicle showroom as a perspective customer and make a list of the specific element and information present which communicate an image of the outlet and its product/service offerings.

UNIT III

STORE MANAGEMENT

8

STORE LAYOUT AND DESIGN

LEARNING OBJECTIVES

After going through the chapter, you should be able to understand:

- The importance of a store design
- Objectives of a good store design
- The types of retail store design layout
- How retailers can work at creating an environment for positive consumer purchase behaviour.

STRUCTURE:

- Introduction
- What is Store Design and Why is it Important?
- Objectives of a Good Store Design
- Store Layout Design
- Retail Store Design and Layout
- Creating an Environment for Consumer Purchases through Design
- Summary
- Chapter Questions for Discussion
- Activity

INTRODUCTION

Retail store design plays a crucial part in influencing a shopper's buying behaviour. It must have been observed that each retail outlet will be designed so as to attract more shoppers and offer them a comfortable environment for shopping. Since all the retailers exist in a competitive market, they should try to design their store using the various components of the retail merchandise mix such that it will appeal to the target customers and motivate them to purchase merchandise from them.

We start this chapter by trying to understand the meaning of store design, its importance for the retailer and the objectives of a good store design, then store retail design and output and creating an environment for consumer purchases through design is studied.

WHAT IS STORE DESIGN AND WHY IS IT IMPORTANT?

The store can be said to be a product in its own right. The store design and layout will communicate a lot to its customers. For the retailers, the store design will help to create an image in the mind of its customers. This image is like giving a personality to the store – speaking about the merchandise, the advertising and the services being offered here. While working out the store design, the retailer will keep in mind his target customers, their needs and buying behaviours and the merchandise that he is going to sell.

From the consumer's perspective, the store design should be such that it is easy to navigate, through it the display of merchandise and friendly staff be appealing to the mind, bringing out happiness, a sense of belonging, comfort and pleasure in shopping at the store.

There are a lot of elements which help in the creation of a positive image. These include a combination of the exterior design, the interiors of the store, the atmospherics within the store, the image, promotions and (store) themes – all go into designing the store. The exterior display and image the consumer visualises of a store will draw him either towards or away from the store. The exterior of the store can help the retailer to showcase their marquee, special look and campaign to draw the attention of the shopping customers. Eye-catching window displays, impressive building architecture, pleasant and inviting entrance, helpful staff, the attractive location of the store, play an important role in influencing the consumer's perception and image of the store.

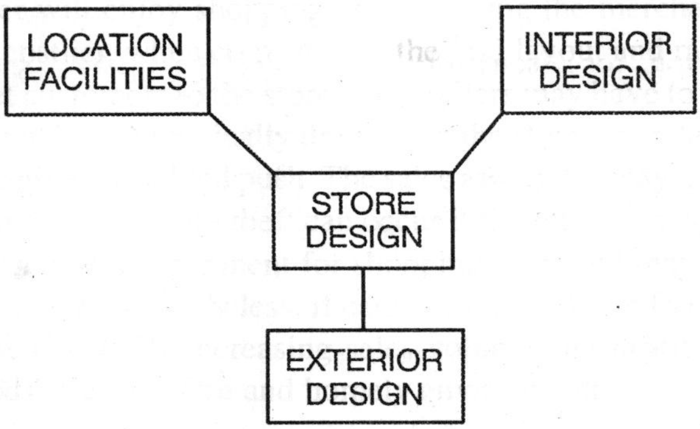

Figure 8.1: Elements of a store design

The store image is a reflection of the personality of the retailer and merchandise available. So, the window displays should be attractive enough to induce prospective customers to be sufficiently motivated to enter and purchase merchandise from the outlet.

OBJECTIVES OF A GOOD STORE DESIGN

The retailer and store manager has to keep the following objectives in mind while working out a good store design:

Store design must be in agreement to the image and strategy followed

Keeping the target customers in mind, the retailer must design his store. For the consumer will be motivated to enter and shop at a store, if the physical environment within the store is matching with the merchandise and prices. Usually, retailers try to ensure that consumers notice the consistency with the store's image and overall retail strategy. Consumers will be induced to purchase from a store if their expectations matches with the merchandise displayed.

Store design should induce positive consumer behaviour

Retailer should make use of attractive in-store layout and space planning. The layout of the store–wide space to move around, attractive display of merchandise, signs to communicate about products, discounts, etc., should be designed into the store, such that it will influence and inculcate a positive buying behaviour among the target customers.

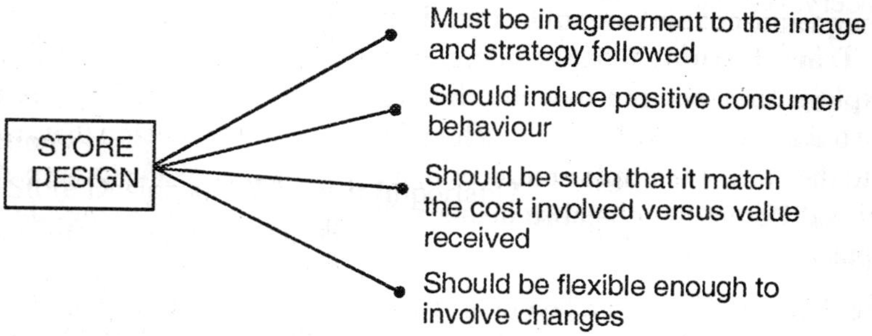

Figure 8.2: Objectives of a good store design

Store design should be such that it match the cost versus the value

The retailer while working on the store design will have to weigh the cost involved versus the value received in terms of higher sales and profits. When working at the store location, visual merchandising, atmospherics, etc., the retailer will workout the costs involved, retail strategy and customer attraction issues. Then he should find a suitable match between costs versus value (higher sales volume and profit margin).

Store design should be flexible enough to involve changes: The store planners must design the store such that it involves maximum flexibility to be modified according to the changes which may occur. Retailers will have to cater to the changes in consumer needs occurring due to fashions, fads, newer needs, etc. Hence, the retailers must design the stores in such a way that they can respond to seasonal changes or go for an image makeover due to a change in the retail strategy without having to go for large-scale innovations.

STORE LAYOUT DESIGN

In order to develop a good store layout, store planners and designers have to ensure the layout should be attractive enough to entice customers have access to comfortably move around the store to purchase more merchandise of their choice. The layout should also facilitate proper display of merchandise suitable to the target consumers tastes

Usually, retailers make a choice from three types of store layout designs:

(a) Grid layout

(b) Race track

(c) Free form

The Grid Layout: The grid layout is visible in most of the supermarkets and discount stores. This layout consists of display of merchandise on flat bottomed surfaces and aisles in a repetitive pattern. Although, the grid is not an aesthetically pleasing arrangement, it is very convenient for customers who need to move throughout the store to locate products of their choice. For instance, when customers do their weekly shopping from 'Star Bazaar', or 'Foodworld' (say) they will be able to move in and out of the specific aisles, easily picking up similar products every week. Since they know where everything (merchandise) is displayed, they do not waste time on such routine purchases (provisions, grocery, vegetables, etc.).

The Race Track Layout: When retailers (department store) want to encourage customers to take time to explore and seek out new and interesting merchandise, they opt for the race track layout. The race track layout also known as a loop layout, is a store design that facilitates customers to have access to the store's multiple entrances and departments. As customers go around the loop layout they notice different merchandise displayed from various angles and thus this store design encourages impulse purchases.

Free Form Layout: Free form layout is also known as boutique layout. In a free form layout, the merchandise and aisles are arranged asymmetrically. This layout can be used in small speciality stores or with the department of a large store. In such a free and relaxed store environment, it is assumed that the customer will enjoy shopping and browsing the merchandise. However, such a layout can workout to be costlier, when compared to the grid layout and race track layout. In order to induce and attract target customers to the store, the retailers may have to invest in costly fixtures. Since the customers may not be automatically drawn into the store, the retailer will have to employ suitable salespersonnel, to give that added push. The sales associates may not be able to monitor and watch the adjacent departments, so more theft can occur if the retailer is not very vigilant. In order to create a homely and spacious environment for shopping, the store may have to compromise on some storage and display space. Nevertheless, if care is exercised, the free from layout design can help to offset the increased costs by increasing sales volume and profit margins, by motivating shoppers to purchase goods in a care-free and homely environment.

Thus, *proactive planning* and *atmospherics* used in the store layout can act upon the emotional state of the customers and are more likely to influence them to enter and purchase merchandise at the stores. *Proactive planning* is based upon the manipulation of the in-store experience by acting upon and responding to the data on store layout in order to influence the consumer's shopping behaviour and experience. The consumers are more likely to enter stores which are made attractive by use of space, colour, walls, pillars, floor coverings, lighting, music, etc. This planned combination of physical messages are known as *atmospherics*. Atmospherics are created by the combination of a whole series of cues and stimulants, *i.e.*, the type of merchandise offered and the way it is displayed can produce the desired store ambience and emotional response from the target customers.

Retailers have realised that background music can be used as a new tool to reach out to shoppers and encourage them to spend more. According to Adrian North, a Psychology Professor at the University of Leicester, England, "There is quite a lot of evidence that music can have different kinds of impact on various kinds of customer behaviour. Music can influence the speed with which people shop, their willingness to spend, their perceptions of value and more". In India also, retailers have realised that the right kind of music can have a positive influence on shopping behaviour and helping them to choose the right music at the right time is what the *Audio Stream Solution* based in Pune does. This audio stream uses sophisticated software, hardware and technology to provide a customised mix of music and branded messages as in-store audio solutions for retailers. Today, Audio Stream Solutions are being implemented at major outlets of *Adidas, McDonalds, Lifestyle, Giant, Ebony, Gold's Gym, Talwalkar's, Fun Republic* and *Globus*. *Barista* launched its in-store radio concept, 'Sound of Barista' using Audio Stream solutions. The reaction to the unique in-store music experiences of the various retailers is given below:

- *Lifestyle* music by Audio Stream solutions ensures the customised music plays throughout the day at Lifestyle stores. It relaxes their customers and builds the ideal setting for a delightful shopping experience.
- Capt. Devendra Bhatnagar, franchisee, *Adidas Exclusive Store* Delhi – Audio Stream's Solutions package incorporates the customer profile (age, gender) with the operating hours and regional taste to make the music match the mood. The customer perks up and so do their staff.
- *Giant Hypermart* Audio Stream has installed the music messaging system in our store at Malad, Mumbai. The added advantage is the preformatted messages that can be played at the predetermined time slots.The retailer looks forward to exploding this as a mainline advertising media in their store put in next line. Read Box 8.1 for understanding how Audio Stream's system works.

Box 8.1 Audio Stream Solutions – In-Store Music System

Audio Stream Solutions is spearheaded by Manmit Shemar, winner of UK's Queen's Award for Innovation, Communication and Technology in 2002. He had designed, developed and implemented one of the most sophisticated satellite data delivery systems for in-store music and messaging solutions across the world. The company is converging the retail, leisure and entertainment industries to enhance the consumer's experience.

How the System Works: It uses the latest optical and telecommunication technology to supply the right music (100-400 tracks) to the retailer and updates it every month.

- The retailers walk-ins are demographically analysed, profiled and segmented depending on the client, outlets, footfall and locations. Due to its close association with music associations (in India and abroad). The latest albums and recordings are easily accessible and often reaches them even before it is released in the market.
- Audio also works with a team of DJs across the country who understand the pulse of the audience in different cities and are responsible for providing a regional flavour to the music.
- The music library is categorised on the basis of 40 attributes such as beats per minute, recall, era and emotion, etc., *i.e.,* depending upon the social behaviour of shoppers. Outlets are divided into daily bands such as:
  (a) On the basis of the time of the day, audience and intended reaction from the customer, songs are slotted into these bands. For instance, during a slack period such as afternoons, fast peppy music is slotted to keep customers in-store and floor employees active.
  (b) Facility of preprogrammed in-store messages which can be changed according to the day, time and audience.
  (c) A in-house hard-disc based set top box or its cost-effective CD based solution which enables the Audio Stream team to change the profile and update the music across retailer networks. This remote control makes it possible to incorporate last-minute changes and messages.

Thus, Audio Stream Solutions is helping the organised retailers to help their customers to have a taste of international shopping experience and information with a growing understanding of intellectual property rights.

(***Source:*** www.audiostreamsolutions.com.)

CREATING AN ENVIRONMENT FOR CONSUMER PURCHASES THROUGH DESIGN

Retail outlets have to work towards enticing impulse purchases, *i.e.,* they have to create an attractive store design which will motivate consumers to visit and purchase goods at the stores. For this, the retailers need to work on the four dimensions of retail design which are design logic, design expression, design execution and design output.

- ***Design Logic:*** This refers to behind the rationale of answering consumers' questions – what do I get in an organised retail shop which is better than an unorganised kirana shop? The answer to this question is to be encapsulated in the store design logic. The design logic has to be analysed and woven into the retail design keeping in line with the consumers' rational and functional needs and desires. The design logic must be relevant to the three human components which form the sociological, psychological and historical background of consumers and this is a part of the subconscious mind where his emotional attachment resides. Thus, the retailer has to consider this critical element in order to motivate consumers to patronise the store.
- ***Design Expression:*** Approaching the retail business with the emotion evoked in a differentiable expressive concept is referred to as design expression, *i.e.,* the retail design should so eloquently express itself that it compels the consumer to experience the need to step inside and purchase all essential items and not just the occasional purchase.

- ***Design Execution:*** The retailers should create and execute the store design that the customer will be surprised with such differentiating execution and then elevate the outlet from the ordinary commodity market. This execution is possible only through combining the rational, functional and emotional content of delivery.
- ***Design Output:*** The design output should be such that it gains sustainable connectivity to the consumer's subconscious mind. This is really a challenge for the retailer because the retail store design must encompass aesthetics, the consumer's desires and mind, an attractive in-shop merchandising design and a striking external character.

The design of the retail stores has to strive to produce an efficient layout with the qualities of ambience which will attract the right customers or target market. Few of the factors which can facilitate this are:

1. **Using of Space Effectively:** Proper planning of territorial areas, break-up store (areas) into logical sales sections and functional areas.
2. **Plan a Productive Layout:** The layout should be planned so as to encourage customers to circulate around the space and visit as many merchandise areas as possible.
3. **Provide Stimulants to Enhance Sales:** Use stimulants such as 'suitable music' which will be pleasing to the ears and liked by a particular age group of customers visiting the stores, enticing them to spend more time at the store and also make purchases.
4. **Make Proper Arrangements and Use Combinations of Lighting:** Lighting apart from being an important mood setter can also produce the desired ambience and when used in combinations can create interesting contrasts through a display area. Proper lighting can influence and create a positive image of the store and its merchandise in the minds of the consumers.

'Usage of different store designs to attract customers'

SUMMARY

Store design is something which will help to create an image or pleasant picture of the outlet in the minds of its customers. It is like giving a personality to the store – speaking about the merchandise, the advertising and the services being offered here. There are certain elements which will help in the creation of a positive store image – the exterior design,the interiors, the atmospherics within the store, the image, promotions and store themes.

The objectives of a good store design must be in agreement to the image and strategy followed, induce positive consumer behaviour, ensure a match between the cost involved and value received and be flexible enough to involve changes. Usually, retailers select a design from three types of store layout designs: Grid layout, Race track layout and Free form layout . Retailers try to work towards enticing impulse purchases by working on four dimensions of the retail design – design logic, design expression, design execution and design output.

CHAPTER QUESTIONS FOR DISCUSSION

1. Why is it necessary for retailers to focus on the retail store design?
2. What are the objectives of a good store design?
3. What are the prerquisites that go into working out the retail store design and layout?
4. Explain how retailers can create an environment for consumer purchases through design?
5. With improved health and grater lifespan, we also have a market segment comprising of senior citizens (say over sixty years). What type of store design will be suitable to attract this category of shoppers to a speciality store? Justify your answer.

ACTIVITY

Visit, Big Bazaar, Pantaloon and the Central Mall in Hyderabad and note down the store design followed by these outlets. Meet the store manager at these outlets and try to find the reasons behind the outlets following the particular store design.

❑❑❑

9 SPACE PLANNING AND MERCHANDISE PRESENTATION

LEARNING OBJECTIVES

After going through the chapter, you should be able to understand:

- The purpose of space planning
- The use of planograms
- The different merchandise presentation techniques and visual merchandising.

STRUCTURE:

- Introduction
- Space Planning Decisions
- Location of Departments
- The Use of Planograms
- Merchandise Presentation Techniques
- Influencing Customer Behaviour through Visual Merchandising
- Summary
- Chapter Questions for Discussion
- Activity

INTRODUCTION

Space planning management and merchandise management techniques are very important for the success of the retail business. In fact space and inventory (or merchandise) are very important resources of the retail firm. It is a very challenging task for the space planners and store managers to allocate the best possible space to departments, products, categories, storage, and also for consumers to move around comfortably while shopping within a store.

In this chapter, we try to examine the importance of space planning by having a look at the assortment planning and merchandise location decision. We also discuss about the methods to effectively present merchandise.

SPACE PLANNING DECISIONS

Allocating of space to various departments categorywise and itemwise is a very complicated and difficult decision for the space planners and store managers. Effective space planning requires to look into two aspects: (a) Help to increase business by ensuring convenience to shop,(b) Ensure merchandise is placed on the basis of the salesperson's work specification.

While working on the space planning aspects, the retailer and store manager will need to have sufficient information on: the nature of merchandise offerings, the suppliers (or vendors), the quantity of merchandise to be carried and displayed, the location of the various departments and the space allocated for the various types of merchandise.

There are two broad objectives of retail space management:

- Effective utilisation of the space for merchandise display and smooth customer movement resulting in increasing productivity and high return on investment.
- To workout a compatible, healthy and rational interface between the customer, merchandise and salespersonnel.

Store planners make decisions related to space based on sales productivity. At times, space planner make an initial estimate based on the following five factors:

(a) To what extent is the merchandise profitable?

In order to ensure optional space allocation, the store and space planner must experiment with different shelf-space allocations and find the combination that maximises profits for the category.

(b) Workout how many SKUs (Stock Keeping Units) will normally be carried in stock based on the planned inventory, turnover and resulting stock -to-sales ratio.

(c) How the merchandise is going to be displayed so as to attract customers attention?

(d) Examine how to locate department and specific merchandise so as to facilitate inpulse purchases and complementary products.

(e) Allocate space based on what items (merchandise) the retailer wishes to emphasise more on.

While working out the layout for the store, the space planner will keep in mind that the customers must feel comfortable and be encouraged to move around the store and at times even be induced to make impulse purchases. It must be borne in mind that the customers may include women, children, the elderly and even disabled persons who may visit the store. So, the space planner must keep in mind the needs of the various categories of customers, likely to visit the store. The store manager has to design and plan the space keeping in mind the merchandise that the retailer intends to sell in the store for the targeted customer audience. The type of display of merchandise, the fixtures to be used and specific arrangements (say, provision for a suitable seating area, if customers are expected to spend some more time in the store) have to be taken into consideration during space planning.

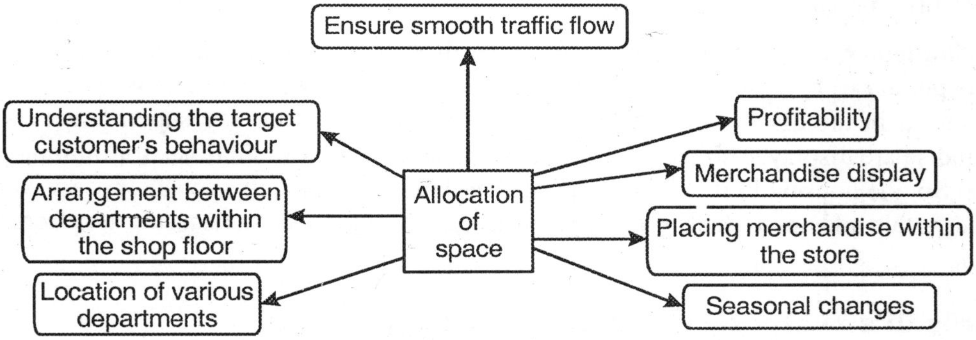

Figure 9.1: Considerations while doing space planning within the store

Location of departments

The retailer should see that the departments where customers would like to shop are strategically located in order to maximise the entire store's profits. However, it may not be possible to have every department located in the best location to ensure more customer traffic flow. So, it is imperative that the retailer has to consider additional demand generating factors and the interrelations between departments when determining their locations.

Benefits of relative location

The best location inside a store can depend upon the floor location, the position within the store, its location in relation to traffic asiles entrances, escalators, etc. If the store is multilevel, a space's value reduces, further it is away from the entry level floor. In large stores, men's departments are located on the entry level floor itself, for they are not known to be enthusiastic shoppers like women. The position at which the store is located, within a floor is very important. *The usually attractive store locations like closet to the store entrances, main aisles, escalators and elevators are the ones which induce people to move into the store and have a look at the merchandise.*

Typical display locations

There are certain products which can be called *impulse purchases* which are displayed, by the retailers at locations which will immediately catch the attention of the prospective customers, like in the front (near the entrance of the store). Such products could be deodorant, perfumes, make-up products, etc.

Specific demand products/services: There could be certain expensive speciality goods like exclusive furniture, spa, beauty saloons, etc., which are located on off beaten roads (not necessarily in main or high traffic moving areas). For such products or services the customers will seek out the availability and would not mind even if such stores or departments selling these are not located in prime locations.

Seasonal products: There are certain seasonal products such as — raincoat or woollen shawls, sweaters, etc., which are in demand during a particular season. For such products, space is adjusted within the department itself. For example, once rainy season products have been sold, this space will be absorbed by winter wear.

Complementary products: Retailers often display complementary products to encourage multiple purchases by customers. For instance, customers who want to purchase printers may also be interested in the display of computer and its related items. Or say supermarkets where the merchandise are displayed so that it becomes a one-stop-shop with facilities for multiple products choices. So, the housewife is able to purchase her daily requirements such as grocery, vegetables, etc., and certain add on products such as personal care products, cosmetics, etc., also from the same location.

Envirosell's evaluation of a departmental layout

New York-based consulting firm, Envirosell, have suggested ways of working out the layout of a store. Apart from the usual hidden view cameras, the firm had opined to make use of the *'track sheet',* a sheet of paper given in the hands of ***trackers,*** who follow shoppers and note down their consumption behaviour . The following observations were made with the help of the above tool:

- Shoppers abandoned their search for some specific items if they felt that their personal space is being invaded.
- Positive consumer behaviour was observed when shoppers could have easy access to the merchandise.
- Place the merchandise so that it catches the eye of the shoppers, as he (or she) enters the shop.

THE USE OF PLANOGRAMS

A planogram is a map used by retailers to determine where the merchandise should be located within a department. A planogram is a diagramatic representation created from photographs, computer output or artists' renderings that will indicate where each Stock Keeping Unit (SKU) should be placed. The planogram will help the retailer to visualise and make the in-store appealing so that the customer finds it pleasurable to shop at the store. Electronic planogramming will require the retailer incorporate information such as model numbers, product margins, turnover, sizes of product, packaging, etc., into the planogram. Then the computer will plot the planogram based on the retailer's requirement. For instance, if the retailer wants to display products with high profit margins in the prime and best locations, the computer will determine the shelf-space priority accordingly. It is said that with the advent of computer graphics and 3D technology, it will not be far when planograms are used to design and also tested and modified, in a 'virtual' shopping environment.

Usually, factors such as product sales, movement of the merchandise within a product category, space management, etc., are taken into consideration while using the planogram. Planograms can workout the exact square feet area required for the various products and the exact number of products to be displayed in a particular area.

If a retailer has more than one store in a broad area or city say, a planogram can be used to ascertain how displays are to be done across the city. This retailer can use consistency to display the merchandise across the stores in all the locations. Customers may feel happy to see consistency across in all the shops and this could result in building consumer trust and brand loyalty.

Merchandise presentation techniques

There are four matters which have to be taken into consideration by retailers for effectively presenting merchandise to the customer.

(1) Merchandise needs to be displayed in a manner consistent to the store's image.

(2) The nature of the products to be displayed has to be considered while taking decisions on how it is to be displayed.

(3) Packaging often indicates how the product is to be displayed.

(4) The product's profit potential is to be considered while taking display decisions.

Given below are certain merchandise presentation techniques:

• Some retailers adopt an ***idea-oriented presentation*** method, *i.e.,* they display and present merchandise based on a specific idea or image associated with the store. For example, *Style spa* present and display furniture in room settings, to help customers to gain an idea on how it would look when used in their homes.

• A very common method is to organise and ***display merchandise itemwise*** or by style. Many of the discount stores, kirana (or grocery) stores, apparel retailers, etc., organise the stock of merchandise categorywise, say when one enters the 'Lifestyle' or 'Shoppers' Stop' stores, we get to see how the retailer has organised and displayed apparel categorywise and itemwise. Since the customer knows of the desired size, he (or she) will find it easy to locate the items if they displayed in this manner.

Some retailers display merchandise using various colour combinations to attract or draw the attention of the customers.

• **Price categories** are used by certain retailers to organise the merchandise. In such stores all products within a certain price line are merchandised together. So, the retail consumer or buyer has more flexibility and may purchase some merchandise a little below or above the expected cost for a price line. Thus, the customer has got the liberty to find the merchandise at the price desired by her.

• In supermarkets and stores such as *Big Bazaar, Nilgiris, Reliance Fresh, Food world* merchandise is presented *vertically using walls and gondolas* to match the customers eyes natural movement as she does her shopping. Many of the stores offering grocery display national brands at eye level and store brands on lower shelves enabling customers to scan from eye level onwards.

• Sometimes the retailers (gift stores or book retailers like *Sapna Book House,* Crosswords) use a ***frontal presentation*** to display merchandise so that the retailer can expose as much of the product as possible so as to catch the eye of the retail customer. For instance, most book stores will display attractive book cover of books to induce the customer to enter the shop. Similarly, a frontal presentation can be used on a rack of apparel by displaying one item out to show the merchandise.

Fixtures and endcaps

Fixtures apart from serving the purpose to efficiently hold and display merchandise can also help to define areas of a store, as well as encourage customer flow inside. The fixtures used by retailers should match the floor coverings, lightings and image of the store. Some of the commonly used fixtures are straight rack, capacity fixture, feature fixture and gondolas. *Endcaps* are the products which are displayed at the end of the gondola or floor fixture where space is available. Some retailers use endcaps to display products at the end of the gondola where some others make use of shelves for displaying merchandise. The purpose of the endcaps is to use the space for organising certain promotional or seasonal items to draw the customer's attention and motivate them to make impulse purchases. Often one gets to see items displayed close to the cash counter, which can induce sudden purchase decisions among retail customers.

INFLUENCING CUSTOMER BEHAVIOUR THROUGH VISUAL MERCHANDISING

Advertising can encourage customers to visit the store but, very often it is the way in which merchandise is displayed at the outlet that could make a difference between making a sale or not. Retailers make use of visual merchandising such as visual materials and window displays to stimulate sales.

Visual merchandising can be defined as a non-personal in-store presentation and exhibition of merchandise along with printed forms of communication used to stimulate sales.

From the above definition it can be seen that visual merchandising is a non-personal form of communication used by the retailer, which helps to:

- bring about maximum product exposure.
- use displays which enhances product appearance and induces interest.
- use display cards and posters which will provide sales and product information to customers.
- ensure security and allow storing of stock.
- generate additional sales through impulse buying.
- work as a reminder for customers – informing customers about the various store offers in the form of a message, directly related to the product.

It is estimated that the average person on the street spends less than 11 seconds considering a window display as window shopping. Thus, since window is the eye to the soul of the store, the retailer must use displays to clearly communicate with the customers on how the store can meet their requirements. Today, the retailer has to exist in a highly competitive world of high street retailing, so the importance of window display cannot be underestimated. With the emergence of brands, mega malls and superstores, the evolution of 'window display' and 'display person' is becoming very important.

(A)

(B)

Bookstore Odyssey, uses visual appeal in the form of:

(A) Graphics to indicate the book likely to suit the consumer's mood.

(B) Use of pleasing colours and ambient lighting within the bookstore to entice shoppers to have a look at the book collection.

Thus, the purpose of visual merchandising (VM), is to create the first impression by which potential customers are induced to enter the store. At the same time the VM should use window displays to convey messages about the brands, quality and price too. Thus, in an effective window display, dramatic lighting works as a 'silent salesperson', attracting and drawing consumers inside the store.

Visual merchandising, using a 'creative' and a 'different from others' approach through window display can communicate the store's very essence to catch the shopper's eye, stimulate their senses and lure them to have a look at the product offerings inside the store.

Apart from attractive window display some of the other elements which can work as a part of visual merchandising include:

- ***Use of signs and graphics*** in suitable colours to present a pleasing overall visual presentation to communicate with customers and help them to find the suitable merchandise.
- ***Have an appropriate lighting*** to highlight merchandise, capture the shopping mood and enhance the store's image.
- ***Use suitable colours*** to highlight the retailer's image and create the right shopping mood and environment.
- ***Usage of suitable music*** can attract the customers to the shop and changing music in the different parts of the store can help to alter a mood or appeal to different markets. Read Box 9.1 on this aspect.
- ***A good scent or smell within the store*** can have a positive impact on impulse buying behaviour and also lead to customer satisfaction.

Box 9.1. Design and Customer-service

With more and more players becoming organised retailers, they have realised the importance of planning and foresight to innovatively use design that can catch the Indian consumers' 'eye'.

Audio Stream Solutions in conjunction with *Kaya Skin Clinic* will soon launch a 'Speciality Music Solution' across all the Kaya Skin Clinics in India. The Speciality Music Solution will provide the right ambience to the environment. The company, in conjunction with *Pepe Clothing India* is in the process of finalising a deal on the launch of in-store music solutions across a number of outlets in India. Audio Stream Solutions opines that the in-store music solutions will provide outlets like Pepe Clothing and Kaya Skin Clinic the right atmosphere to increase footfalls and profit margins whilst entertaining their customers. Sophisticated equipment at the outlets provides unique hands-free demographically profiled music, and targeted music and messaging. The music and messages are sourced, produced and distributed digitally for major branded retail, corporate and leisure chains in the multiple business sectors using the latest optical and telecommunication technologies.

They are also in the process of finalising the launch of a speciality lounge and piped music solution across hotels in India. The first such deal which will soon be finalised is with Sun 'n' Sand.

Information Courtesy—Audio Stream Solutions.

(***Source:*** *Retail Biz*, October, 2004)

Most of the retailers are using VM and store design as a part of their marketing mix strategy. The *Ebony Stores* have a dedicated VM team, with allocation for monthly budget also. Plans are worked out every three months and all events, festivals and seasons accounted for. Then depending on the location and target audience, the concepts are replicated across stores, although these are worked out according to the local interests.

According to Mr. Rakesh Malhotra, COO Ebony Retail Holdings "VM is a science that must be thoroughly studied and practised", and further adds "Jo diktha hai, woh bikta hai"– this is the entire premise of visual merchandising. For, what the consumer sees, he or she will buy. Studies suggest that retailers have a precious three minutes to entice the customer into entering a store and it is well-known that the consumer has a wandering eye. This means that it is vital for the retailer to, in these precious few minutes, ensure the attention is captured to succeed in selling to him/her. Thus, the retail design encompasses more than the store layout, a colourful window display.

Customer-service in the form of convenience and service can contribute to the consumer's perception of the shopping environment. This requires a clear understanding of the target consumer's in terms of their colour choices, style preferences and display options. Depending on the audience or customer profile, the necessary visualisation changes can be effected. Experts have opined that a strong retail design strategy can bring about a 15-20 per cent impact straightaway and simple things such as change in texture, colour, lighting and display can do wonders. Box 9.2 on VM makes interesting reading.

Box. 9.2. Catching the Consumer's Eye

Mani M. Nagasubramanian, MD, RD&M, a Bangalore-based retail design company says, "Retailers' design efforts must motivate in men and women (shoppers as well as employees) the qualities that are stimulants of progress. This would require confidence in one's abilities, curiosity, inventiveness, a sense of dynamism, action and of risk, a desire for conquest, a taste of hardwork, aesthetic sensitivity, solidarity and a respect for difference".

As the industry is fond of saying, the difference is going to be 'experience'. The oft-repeated factors of value and quality will soon be on par at most stores. In such a situation, it is design that promises to play the role of a key differentiator. Retailers, though, are not unaware of these trends. Says Mr. Malhotra, "Most retailers today understand VM and store design's significance and are working accordingly".

R. Kannan, CEO, RAMMS India, a retail design consultancy with a leaning towards FMCG has a story. Traditionally, it has always been FMCG companies who have tried to attract consumers with attractive POP displays at the retail outlets they were present in. In organised retail formats, supermarkets like *Foodworld* do not place much significance on VM and prefer to concentrate on 'value'. Posters that companies put up within the outlets are now charged for space but the system is still not organised.

He believes that sectors other than retailing are doing much better at embracing effective VM. "Nowadays, the telecom and consumer durable players seem to be employing VM quite spectacularly. Here VM is more planned, with attention paid to the space available, the kind of traffic that the store sees and its audience", he says.

POP displays were never thought of as a medium but today, it is part of the marketing mix. Considering that 75 per cent of purchase decisions are made at the point of sale, one cannot afford to ignore its impact. Says Mr. Kannan, "Since the idea is to stop and seduce the consumer, a gondola created to display soap may just persuade her to buy that particular brand".

Most FMCG companies including HLL, P&G and ITC have accepted the inevitable and regularly come up with innovative concepts.

Changes are taking place everyday. "Today's signage is very different from what it was a few years ago. So, will it be with design", says Mr. Kannan.

(***Source:*** *Retail Biz*, June 2004, pp. 14-15.)

SUMMARY

Space planners and store managers have got a very challenging task of allocating the best space to departments, products categories, storage and also for customers to move around comfortably. Effective space planning requires the store manager to look into two aspects:(a) Help to increase business by ensuring convience to shop, and (b) Ensure merchandise is placed according to the salesperson's work specification.

It is very necessary for the retailer to see that the departments are strategically located for the convience of the target customers. Such a location will also help to maximise the entire store's profits. Retailer make use of a planogram, which is a map which will help them to visualise and make the in-store appealing such that customers will find it pleasurable to shop there. Some of the commonly used merchandise presentation techniques are: idea-oriented presentation, display merchandise; itemwise, display by price categories, using walls and gondolas, frontal presentation and by using fixtures and endcaps. Retailers also make use of visual merchandising to increase sales. Visual merchandising can be defined as a non-personal in-store presentation and exhibition of merchandise along with printed forms of communication used to stimulate sales.

CHAPTER QUESTIONS FOR DISCUSSION

1. What are the specific features to be considered if space planning is to be done for a department store and a supermarket?
2. Briefly explain the following terms meaning as well as their role in space planning:
   (a) Planograms
   (b) Fixtures and endcaps
3. Why it is necessary for the retailer to indentify the "right" location of the department?
4. Explain the importance of visual merchandising in retail management.

ACTIVITY

Visit any retail outlet you frequently go to purchase apparel and try to find out from the store manager and retailer:

(a) What methods are being used to allocate space to the various merchandise?

(b) What methods or basis are used to evaluate the profitability of space?

❑❑❑

UNIT IV

LOCATION STRATEGIES

10 RETAIL LOCATION STRATEGIES

LEARNING OBJECTIVES

After going through the chapter, you should be able to understand:

- The types of locations available to stores namely shopping centres and freestanding sites.
- The location and retail strategies
- The factors affecting the demand of a region or trade area.
- Factors affecting the attractiveness of a site.

STRUCTURE:

- Introduction
- Shopping Centres
- Free Standing Sites
- Location and Retail Strategies
- Factors Affecting the Demand for a Region or Trade Area
- Factor Affecting the Attractiveness of a Site
- Summary
- Chapter Questions for Discussion
- Activity

INTRODUCTION

For a retailing firm to be successful, the retailer will have to take decisions on selection of merchandise, pricing policy, layout and presentation, retail marketing and so on. However, all these decisions will be dependent on the ideal location of the outlet. There are certain 'Considararetions' to be noted when adopting a systematic approach to identify a suitable location. These considerations are consumer's choice of preference (location), gain long-term competitive advantage, the existing (or current) social and structural changes, the investment and rental costs and legal and political guidelines. Thus, the retail location strategy is very important for it conveys a certain image of the store and can influence the merchandise mix as well as the store interiors and visual merchandising.

The retailers can select a location from a shopping centre or a freestanding site. In this chapter we discuss about these two locations. We also try to examine location and retail strategies, factors affecting the demand for a region or trade area and those which affect the attractiveness of a site.

SHOPPING CENTRES

A shopping centre is a group of retail and other commercial establishments that is planned, developed, owned and managed as a single property.(Weitz. A. Barton, Levy Michael, Retailing Management, 5th edition, 2003.) Shopping centres are attractive for consumers because they are able to make purchases from a huge assórtments of merchandise available at the stores. So, when many stores are put up under a single roof (Shopping Mall), it helps to create a synergy which will help to attract more customers.

In India, typical shopping centre, which is a planned one will comprise of a group of architecturally designed, owned or managed stores, all operating under a single roof, with balanced tenancy and having parking facilities. Broadly, these can be classified into the following categories:

(a) Regional shopping centres or malls
(b) Neighbourhood/Community shopping centres
(c) Specialised markets
(d) Periodic markets.

Regional Shopping Centres or Malls

Regional shopping centres or malls are very large planned shopping centres, very often anchored by a few (two or more) major departmental stores, with enclosed malls, a large trading area and involvement of high monthly rentals. Some of the such popular shopping centres or malls are Forum Mall, Ansal Plaza in Delhi, Crosswords in Mumbai, etc. Generally, in India, the tenant mix and size of the shopping centres tend to vary according to suit the needs of the target customers. Similarly, the patterns of shopping behaviour displayed will also depend upon the lifestyle of the consumer.

The ***advantages*** of shopping malls are:

- In many of the malls, the consumers are able to experience a pleasure of combining shopping with entertainment. So, it becomes an enjoyable experience.

- Malls usually contain a complementary tenant mix and the customers are able to have a one-stop shopping experience with a well balanced assortment of merchandise.
- The retailers in a mall as well as the customers do not have to worry about the external environment. Typically, the mall tenants will see a certain level of homogeneity with the co-existing stores. Since the mall managers will decide on the common areas functioning, they will have to abide by the uniform hours of operation started, space used for external signage and so on. Customers can also enjoy shopping since these malls are fully enclosed and hence protected from the external weather.

Although shopping centres are an attractive option in front of the retailers, they also have *certain disadvantages:*

- Mall rentals are usually very high, so retailers who require larger stores (or space) prefer to setup an outlet at other locations.
- Some tenants may not feel comfortable having to operate within the restrictions related to "store timings" or usage of window displays.
- Since competition is instense within the shopping centres, it may be difficult for small speciality stores to operate and compete with large department stores.
- Mall are also facing increasing competition from other types of retail alternatives, from where the customers are comfortable to purchase such as the internet, catalogues, etc.

To tackle some of these issues, mall owners are allowing entertainment opportunities (games, movies, etc.), along with the shops or stores selling merchandise. It is believed that if people are encouraged to spend more time at the mall they are likely to spend more money there.

Neighbourhood/community shopping centre

In order to cater to the needs of the people in a neighbourhood, there could be a community (or neighbourhood) shopping centre. Such shopping centres will have a balanced mix of a few grocery stores, a chemist shop, a few stores selling convenience goods, a variety shop, a small jewellery shop and a few other stores.

Specialised Markets

Apart from the general markets, in India we have certain specialised markets famous for a particular product category. In such places, an established retail area is already operating, so a prospective retailer need not put in extra efforts. Since customers are already aware of this market and visit it for purchasing the particular merchandise. For instance, the K.R. Market in Bengaluru for vegetables, and flowers, in Chennai the 'T Nagar' for ready-made garments, in Ahmedabad 'Dalgharwad'for clothes and so on.

Periodic Markets

Another type of market found in most of the cities in India are the 'periodic market'. The retailers who sell their merchandise in this market have mobile setup which is shifted from one market to another depending upon the day of the week. Often such markets are kept open in the evening hours and are patronised by customers belonging to the lower middle income class or below. These markets provide convenience and low pricing and especially help to meet the requirement of a large population (often migrant labourers who have moved from rural to urban areas in search of a better living). Although this is a popular rural retail format, it is now very popular in the Indian cities also. For the customer, in such a market, merchandise is available at low prices and at convenient hours. While for the retailer, it helps to attract customers from large trade areas, with limited credit transactions, limited infrastructure related costs and carry low overheads.

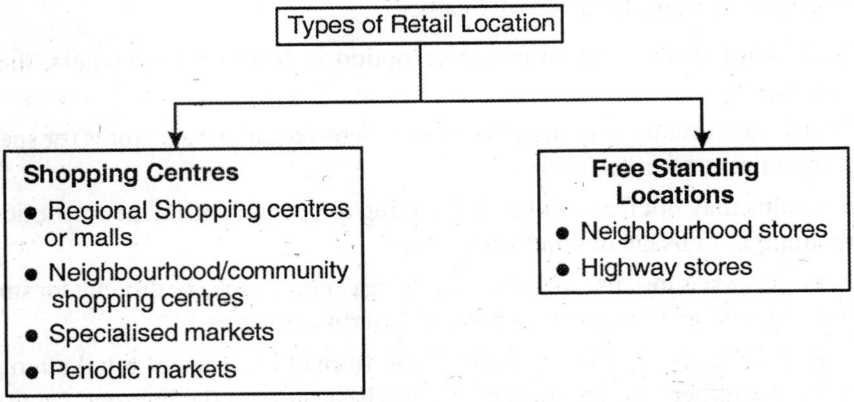

Figure 10.1: Various types of retail location

FREESTANDING SITES

There are freestanding location sites where such retail outlets do not have other stores in the near vicinity. Such freestanding sites are not connected to other retailers even though they may be located adjusted or close to malls. Retailers who need to have large space for retailing purposes, such as the hypermarkets freestanding grocery shops, etc., can be called freestanding location sites. Such retailers need to have their own pulling power and promotional activities in order to attract their target customers. Some of the ***advantages*** of freestanding location sites are:

- No direct competition
- Greater visibility from roads
- Less rentals
- More convenience for shoppers
- Easy parking facility for customers
- Unlike shops in malls, freestanding sites face lesser restrictions on display of signs, hours to be kept open, etc.

Such freestanding location sites also having certain ***disadvantages:***

- Lack of synergy with other stores, so they have to work very hard to attract customers to their freestanding location
- No shared costs as in a shopping centre and so the retailer will have to bear all the costs alone.

- Such free destination location sites will have to work a lot to offer customers different or unique merchandise, price offers, promotion and services in order to induce them to enter the store.

Freestanding location stores can be classified as neighbourhood stores or highway stores.

Neighbourhood Stores

Neighbourhood stores can easily be located in residence areas and serve a small locality. Some of these stores are like the kirana stores which sell groceries and provisions to a locality. With most of the cities and towns expanding, even large organised sector stores are seen operating at-free standing locations in suburbs or away from major market areas. For instance, the **kidskemp, kempfort** or the **Lifestyle stores** in Bengaluru can be called freestanding stores located away from the major markets of the city.

Highway Stores

In order to attract customers who drive across on highways, some stores are located along these roads or at the intersection of two highways. Such stores can easily catch the eyes of the persons using the highway. The *dhabas,* outlets attached to petrol bunks on the highway, etc., are a few examples of the highway stores.

LOCATION AND RETAIL STRATEGY

It will be interesting to examine why retailers select the particular location for their store. Let us have a look at the location strategies for different types of retail outlets.

Department Stores

Department stores are usually located as standalone stores in Central Business areas or in malls or shopping centres. Such locations help to draw a lot of target audience because of the size of the store *(Pantaloons, Shoppers' Stop, Lifestyle, etc.),* and the variety of merchandise to select from. Central Business areas can have a lot of potential customers working in that area too. When department stores are located in malls, it becomes an attractive location because of the presence of entertainment and recreation facilities there. Moreover, as mentioned earlier in the chapter since the malls are covered and all the stores within it are protected from the vagaries of the weather also it can be attractive location. Further, the tenant mix at a malls are such than the stores will appeal to potential customers who are looking out for one-stop destination for shopping a variety of things.

Speciality Stores

Speciality stores carry products for which the consumers may prefer to spend time comparing alternatives. These stores generally focus on one type of (special) merchandise. Some stores may stock exclusive high-end products say *Louis Vuitton.* While at the other end there could be stores selling products such as *Flying Machine Jeans* to the price-conscious customers. Often these types of stores have almost similar buying, marketing and merchandise display strategies making it easy for the target customers to compare alternatives. Such speciality stores are located in Central Business areas (or districts), main street locations most of the luxury malls, lifestyle centres, fashion malls, etc. Such types of locations have a lot of floating population who come with a specific intention of purchasing goods by enabling them to compare across stores or to make good of the entertainment and recreation opportunities available. Speciality retailer examples could include *Time Zone, Tanishq*, etc.

Category Specialists

These are giant retailers who have dominance in one area of merchandise like Office Depot, Home Depot, The Sports Authority, etc. Such category specialists are very likely to be located in power centres or in a freestanding location as their locational needs are different from that of the the the department or speciality stores. Customers consider category specialist stores as destination stores, where the typical merchandise, selection, presentation, pricing, etc., induce customers to visit the outlet. The reason for selecting such power centres or freestanding location site is that customers wanting to purchase specific products like say sanitaryware, electronic goods, sports goods, etc., will seek out the store irrespective of the location.

Grocery Stores

Grocery stores are found at locations which facilitate convenient shopping for day-to-day needs of the consumers in the near neighbourhood. Usually for purchasing groceries and provisions, people are not keen to travel to far off places. Such grocery stores are located on strip centres, where the retailers are also not very high and customers in the neighbourhood are able to either walk down to the shop or park their vehicles near the store for a short period. The two main advantages of the location of the grocery stores are:

(a) Availability of convenience products (such as bread and milk) for which consumers do not want to spend considerable effort in prior information and search

(b) Location is easily accessible by target customers without having to travel long distances.

FACTORS AFFECTING THE DEMAND FOR A REGION OR TRADE AREA

Every retailer strives for selecting a trade area which will induce more customers to visit his store and also generate high sales for him. So, while assessing the demand of the trade area, the retailer will have to consider the following:

Identify Market Potential

While working out the potential market demand for their range of product-line the retailers should ideally take into consideration:

- The target population's characteristics
- The average household purchasing power of an area.
- Suitability of business climate
- Level and nature of competition

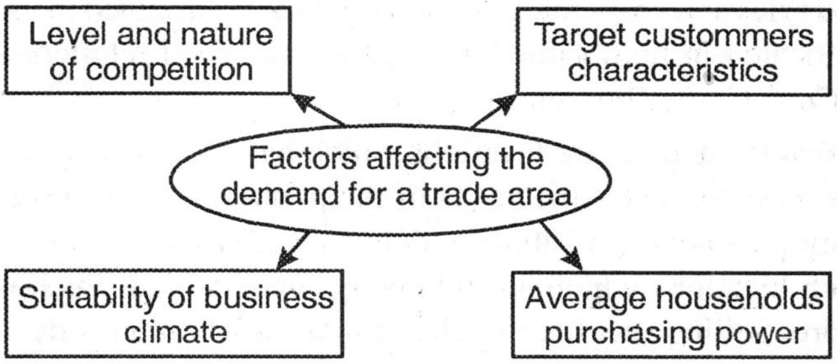

Figure 10.2: Factors which will help retailers to workout the market potential

(a) The target customers characteristics

There are typical target customers characteristics such as geo-demographics, psychographics and behavioural characteristics which can be used by the retailer to segment his market. This information can be obtained from secondary and primary sources. The retailers can get to know the population size in terms of the number of households, their income distribution, number of male and female population, occupation, educational qualifications, customers lifestyles, store loyalty and patronage trends, etc.

(b) Average household's purchasing power

Information related to the areas household's purchasing power (on an average basis), how do the household's spend their money, the distribution of household income, etc., can help the retailer to take decisions on how to stock and display his merchandise.

(c) Suitability of business climate

The retailer needs to examine a market (or trade areas) employment trends because a high level of employment in a particular area will indicate an increased purchasing power ability of the target market. For instance, Sarjapur road area (in Bengaluru) has become a desirable retail location because of its proximity to many of the well-known corporate houses (*Wipro,* etc.)

The retail location analysts also need to determine for how long such growth will continue and to what extent it will affect the demand for their products. Alongside , the retailer also needs to ensure a strong retail environment with the ability to view the existing business climate and foresee the likely changes to occur in the future, if growth is diversified in a number of industries.

(d) Level and nature of competition

The demand for a retailer's products and merchandise can affect the level of competition. The level of competition can be defined as saturated, unsaturated or over-stored trade areas. A saturated trade area offers customers a huge variety of merchandise products at competitive price. Even retailers who find location characteristics to be compatible to the marketing mix element used by them will set up their stores in such locations. Retailers putting up stores in such saturated trade areas try to develop methods which will help them to have healthy competition. They feel such locations can help in high footfalls will can result in good sales and profit margins with the help of sustained marketing efforts. Examples of retailers located in high saturated areas are the food retailers like *McDonalds, KFC, Domino's, Café Coffe Day, etc.*

An understored trade area are locations which have too few stores selling specific goods and services so as to satisfy the needs of the population. For instance, Foodworld's early entry in developing areas (or suburbs of cities) was based on a location strategy of opening stores in such locations which are relatively understored. Such understored trade areas have few stores selling specific merchandise to satisfy the needs of target market's needs efficiently.

An overstored trade area are those having many retailers in a specific product category. For new entrants wanting to set up shops in such locations it will require lot of investment and efforts to attract customers. In India, such overstored trade areas can be said to be the typical traditional market with limited space and high rentals.

FACTORS AFFECTING THE ATTRACTIVENESS OF A SITE

Retailers will have to consider the following factors while ascertaining the attractiveness of a site. These factors include:

(a) Type of merchandise to be sold

For retailers dealing in convenience goods, the traffic or number of people visiting the store is important. ***Convenience goods*** are often purchased on impulse from easily accessible stores while shopping. So, the location of the store should be such that it is easily visible from outside and also easily accessible for the customer. In case of ***shopping goods,*** more than quantity (number) it is the quality of customers which matter. This could probably be the reason for the emergence of the 'exclusive factory outlets' in many of the cities. ***Speciality goods*** can go in hand with shopping goods and so retailers dealing in them prefer to locate the store where the establishments close or next to their outlets, are selling merchandise which are compatible to their goods.

(b) Cost involvement

Cost is a very important consideration in location decisions. While working out the cost of the space for locating the store many aspects have to be looked into: rent/lease payment, utilities, decoration and visual merchandising costs, safety and security, insurance, etc. The cost factor will vary depending upon the type of transactions. Since rentals for commercial establishments are high, many retailers go for lease agreements and those who can afford, own the place which is considered to be prestigious in the business community. There are certain retailers who operate in periodic market (mentioned earlier in the chapter) who do not own the place where the merchandise is sold but prefer to pay a small rental for their location setup in each market. This arrangement will suit their model of selling merchandise at very low margins.

(c) Location of competitors

While selecting a location site for retailing purpose, the number and the type of competition also need to be looked into. When a retailer is planning to offer quality as well as price on par with competition, they will prefer location sites close to complementary business which will help to attract customers to the store.

(d) Accessibility and traffic flow

A very important consideration which will make a location site attractive is if it facilitates accessibility and ease to traffic flow. If the target customers find that the location of the retail outlet is easily accessible, close to residential areas, doesn't cause traffic congestion, etc. Then it can easily become a preferred shopping destination for them.

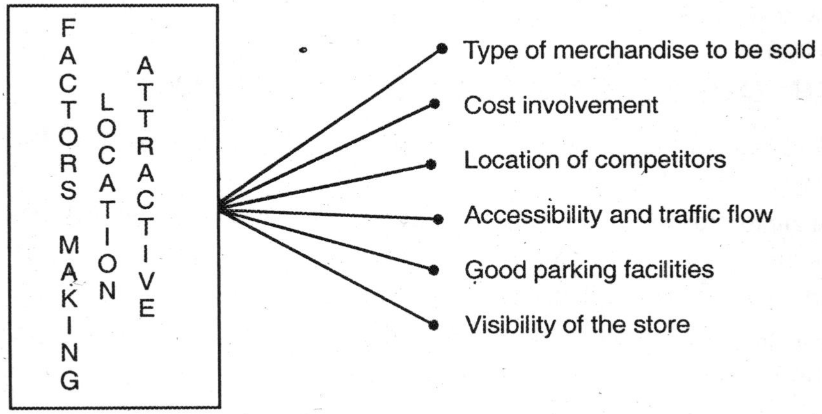

Figure 10.3: Factors which make a location site attractive

(c) Good parking facilities

A location can workout to be attractive for the customer if they feel that the retail outlet has got sufficient space marked out for parking vehicles. The retailer on his part must evaluate the parking facility by working out the ideal parking capacity (number of vehicles that can be parked) and parking configuration (how the parking lot is laid out).

(d) Visibility of the store

A retail outlet location should be attractive enough to induce prospective customers to visit the store. This will occur only if the store is sufficiently visible to all prospective customers, be it all those who are passing by or window shoppers or regular customers.

The retail outlet should have sufficient visibility so as to encourage customer pull within the store.

SUMMARY

All the decisions taken by a retailing firm right from the selection of merchandise, layout and presentation and so on will depend on the ideal location of the outlet. The retail location strategy will help to convey a certain image of the store. Retailers can select a location from a shopping centre or a free standing site. A shopping centre is a group of retail and other commercial establishments that is planned, developed, owned and managed as a single property. In India, the shopping centre can be classified into: (a) regional shopping centre or mall, (b) neighbourhood/community shopping centres, (c) specialised markets, and (d) periodic markets.

Freestanding location sites are retail outlets which do not have other stores in the near vicinity. Such retailers need to have their own pulling power and promotion activities in order to attract their target customers. Freestanding location sites can include neighbourhood stores and highway stores.

The factors affecting the demand for a region or trade area are: the target population's characteristics, the average household purchasing power of an area, suitability of business climate and the level (and nature) of competition. The factors which can affect the attractiveness of location site include: the type of merchandise to be sold, cost involvement, location of competitors, accessibility and traffic flow, good parking facilities and visibility of the store.

CHAPTER QUESTIONS FOR DISCUSSION

1. "The success of a retail outlet greatly depends upon its location site." Do you agree with this statement? Why?.
2. What are the advantages and disadvantages that can be associated with "shopping centres" and free location standing sites?
3. Briefly mention and explain the various types of retail locations.
4. Give a short note on the various factors affecting the demand for a region or trade area as well as those affecting the attractiveness of a site.

ACTIVITY

1. Meet the kirana or grocery shop near your residence and ask the owners what were the major decisions taken for setting up the store at that location.
2. Meet the store manager's of:
   (a) A freestanding site (say *Big Bazaar*)
   (b) An outlet at the shopping centre (say Landmark)
   (c) A local store selling fashion accessories near the Charminar area (at Hyderabad) and find out the various factors taken into consideration while setting up the outlet there.

❑❑❑

UNIT V

RETAILING IN INDIA

11 RETAIL IN INDIA

LEARNING OBJECTIVES

After going through the chapter, you should be able to understand:

- The existing retail scenario in India
- Factors affecting retailing in India
- Regionwise analysis of Indian Retailing
- The key challenges and retailing opportunities in India

STRUCTURE:

- Introduction
- The Existing Retail Scenario in India
- Factors Affecting Retailing in India
- Regionwise Analysis of Indian Retailing
- The Key Challenges and Retailing Opportunities in India
- Summary
- Chapter Questions for Discussion
- Activity

INTRODUCTION

Retailing has played a key role in world economy be it in the US, Europe, Japan, China or India. Retailing has been in existence since quite sometime in India. But this industry was largely dominated by the unorganised sector comprising of small, independent, self-owned shops. Apart from these there were many unaccounted number of low-cost kiosks (like the local tea stalls, food centres, saloons (or barbar shops), etc. However, the retail industry witnessed a major revolution from 1991, when the first organised retail chain "Shoppers' Stop"opened its first outlet in Mumbai. Thereafter, with many other organised retailers entering the industry, the Indian retail industry has been growing very fast. Today, we get to see the coexistence of the organised retailers along with the conventional kirana stores, minidepartment store on the roadside, the local (on the road) eatery, etc. In fact, even the traditional retailers have gone for a revamp – organising their merchandise, attractive display, having promotional programmes, free home delivery, loyalty offers for frequent shoppers and so on. Thus, it will be interesting to have a look at the changing phase of the retail industry in India.

This chapter commences with a brief discussion on the existing retail scenario in India. Then we have a look at the factors affecting the retailing industry, regionwise analysis of Indian retailing and the chapter concludes with examining the challenges and opportunities in the Indian retail market.

THE EXISTING RETAIL SCENARIO IN INDIA

Retailing in the form of the barter system had been prevalent in India during the olden times. This was followed by the *Haats, Melas* and *Mandis,* which continues to be existing in many parts of India even today.

Traditional formats

Haats are periodic markets (covering around 20-50 villages) and is popular in the rural India. The location for the trade market witnesses a public gathering of buyers and sellers at fixed times and fixed locations. Almost all the states in India hold *Melas* (or fairs) which could range from commodity fairs to religious fairs. Estimates indicate that the average outlets in every mela would be more than 800 and the average sale per mela would be around ₹ 1.43 lakh. *Mandis* are markets setup by the state government, as a platform for the farmers to sell their agricultural produce directly to buyers.

Established formats

We also have the *PDS* or the *Public Distribution System* which can easily be referred to as the single largest retail chain existing in the country. The PDS helps in the distribution of essential selective cereals, (rice and wheat), sugar and kerosene at subsidised prices to ration cardholders. The PDs helps to regulate supply and distribution of (and trade and commerce in) essential items so as to maintain supplies and also ensure equitable distribution and their availability at fair prices in accordance to the essential commodities Act, 1955 and the subsequent control orders. The PDS was first started in 1939 in Bombay (now Mumbai) and is continuing to function even today, although now they are popularly known as the fair price shops or FPSs. Another example of organised retailing format are the *super bazaars* and *kendiya bhandars* which follow a user-friendly store format, where huge variety of merchandise are sold at reasonable prices. However, these outlets are known for offering average customer-service, follow bureaucratic timings and are poorly maintained.

In April 2000, *Mother Dairy Fruit and Vegetable Limited (MDF&V),* a wholly-owned subsidiary of NDDB (National Dairy Development Board) was formed to be involved in the marketing and distribution of milk, milk products and horticulture produce. The company sells ice cream under the brand name *'Mother Dairy'* and horticulture produce in fresh, frozen and processed form under the brand name *'SAFAL'* through a chain of retail outlets across the country. The objective of having the processed products branded under the name 'SAFAL' is to ensure that the consumer gets the highest quality produce at a reasonable price alongside ensuring the most remunerative price to the farmer.

Over centuries, India has developed a wide collection of arts and crafts and artisanal items (ivory, brass, gold, silver, copper, silks, carpets, precious stones, etc.), which are sold to tourists and local customers through the *Central Cottage Industries Emporium* (CCIE). Through the CCIE, the government has provided the artisans and craftsmen an alternative retail channel which are considered to be attractive urban markets and a platform for them to get the right exposure and at right prices too. The Central and State Governments run various cottage and handicraft emporiums across the country. These emporiums retail a wide variety of product categories procured from different parts of the country.

We have the *post offices* which has among the largest network of outlets across all states and union territories in the country. They are retail outlets helping customers to communicate with relatives and friends using various written communication methods.

In 1957, the government established *The Khadi and Village Industries* (KVIC) retail stores to act as a custodian of cooperative institutions and an incubator for the village industrial units. Simultaneously such government established retail chains can also provide effective marketing infrastructure to small-scale industries involved in the making of handicrafts and local goods.

Till the 1980s consumers did not have much purchasing power, with limited investments taking place and a lot of government restrictions and protective measures for certain industries, not much industrialisation took place. However, from 1991 onwards, with the opening up of our economy and liberalisation, the Indian economy has come to be accepted as a "market-friendly" one.

Emerging formats

We get to see on a general basis the kirana shop, mom-and-pop store, general store, the chemist shop and family owned retail stores. The *kirana* (or grocery) store is usually located in neighbourhood (residential areas) or central business districts and keeps a stock of non-packaged, unbranded/generic commodities such as rice flour, pulses, etc., along with branded and packaged fast moving consumer durables (FMCGs). *General stores* keep stocks of branded and FMCGs and are located prominently in neighbourhood centres and residential areas. The *chemist shop* apart from stocking pharmaceutical products, sells branded personal care products, health foods, etc.

Apart from the above retail outlets there are a large number of small unorganised retail players such as the paan-beedi stores which stock products in sachet form, batteries, soaps, bakery items and confectionery, tea/coffee/juice stalls, ice cream parlours, electrical, furniture, hardware stores and boutiques. There are also some people who can be said to be a part of the *unorganised sector* such as the large number of the hawkers, push cart pullers stalls within the main markets or localities and street corners and even the many door-to-door vegetables or snacks selling vendors.

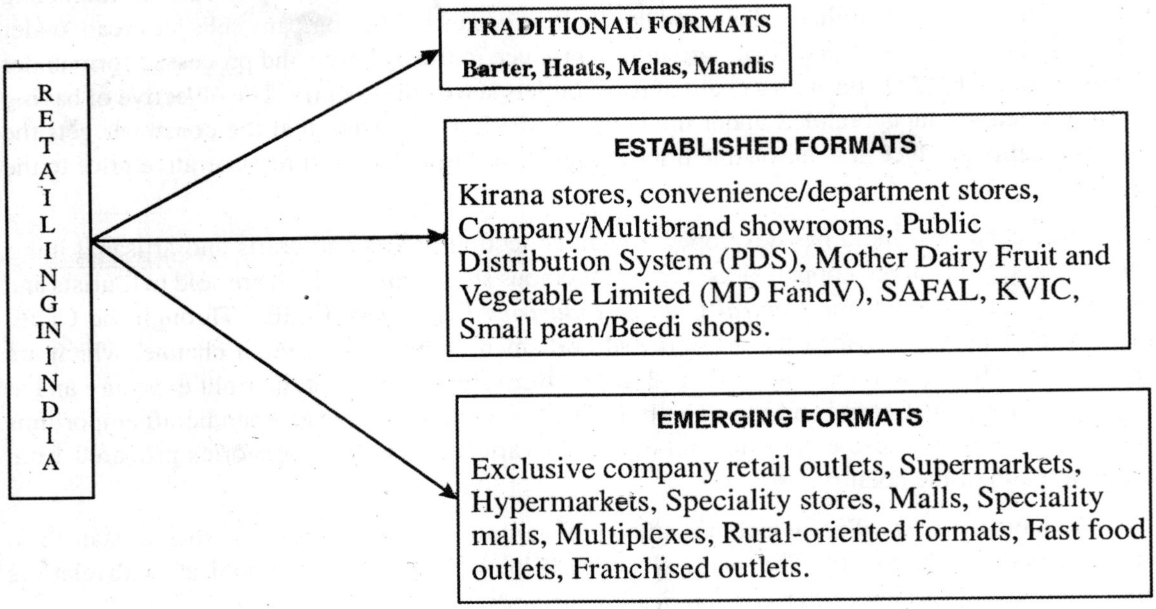

Figure 11.1: The retailing scenario of India

Post-liberalisation the retailing formats have become more organised with the induction of a lot of professional management and efficiency in the value-chain. The customers stood to gain with the proliferation of both Indian and foreign brands, both enjoying strong brand equity. The independent retail stores like *Akbarally's, M.K. Ahmed and stores, Nalli's showrooms,etc.,* cater to the typical needs of the customers.

Franchising through showrooms or services like *Pizza Hut, McDonalds, Marks and Spencer, Subway, Arvind, Colour Plus, Madura Garments, Ayush* (HLL), etc., is gaining popularity and as a means for the companies to expand their network across many market areas.

Another major organised retailing format in India are the chain of stores. Long back this trend was visible in the textile industry, retail chain of Reliance through its *Vimal showrooms* and the *Garden Vareli showrooms* of Garden Silk Mills (Surat). Then with the growth of textile retail, many ready to wear (ready-made) branded apparel gained popularity. For instance, *Indigo Nation, Peter England,* etc., which were available for customers through their branded menswear showrooms.

The boom in the organised retailing in India can be attributed to the changes occurring retailing in the socio-economic status owing to the rising disposable incomes of the growing middle-class in the society. This middle-class was seeking value for money products. Even the women (many of whom have taken to work) who was donning many roles of a working housewife started expecting and demanding more products choice, a better shopping ambience, more convenience, preference for a one stop-shop destination (with entertainment facilities and ample parking space). This has led to the growth of the departmental stores, speciality stores, supermarkets, malls, etc.

It can be said that organised retailing has been gaining momentum because of the influence of certain factors like increase in the purchasing power of consumers, availability of a variety of options, increased brand awareness, consumers seeking equality products and the modern supply and distribution management solutions.

Even with wider global exposure, there has been an increase in the demand for lifestyle products. This has resulted in the emergence of lifestyle and fashion specialist branded retailers like *Lifestyle, Shoppers' Stop, Globus, Westside, Landmark Stores,* etc., books, music, gift retailers like *Crosswords, Sapna Book House, Planet M, Music World, Archies, Feelings,* etc., exclusive health and personal care retailers such as *Ayush, Kaya Clinics, Health and Glow,* etc. All these retailers offer customers an exclusive shopping amblence and pleasant shopping experience with a wide range and variety of products to match the particular target market's needs.

The advent of malls in major metros and cities gave birth to the concept of retailing with entertainment an enjoyable experience for the whole family. The success of huge malls such as *Spencer Plaza* (Chennai) *Central Mall* (Seamless mall in major cities) *Crosswords* (Mumbai), *Ansal Plaza* (Delhi), *Forum Mall* (Bengaluru) have motivated a number of developers to join the retail bandwagon. Now mall developers are setting up base in many upcoming smaller cities too (such as Surat, Jaipur, Lucknow, Cochin, Chandigarh and so on.)

The growth and acceptance of organised retailing has led to the market being filled with local, national and international retailing chains trying to woo their customers and gain space for themselves too in the market.

A look at the food and grocery segment will indicate the rise of supermarkets and grocery chains like, *Foodworld, More, Fabmall, Nilgiris,* etc., *speciality* retailers like *Viveks, Girias, Pai's, Adishwar's,* etc., fastfood chains like *McDonalds, Domino's, Pizza Hut, Subway,* etc., and coffee chain outlets like *Barista, Cafe Coffee Day,* etc.

Table 11.1: Types of store formats

Type of Retail Format		*Description*
Convenience Store	:	Ideally located close to residential areas to enable target customers have easy accessibility and select convenient merchandise such as beverages, ready-to-eat snacks, grocery, etc. For instance, the friendly neighbourhood grocery stores.
Chain of Stores	:	A single retailer establishes a chain of stores with its exclusive-store design, synergistic merchandising plan, promotion and service strategy and so on. For instance – *Raymond* chain of stores, *Khazana Jewellery,* etc.
Franchise	:	Retail stores owned and operated by individuals on behalf of, and licensed by a big supporting organisation. For instance, *Pizza Hut, Baskin Robbins, Aptech, NIIT, Nirulas, McDonalds,* etc.

Speciality Store	:	Retail shops displaying merchandise which have narrow product-lines, specialising in a particular type of merchandise and offering specialised services to customers. For instance, *Carbon* from Peakok Jewellery, has its own exclusive stores selling fashion accessories and jewellery, or *Park Avenue,* from Raymonds is a men's speciality store.
Departmental Store	:	A store having several departments such as clothing, personal care and cosmetics, books and stationeries, houseware goods, electronics, etc., all under a single roof, although individually functioning as a Strategic Business Unit (SBU). These stores are large in size (or area) more often owned by large or national chains. For instance, *Lifestyle, Shoppers' Stop, Pantaloon, Westside, Ebony,* etc.
Supermarket	:	A store which is departmentalised, with self-service offering groceries, limited non-food items such as health and beauty related items and general merchandise. For instance – *Foodworld* outlets, *Nilgiris* (in the South), etc.
Hypermarket	:	Hypermarkets are very large in size, carry grocery, hardware, appliances and other general merchandise, with self-service facilities, usually located in warehouse type structures with large parking facilities. For instance, *Trent's* (a Tata Enterprise) *Star India Bazaar, Giant* (RPG Group) and *Big Bazaar* (Pantaloon Retail India).
Shopping Mall	:	A shopping mall is an arrangement of retail stores and providing the right mix of shopping, food courts and entertainment and parking facilities. The retail space is shared by an anchor stores and other retailers (tenants), who will pay the developers of the mall – rent or lease payment for putting up the shop within the mall premises. For instance, in Bengaluru – *The Forum, Central, Sigma Mall*, etc.
Shopping Plaza	:	The shopping plaza will be a configuration of many tenants using space of 1,000 sq. ft. or so for putting up stores within a single building. For instance, *Fountain Plaza (Chennai), Modi Arcade Plaza* (Bengaluru), etc.
Discount Stores	:	Discount stores retail a broad variety of merchandise, offer limited services and at low prices. For instance, *Subiksha* and *Margin Free Supermarket.*
Factory/Seconds Outlet	:	The factory stores are owned and operated by the manufacturers who sell discounted merchandise or factory seconds or cancelled orders to consumers at low prices. For instance, the *Bata factory Outlet, Indigo Nation/Peter England* factory outlet, etc.
Kiosk	:	Kiosk as a store often is a concession format store placed within a mall/shopping centre, a bus station, airport, etc. It is

a free standing pavilion open on one or more sides. For instance, in a bookstore kiosk, customers are provided with on-line catalogue service to help them to identify titles and read reviews before making a purchase decision.

FACTORS AFFECTING RETAILING INDIA

The factors which affect the retailing industry in India are given below:

Consumer Pull

Consumer pull is probably one of the largest influencing factor which has contributed to the growth of retailing in India. Both the traditional as well as organised retailers are trying to offer products and services to match the needs of both the middle and upper middle-class customers. These customers are seeking value-added products at decent prices and convenience while shopping. The modern retailers on their part, by offering a wide range of products, good ambience, proximity, value-added services such as credit, etc., are making themselves attractive and appealing to all classes of society. For instance, *Haiko Supermarket* (Mumbai), offers their customers a care-lobby near the entrance of the store and other services like wheel chair for handicapped customers to enable them to shop. Simultaneously, another key component affecting the retailing industry is the growing population both in the rural as well as urban markets. Further, there has also been a steady growth in the number of double-income households and high income populations. Customers who fall in this bracket often spend a reasonable amount (around 55 per cent of their take home salary) on food and grocery. The retailers are trying to meet the demand for higher quality or high priced consumer goods through their outlets. Malls such as *The Forum* (Bengaluru) are able to attract customers by providing the right ambience and wide range of quality merchandise to choose from.

Changes in the Social Structure and Consumer Behaviour

The retailing industry in India is emerging along the lines of the economic evolution of the society. The society consists of the urban woman, today who is highly educated, professionally qualified and working (with a high disposable income). Apart from being hard-pressed for time – stretching herself to maintain the right balance between home and work, she is also a part of the nuclear family household. With an increase in such double-income households and working women segment, consumers are looking for a different lifestyle. Such customers, while shopping are looking for the convenience of one-stop shopping, *i.e.,* speed and efficiency (to take care of their limited time) seek more information, variety, quality products, hygiene, attractive shopping ambience and good customer-service. These customers are seeking 'value for money' for the goods purchased. These needs of consumers are taken care of while shopping at convenience stores, departmental stores, supermarkets and so on.

With nuclear families concept gaining acceptance, especially in urban areas, it is very common to see the entire family going for shopping together. These customers are interested in shopping places which have the right mix of shopping, eating joints and entertainment. Shopping malls with their varied mix, distinct identity and tenant mix are able to offer customers a great and complete shopping experience for the entire family in an environment where there is variety and choice.

Today, the malls being more organised in terms of categories, formats, movies and food courts have not only added convenience but also a fun element to the shopping experience. Such shopping, environments when customer care initiatives, special offers, events and promotion are taken care of by retailers, not only help in creating a differentiating factor but also provides different value propositions to the consumer.

Shopping complexes appeal to customers because of the availability of a variety of products, at reasonable costs and a one place shopping experience.

Retail outlets such as the *Nilgiris* help time pressed customers to purchase vegetables and household items at convenience and at competitive prices.

Reliance retail at petrol station

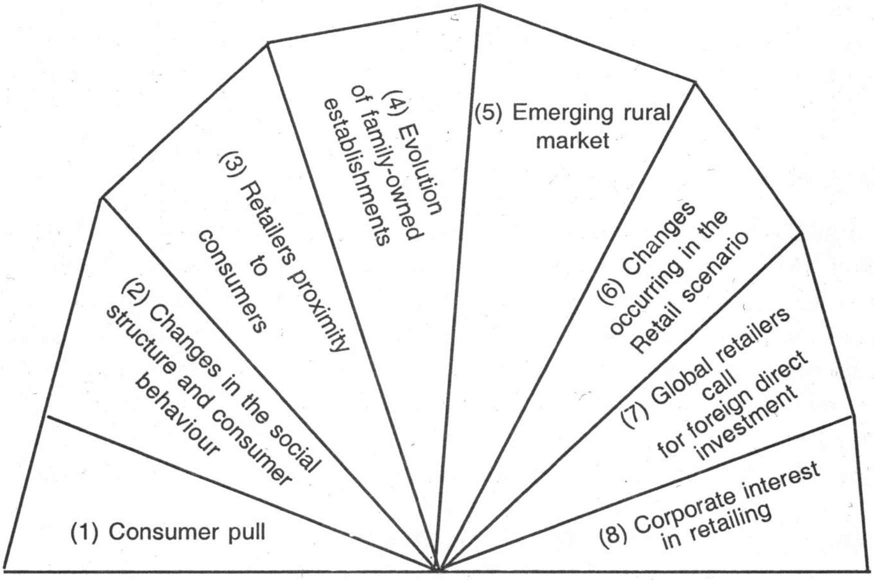

Figure 11.2: Factors influencing the growth of retailers in India

Retailer Proximity to Consumers

The supply-chain management starts from the manufacturers, who will manufacture products on the basis of consumer demand and need. Subsequently, the goods will reach the hands of the consumer through the distributors. With the evolution of the market, now retailers are the ones who provide the vital link between the manufacturers and the customer in the supply-chain. Retailers, because of their proximity to customers are in a position to get a pulse of the market tastes and communicate the same to the manufacturers. For instance, food retailing is still at the nascent stage of development. Initially, the food retail formats were largely influenced by the Western counterparts. But based on the feedback given by retailers to the manufacturers, the trend is slowly changing, as customers now prefer to touch, see and feel the product before they take a buying decision. In fact, the Indian food consumption habits do not comprise much of packaged foods. So, keeping in mind the tastes of Indian consumers' organised food retailers like *Foodworld, Reliance Fresh, Namdhari's, Nilgiris,* etc., offer fresh and quality vegetables and grocery items.

Even retailers such as Ramchander Aggarwal has been successful in running a chain of *Vishal Megamart Stores*, only because he was able to read what his category of customers were looking for when going for shopping.

Evolution of Family-owned Establishments

Till organised retailing revolution started emerging along the lines of economic evolution of society, most of the customers used to make their purchases from the local family-run businesses. These shops offered customers convenience and a wide range of products at competitive prices.

However, today's consumers, through exposure (*via* media), increase in the per capita income and being double income households are looking for a different lifestyle and shopping experiences. Such needs of the new age customers are being met through the various organised retailing formats such as '*Pantaloon's Retail Stores, Vivek's Exclusive Showroom,* etc., who have found that they can dramatically increase their customer brand interaction and transactions by creating an overall retail 'experience'.

A Emerging Rural Market

The rural market in India is fast emerging as a retail consumption area. The total size of the rural market for FMCG products is ₹ 41,550 crore when compared to ₹ 37,130 crore of urban India. The rural customers is now more aware and open to experiment in key product categories like FMCG and consumer durables. The rural middle-class is steadily increasing. In fact, the middle to high income households in rural India are now 17 per cent of the total rural population and are growing at the rate of 7 per cent. Thus, realising the huge potential in rural retailing, retailers are trying to work-out rural retail formats, using innovative marketing strategies to reach and serve rural customers across different income groups through cost-effectiveness and efficiency.

Changes Occurring in the Retail Scenario

In order to take care of the consumer acceptance of organised retailing, retailers are involved in finding the means to incorporate maximum innovation with minimum fuss, maximum customer focus with minimum price intervention and maximum value for money with minimum people problems. Some of the retail actions taken by retailers are introduction of designs labels, revenue sharing formulae, new Return On Investment (ROI) models, enhancing the sales staff quality and increasing overall operational efficiencies.

Department stores such as *Pantaloon, Shoppers' Stop, Westside* have started selling designer wear. These designer wear going by the brand names '*Buzz*', *Springboard,* etc., have helped in creating a store image and is widely accepted by the customers.

The malls are trying to attract customers with *display of designer pret and wear* all lined with new and veteran brand tags. Malls such as *The Forum* are using the *revenue sharing model.* This is a kind of long-term working arrangement with the tenants regarding revenue sharing and minimum guarantee, (*i.e.,* to the extent of exposure to the real estate cost). As per this revenue sharing model, it is a win-win situation for the space occupiers and mall promoters as the former will be viewed more as promoters rather than as tenants.

Another area of action is where retailers are going for *tie-ups with foreign players.* For instance, *Piramals,* the promoters of retail chains *Crossroads* and *Pyramyd* are in talks for a possible strategic tie-ups with Australian and Far East retail giants. Says Urvi Piramal, Executive Vice-chairperson, Piramal Holdings, "Initially it will only be a technology tie-up. Whenever foreign equity is allowed in the retail sector, we may look at expanding the scope of the tie-up to include financial participation as well".

Retailers are considering the hiring of a *retail specialist* – one who is a process integrator with specialised domain knowledge of the retail industry and is able to combine consumer experience, point of sale and supply-chain.

Franchising is another format of retailing. Two factors which are attracting even global companies are – (*a*) flourishing class of urban consumers possessing a considerable amount of disposable income, and (*b*) the continuous growth of the economy. Post-liberalisation, apparel and fashion retailing were one of the first sectors to take-off, for example, *Vimal Stores, Bata, Liberty, Raymond, Zodiac,* etc. But today, there are other brands like *Arvind, Madhura Garments, Nike, Reebok and Rockport, Indus League, Levi's, Adidas, Colorplus, Benetton, Wills Sport, Provogue,* etc., who have widespread franchise networks. In spite of the Indian government's current investment regulations barring foreign investment in the retail sector, there are global companies such as the *Marks and Spencer,* who are entering the Indian market through franchising arrangements. Even the existing retailers like *Viveks, Foodworld, Tanishq, Ayush. etc.,* are expanding.

Going by the consumers' preferences and liking of the various formats of retailing such as supermarkets, hypermarket, malls, speciality chains, etc., many of the large retailers such as *Raymond, Titan,* etc., are thinking of extending into chain of stores, to take advantage of consumer's acceptance of private (branded) labels.

Global Retailer's Call for FDI (Foreign Direct Investment)

FDI has helped to organise retail to grow substantially in countries such as Thailand, Malaysia, Brazil, Poland, China, etc. However, the Indian government has still not framed a clear-cut policy on opening up the retail sector to foreign direct investment, fearing that it may lead to harming small retailers. To counter this view and dispel the government's fear, many global consultants had come together. US consultant A.T. Kearney says, "FDI in retailing will not harm the interest of small retailers as large organised players will not cover more than 10 per cent of the retail space. Thus, leaving a lot of space for small players in the country." Meanwhile, at the parliament review meeting the government hinted at a series of policy changes, including a relook at the issue of foreign direct investment (FDI) in retailing. For this, creating an effective supply-chain from the producer to the consumer is critical for the development of many sectors. Thus, the opening up of the retail sector will help in the growth of allied industries such as construction, logistics and supply-chains.

1. Recently it was reported that the Government of India is likely to come out with a proposal, which would allow FDI upto 5 per cent in multibrand retail. Initially, only those foreign retailers who first invest in supply-chains and other related back-end infrastructure would be allowed to setup multibrand retail outlets. The reason for this is that retailer must have already created jobs for rural India before venturing into multibrand retailing.
2. Such a move will benefit retailers such as *Wal-Mart* and *Metro*, for Wal-Mart operates a 50:50 cash and carry joint venture in India Bharti Retail, whereas Metro has fully-owned stores. (*Times of India*, Bengaluru, 29-10-2010).

Corporate Interest in Retailing

Unlike the past when retailing was not an attractive market for corporate, today they are taking initiatives to invest. *Reliance Industries Limited* (RIL) has unveiled a slew of new initiatives including its intention of setting up many retail outlets (a part of the petroleum retailing business) across the country.

It has already opened a few petrol outlets in the country. Anglo-Dutch oil major *Shell* group has made a return to India after a gap of nearly three decades and opened its first petrol pump in Bengaluru. Shell has a licence to open up to 2,000 petrol pumps in the country and will invest ₹ 250 crore in phase-I of its retail plan that focuses on setting up petrol pumps in the South. *Oil and Natural Gas Corporation* (ONGC) is working out plans to setup petrol pump outlets in Gujarat at Ahmedabad, Baroda, Bharuch and Ankleshwar, where it plans to setup a minirefinery.

Reliance Industries after completing its first phase of setting up retail petroleum product outlets and *Reliance Infocomm* stores is planning more retail ventures. The Ambani enterprise is planning to cover the entire retailing *Ankit* including setting up shopping malls and hyper malls all over the country.

Nirma and *OP Lohia group* were vying for a stake in the Trinethra food and grocery chain based in Andhra Pradesh. *Piramal Holdings* had sent out teams to markets like China, Malaysia, Indonesia and Hong Kong to explore sourcing opportunities inherent in products like toys, gift articles, fashion accessories, food and household products for its retail formats – *Crossroads, Piramyd* and *Jammin.*

Thus, presently, the retailing industry is attractive for all – the existing unorganised and organised retailers, corporate and global retailers. All are trying to develop the right proposition of suitable prices and benefits to the customers, so as to achieve the economies of scale as well as profits in the long-run. Since it is a long haul ahead only retailers who are able to understand the customers' requirements and act accordingly will be able to survive and succeed.

REGIONWISE ANALYSIS OF INDIAN RETAILING

As it is already been mentioned in the text earlier in India the retail market comprises of the unorganised sector as well as the organised sector. The unorganised market which includes the local bania, or kirana shop, the paanwala and the vegetable vendor have been practising retailing since a very long time. Although they may not use technology, they know their customers by name, and also offer services such as free home delivery and credit facilities. The developed countries are of the view that in India, the retail trade is still in a developing stage. However, one cannot ignore the fact that not only agricultural products but even consumer durables and nondurables are made available to consumers even in the corners or remote regions across the country in the absence of the so-called organised retail firms.

South India Retail

There are certain key elements which differentiate South India from other regions in the country. These are: higher literacy rates, lower population growth rates, and higher levels of urbanisation. Bijou Kurien, President and Chief Executive, (*Lifestyle, Reliance Retail*), has opined that diversity in language and ethnic and cultural practices as well as higher price and brand sensitivity of customers induce retailers to adopt distinctive retail strategies for the different places in the South.

South India has always been in the forefront of the retail revolution, with several firsts to its credit. For instance, the largest toy store *Kempfort,* the largest film city, *Ramaji Film City,* and even the first mall in the country, *Spencer's Plaza* in Chennai. The huge potential that South India offers can be seen from the example of *Viveks* which achieved a turnover of ₹ 100 crore in just 105 days (in 2009). There are many South based retailers who started out in a small way in one city and then over the years expanded to multiple locations and multiple cities in the region. *N Supermarkets* is aiming to open 60-70 stores over the next five years in the South. *Viveks* plans to expand across the country with 100 more stores across the South and West over the next five years. Another retailer *Witcos* was planning to open five more stores in Bengaluru and then enter the Hyderabad market.

At the India Retail forum *The Shop,* an Images Group event, the participating retail firms heads had felt that the gap between the South and North markets were narrowing. Further, there was a general consensus that Westernised fashion brands do not require a change in strategy for different markets. However, brands that compete in the traditional or ethnic market segments were required to customise their merchandise, pricing strategy, and marketing communication strategy for each market. (***source:*** www.indiaretailing.com)

Few examples of some retailers (in diverse market segments) who are expanding markets down South are given below:

- **Reliance Retail** launched its first small electronics store "Reliance Digital" in Tamil Nadu, to sell the private label of Reliance accessories, consumer electronics and home appliances.
- Global ice cream brand *Swensen's* opened its maiden Indian outlet in Bengaluru at Mantri Mall in June 2010, and has long-term plans to open 50 outlets in South India over the next 4-5 years. The other cities it plans to open outlets (besides Bengaluru) are Hyderabad, Chennai and select cities in Kerala.
- **Joy Alukka and Sons** is planning to make its brand visibility in 2012-13 by keeping aside an investment target of ₹ 550 crore and is targeting the states of Tamil Nadu, Kerala and Karnataka by opening 12 stores to consolidate its position and is aiming at earning a sales turnover of ₹ 1,025 crore by then.

Apart from the above moves made by various retailers, there are many organised retailers who have established themselves in various markets down South.

In food category retailing, the popular names are: *Spencer's* Food Stores, *Nilgiris,* RPG's *Foodworld, Giant* and *Varkeys. Subiksha* had operated on the discount store principle, opening its first store in Chennai before expanding to the other South Indian states. However, due to some financial problems, the firm discontinued its operations and closed up all its stores. *MTR* (Mavalli Tiffin Room) is another speciality food store which opened its first department store in Bengaluru in 1976 for retailing groceries and other household general items. Thereafter, it has grown offering a wide range of product categories which have a consistency in good quality under the MTR brand name. It has made a successful presence in South India as well as in the US, UK, middle-east countries and South Asian countries too.

Many of the fast food chains such as *McDonald's KFC, Domino's, Pizza Hut, Subway* apart from the local restaurants (*Kamat and Shanthi Sagar* group in Bengaluru and other parts of Karnataka, etc.), have popular eating outlets across the South Indian markets.

There are clothing retailers who own impressive showrooms. These outlets offer unstitched and ready to wear products apart from the popular ethnic wear (Sarees, dhoti, Veshti) and have established themselves as successful retail chains such as *Nalli, Kumaran,* etc. Other leading exclusive company showrooms with trendy and attractive ambience to enhance the shopping experience of their customers include *Raymonds, Maduura Coats. Grasim, Globus,* etc.

In footwear retailing *Liberty, Bata, Boots,* etc., apart from the local retail multibrand stores are some of the popular retail chains operating in the major cities across South India. The other popular department store chains in the major cities like Chennai, Hyderabad, Bengaluru are the *Shopper's Stop, Pantaloon Retail, Lifestyle,* etc. For durable products *Titan* offers its watches targeted at various customer segments using different formats such as independent retail outlets, franchised stores, company owned stores, exclusive and discount stores.

Retail Sector in the East of India

KOLKATA

It will be apt to say that the retail sector in the Eastern India is Kolkata centric. Although now the retail revolution has also spread to the other major cities like Patna. The shopping trends have witnessed a pleasant change during the past few years from the conventional trader run standalone shops to more organised and large retail formats. Today, the customers are also looking for variety, value and convenience in a more comfortable shopping environment. This is evident from the surge indulged to by the consumers on branded products. In fact, the city's *Music World* outlet had even recorded the highest earnings per square feet amongst all the outlets in the country during *2008.* Kolkata is an attractive metro market for the retail industry because it is considered to be the principal retail-and-services market to the eastern and north-eastern states of India, thereby serving as a centre of trade and commerce for the region. The other factors favouring Kolkata as a retail marketing centre are:

- Proximity to Bangladesh (with a population of more than 13 crore prospective customers.)
- The Kolkata port and Haldia port can workout to be suitable gateways for products which can be supplied to countries like Nepal and Bhutan.
- NCAER (National Council of Applied Economic Research) report which indicate the rising disposable income in the hands of the consumers.

Some of the prominent retail chains which have already established their presence in the Kolkata market include *Music World, Westside, Dominos, Pizza Hut, Shoppers' Stop, Wills Sport, Barista* and *Pantaloons.* Apart from these retailers there are a large number of traditional specialised markets like the *Bourrabazar market, Bagri market, China Bazar, Lake Market, and Chandini market,* etc. There are certain high street markets which offer a variety of stationery items, dairy products, electronic goods and appliances, wooden furniture, Jewellery, textiles, fruits, spices, etc. These markets are at Park Street, Camac Street, Esplanade area, Shakespeare Sarani and Gariahat.

The local retail chains which are popular in Kolkata are *Arambagh Hatcheries Ltd.,* (leads in marketing poultry products and their outlets offer quality and low MRP food and other FMCG items). *Khadim's* (provides good quality footwear and leather accessories at affordable prices and has exclusive showrooms in Bihar, Jharkhand, Tripura and Odisha in the East, apart from West Bengal) and *Sree Leathers* (offers comfortable footwear to customers through its various outlets in West Bengal, Odisha, Bihar and other international markets of the Middle East, Singapore, Greece, Germany, etc.

There are the *Nicco Park*, termed as the Disneyland of West Bengal offering a variety of unusual and exciting games and rides and *Aquatica,* an eight acros waterpark at *Rajarhat* in Kolkata.

The other successful medium and large format branded and nonbranded shopping complexes/ malls in Kolkata are: *Forum Mall, 22 Camac Street, Metro Plaza, Emami No.1, City Centre, Enclave, C3-The Market Place, Fort Knox, Gariahat Mall, Metropolis, etc.*

BHUBANESHWAR

Bhubaneshwar is another city in the east which attracting a lot of retailers. With IT companies like Infosys, etc., setting up offices here, there has been a rise in a new breed of customers with high disposable income. This city has two faces of retailing, (a) a traditional store evolving with time and (b) Mall culture. The well known retail formats include: *Satyam Shivam Sundaram* (an established multibrand department store famous for its textiles and ready-to-wear garments offerings) *Forum Mall* (with outlets of *Big Bazaar* (anchor store) *Pizza Hut, Moustache, Dukes, Sree Leathers, Baskin Robin,* among others. *The Forum Mall* also has a floor dedicated to food courts and entertainment zone. This mall has received positive response as a well received shopping destination for people from Bhubaneshwar, Cuttack and other towns in the state.

The retail revolution is also affecting the lifestyle of people from smaller towns like Bhagalpur (in Bihar) having its own shopping mall, a shopping centre called "*Sriyash Aap Ka Apna Bazar*" among others. Thus, retailing has integrated into the lifestyle of the people of the East by working out retail format suitable to the customers of this area based on how they would like to work and live.

Retail in North India Region

North India especially the New Delhi, Gurgaon, Punjab, Chandigarh, etc., are as where organised retailing has caught up with the customers interests. The North Indians with growing purchasing power, interested in shopping with convenience and good attractive ambience, changing lifestyle, etc., has accepted organised retailers in many of the market segments and in different formats.

In this region traditional retailers coexist along with organised retailers. The early signs of food retailing started sometime during the eighties. For example, the well-known food stores, *Morning Stores and Modern Stores,* cooperative stores such as *Kendiya Bhandar,* in Delhi have been very successfully running many more outlets at strategic locations in the city. Another example is of the popular '*Sabka Bazaar*' in Delhi.

In the food service sector there are many restaurant chains (both Indian and foreign) and fast food chain and local joints which are popular with the North Indian tastes and preferences. These include US fast food chains – *McDonalds, KFC, Domino's Pizza, Pizza Hut* as well as local chains such as *Nirulas* and *Pizza Inn.*

There are also certain traditional eating joints or retail outlets quite well-known for their specialised preparations, customised according to local tastes and operating low costs in Central Business Districts (CBD) and neighbourhood centres. A brief view of a popular CBD in Delhi, the Chandini Chowk. Most of the eating joints here were started long ago, handed down father to son and some of these being handled by the 4th or 5th generation. Each of these outlets focus on quality very minutely and have their own recipes, not similar to even in flavour though they may be located very close to each other.

The Ghantewala Halwai is one of the oldest sweet shops in Chandini Chowk, more than two hundred years old, known for the quality of sweets available especially the popular *Sohan Halwa. Natraj's Dahi Bhalle* well-known for a typical Punjabi delicacy prepared from dahi (curd) and bhalle (a doughnut shaped item made from ground pulses) apart from a big list of South Indian and North Indian traditional food dishes. *Kanwarji Bhagirathmal Dalbhujiawallah* an outlet more than one hundred and fifty years old and popular among its loyal customers for its namkeens and sweets. *Gianiji ka Falooda* is another popular eating joint started at the time of India's independence famous for its *rabri Falooda* and ice creams.

Near the Fatehpuri mosque there are two more famous confectioners *'Meghraj and Sons' and Chainaram',* dating back to more than hundred years ago and famous for their exotic Indian sweets and other fried food stuff.

In the *health care category* there are chain of hospitals apart from the local chemists and pharma stores to cater to the health and well-being of their customers. The *Apollo Hospital, All India Institute of Medical Science (AIIMS),* (New Delhi) have round the clock facilities for providing medicines and other health and body care related products. The Apollo Hospitals group have many round the clock retail outlets to help customers purchase medicines and other health related products. In fact, *Apollo Health and Lifestyle Limited (AHLL)* is planning to establish a nationwide chain of primary health care centres through franchisees as a one-stop solution to the primary health care needs of the family as a whole.

In the *beauty care service* sector, there are a few popular organised retail formats in Delhi, Punjab, etc., such as *Shahnaz, Lakme Lever, VCLL and Health and Glow* outlets which focus on working as sales counters for beauty products, beauty advisors and dealer aids. Then there are *Lakme Beauty Saloons, Kaya Skin Care Clinics* and even multilevel marketing players such as *Avon, Oriflame* and *Amway*, in many of the major cities in the north to tap the cosmetics products market.

Dr. Morepen acquired *Lifespring* (the renowned chain of health and beauty stores from Total Care Pvt. Ltd.), with plans to expand its franchise into a retail format with stores spread across high retail density areas in Delhi.

There are many clothing and footwear shops found in the shopping centres and markets in many of the cities and towns. Most of these shops are a mix of traditional and modern outlets. The traditional outlets are usually family-owned with not much emphasis on alluring displays, or advertising but with a strong customer relationship which works in their favour. This set of retailers depend upon local wholesalers or traders from places like Ludhiana, Lucknow, etc. for specific kind of clothing and Agra, Jaipur and Kanpur for footwear. These retailers position their stores as outlets with 'Value for money' due to economical pricing, quality, variety of merchandise and other services such as credit facility, home delivery, alteration, return, etc. Some of the established retail chains include *Meena Bazaar* (Delhi), *Saat Footwear (Ludhiana), Delco* and *Metro* (Delhi).

The well-known organised retailers who operate through various formats in the major cities in North India include *Raymond, Gwalior, Grasim, Madura Coats,* the state-owned *KVIC* runs the khadi chain of stores, *Bata stores, Liberty stores, DCM Benetton chain, etc.* Department store chains such as *Shoppers' Stop* has outlets in Delhi, Gurgaon and Jaipur. *Arcus Home Store Chain* has an exclusive arrangement with the Gurgaon based developer Unitech and sells a variety of products including sanitary ware, electrical items, furniture, ready-made kitchen items, paints and white goods through its Gurgaon store.

Apart from these there are malls *Ansal Plaza*, etc., which offer a one-stop destination of shopping with entertainment to its shoppers.

Kapsons, one of the leading North India's Lifestyle fashion retailer, having 68 retail outlets in Punjab and Chandigarh wants to open six more mega fashion stores within the next two years in New Delhi, Bathinda, Chandigarh and in Panchkula, Haryana, along with a big warehousing facility in Mohali.

Bharti Retail has 59 *Easy Day Stores* outlets in Punjab, Haryana, Rajasthan, Uttar Pradesh and New Delhi. It has also opened three compact hypermarkets in Punjab under the Easy Day Market. Bharti's Easy Day and Easy Day Market stores source fresh produce from Bharti-Wal-Mart, the company's joint venture with the US retail gaint Wal-Mart that opened its first best Price Modern Wholesale cash and carry outlet in June 2009.

Retail in Western Region of India

With the economy thrown open to foreign goods India is seeing a plethora of foreign brands entering the country. This can be seen in the ₹ 2,000 crore footwear market in India which has attracted many foreign brands. For instance, *Nine West International* was one of the early entrants with their exclusive outlet at Khar (Mumbai) Atrio Mall, Worli (Mumabi), High Street Phoenix Mills (Mumbai), etc. This brand is targeting the well travelled and fashion-conscious customers who are loyal to the brand. Fashion footwear brand *Bally* started its retail presence in India with opening its first store in Mumbai. This brand has appealed to Indian customers seeking footwear which has classic elegance, luxury, etc., which are the hallmarks of Bally. Another footwear brand targeted at mid-to high-end customers is *Aldo,* which had inaugurated its first store in Mumbai in 2005.

Most of the food retail players in the organised sector have established their name region specific. For instance, *Haiko* and *Radhakrishna Foodland* in Mumbai and *Adani* in Ahmedabad which are in the Western region of India. There are retailers in the food and grocery market also. These include chain of supermarkets like *Food Bazaar, More, Spencers,* etc., which have a national presence. In the food service sector there are the popular fast food chains like *McDonalds, KFC,*

Domino's Pizza, Subway, etc., doing good business in the major urban areas in the western part of India and are now spreading to smaller cities also.

For the consumer durable market which comprises of products like televisions, refrigerators, washing machines, air-conditioners and microwave owens the markets are spread across the states of Gujarat and Maharashtra (in the western region) apart from the other states in other regions. Retailing is carried out through the many acturer's stores like Videocon Plaza, BPL Gallery or through chain stores like Vijay Sales in Mumbai. There are another category of retailers in the consumer durables market such as Sumaria, Kohinoor, Sony Mony Mumbai who though not the leaders in their category, enjoy a strong customer loyalty.

Briefly given below are examples of types of retailers in different product categories, doing very well.

- *"Apna Ghar" is a traditional Indian food joint* based in Pune. It was started by Nana Thorat to provide quality snacks to office goers and college students at affordable rates. Apart from delicious food, the retailer has a strong loyal base of customers because of the place's cleanliness and efficient consistency in service provided.
- *Independent speciality store: "Seasons",* in Mumbai is a retail outlet dedicated to offering Indian ethnic wear and the customers are happy as it is a one shop destination with all ethnic wear right from the 'Haldi' ceremony to the 'Honeymoon' made available under one roof.
- *Kala Niketan, the clothing store:* In Mumbai is a destination in itself and today stands as a store with a world of elegance and extravagance house of some of the most exquisite silk Sarees, fabrics, garments and also chic accessories such as jewellery and bags to match one's outfit. It is said that Kala Niketan is a pioneer of tailor-made sarees and over the years has had a royal clientele to boast of.

In the department store chain category, the western region especially Mumbai, Pune, Nashik, Nagpur, Ahmedabad, Vadodara, etc., have got stores of *Shoppers' Stop, Pantaloon, Lifestyle International, etc. The Future group with its Food Bazaar, Big Bazzar, Hypermarkets, Reliance Fresh, Relaince Retail, Tata's Treat, etc.,* have got their outlets in Mumbai and the major cities and towns in the region.

Mumbai being the commercial capital along with Navi Mumbai, Pune, Ahmedabad, etc., are the city's retailers prefer to open their retail outlets in various formats. This is due to lifestyle preferences, increase in purchasing power with a rise in disposable income of the people residing there.

THE KEY CHALLENGES AND RETAILING OPPORTUNITIES IN INDIA

The organised retailing has slowly gained acceptance across the country and is now in its transition phase and thus has tremendous challenges and opportunities before it. When this industry is in its expanding mode, there are certain challenging forces which have to be tackled to convert them into opportunities. These are briefly given hereunder:

Real estate and infrastructure

The success of a retail outlet greatly depends upon an 'ideal location'. However, often retailers face a lot of problems due to paucity of real estate space in Central Business Districts, due to high price and demand in these areas. Moreover, sometimes the private retailers are not able to take off due to the lack of support of the civic authorities and improper infrastructural facilities. If these aspects are handled properly by the concerned authorities it will encourage many enterprising retailers to open their own retail outlets.

Provides employment opportunities

The organised retailing industry requires the services of trained workforce to be employed in their establishments. Child labour and semiskilled labourers who used to be employed in the unorganised retail industry are being exploited with less pay and long working hours. However, in the retail industry which employs educated and professionally qualified personnel, the retailer will have to abide by the laws, pay as per industry standard and create a condusive working environment. Otherwise, the retailer stands to lose his employee(s) to competitors. Thus, for those who are suitably qualified and interested in pursuing a career in the retail industry, the employment opportunities are many.

Understand the buyers needs better

The retailers outlet is the final place in the channel of distribution when he gets to interact directly with the customer. Since most of the products in a particular category are standardised when compared to the competitors, the retailer when directly serving the customer is able to get a direct feedback about their services and products and also obtain information about their future unmet needs. This will enable the retailer not only to understand his target audience's opinion about the services rendered but also provide a platform for identifying new products and services offerings.

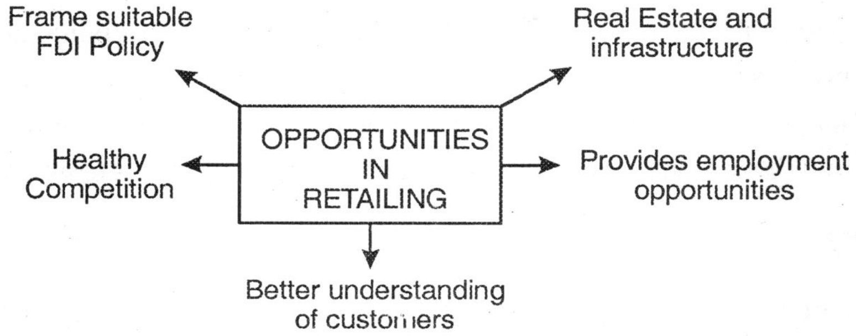

Figure 11.3: Opportunities in Retailing in India

Healthy competition

Since the retailers are offering products with not much differentiation in terms of quality (although it may vary formatwise) in order to survive in the tough retail climate each retailer will have to focus on developing close ties with their target market and foster customer loyalty. Thus, with healthy competition, customers stands to gain with more customised product or service offerings and get access to value-oriented services. Whereas, the retailer will continuously try to seek innovative ways to create stronger and more direct links with their customers.

Frame suitable FDI policy

As per the McKinsey report, with appropriate reforms carried out, the retail sector can generate tremendous employment opportunities for many people. Even though, there are may retail players advocating FDI in the retail sector it is to be noted that merely by permitting FDI in the retail industry it would not be prudent to believe that investments will pour into the sector. The government as well as the retail players advocating the FDI on principle need to workout a suitable framework for FDI such that foreign firms will be interested in investing here. This is the long run will bring in the much needed capital to fuel growth in this sector.

SUMMARY

Although the Barter system has been prevalent in India since a long time, broadly the retailing industry can be divided into three: Traditional formats, Established formats and Emerging formats. There are certain factors which help to understand the retailing scenario in India. These include consumer pull, changes in the social structure and consumer behaviour, Retailer proximity to consumers, Evolution of family-owned establishment, Emerging rural market, Changes within the retail scenario, Global retailer call for FDI (Foreign Direct Investment) and Corporate interest in retailing. The regionwise analysis of retailing was discussed by having a brief overview of South India retailing in, Eastern India, North India and the western parts of India.

The key challenges and opportunities of retailing in India can be seen through: real estate and infrastructure, provides employment opportunities, helps to understand customers better, promotes healthy competition and framing of suitable FDI policy.

CHAPTER QUESTIONS FOR DISCUSSION

1. Briefly describe the various retailing formats existing in India giving relevant examples.
2. Explain the various factors affecting retailing in India.
3. Mention the retailing formats which are popular in the various regions across the country.
4. What are the key challenges and opportunities for retailers in India?

ACTIVITY

1. Move around your city and make a separate list of the retail outlets existing in Hyderabad (old city) and Secunderabad. Obtain information on the retail mix of the various retail outlets.
2. Meet a traditional retailer in the Charminar area and another modern independent retailer doing good business in the city and find out about the retail marketing mixes used by both of them. What differences and similarities do you find in the way the retail marketing mixes are used by them?

❑❑❑

12 CUSTOMER RELATIONSHIP MANAGEMENT

LEARNING OBJECTIVES

After going through the chapter, you should be able to understand:

- The meaning of Customer Relationship Management (CRM)
- The importance of the CRM Process
- The steps involved in the CRM Process

STRUCTURE:

- Introduction
- Meaning of Customer Relationship Management (CRM)
- Importance of the CRM Process
- Steps Involved in the CRM Process
- Summary
- Chapter Questions for Discussion
- Activity

INTRODUCTION

Trading of goods has always been a part of our traditional society but today it is the retail sector which is making significant contribution to the economic development and redefining the shopping habits of Indians. The constantly changing consumer attitudes and buying behaviour is making it difficult for retailers to take their customers for granted. The highly demanding and knowledgeable consumers are compelling retailers to stock a huge product range, offer attractive discounts, in an aesthetically setup environment and so on – all in the hope of having a loyal customer base. But high lead times (for inventory holding) seasonal fluctuations, evolving consumer tastes and sizes are some of the issues creating stiff competition at the marketplace. So, retailers have realised that it is very essential to work towards getting into customer relationship management programmes. For this, they are working out ways to understand the tastes and preferences of individual customers, then chart out strategies and programmes so as to develop a base of loyal customers who will patronise the retailer frequently.

In this chapter we try to understand the meaning of the term 'customer relationship management', the steps which constitute the CRM process and the philosophy behind CRM process which will enable retailers to increase their profitability through effective management of merchandise inventory and that of the outlet.

MEANING OF CUSTOMER RELATIONSHIP MANAGEMENT (CRM)

Customer Relationship Management (CRM) may be referred to as a business philosophy, a set of strategies, programmes and systems which focuses on identifying and building loyalty with a retailer's most valued customers. This means that CRM will work on the principle that retailers have to chart out programmes which will help them to raise their profitability on a continuous basis through building long-term relationships with their customers. This is possible through adopting effective inventory management practices, buying systems and managing the stores so as to achieve the primary objectives of building customer and store loyalty. The primary aim of the CRM programmes will be in the development of a base of loyal customers to frequently patronise the retailer.

In the recent past, the marketplace has witnessed dramatic shifts in the behaviour of customers especially characterised by individual customer expectations coupled with aggressive participation in the buying process. With many global retailers (such as *McDonalds, Metro Cash & Carry,* etc.), having set up shop here to meet the Indian customers' changing needs, the Indian retailers are also going all out to woo the customers by providing a dynamic retail environment along with customer interaction. The basic purpose of CRM is to pave the way for a high customer contact, service and relation with the aim of building long-term relationships with them. With all retailers striving to enter into a long-term relationship with their customers, adopting CRM programmes can help the retailer in a big way. This is because acquiring customers is usually much more expensive than keeping them. This can be measured by working out the cost of acquiring customers, changes in the number of customers, frequent changes in each customer's needs and buying habits.

The benefits of CRM by retailers can be briefly put as:

- *CRM helps in improving customer retention and loyalty.* The customers will spend longer periods at the retail outlet and buy more products which can result in long-term value.
- CRM will help in generating *high customer profitability* through a steady flow of customer purchases from the same retail outlet.
- CRM can result in *reduced cost of sales*, as existing customers will be more responsive and active.
- *Peter Drucker "The basic purpose of an organisation is to create customers and retain them".*

The concept of CRM has been in vogue even before organised retailing came to India. This practice goes back to the days when the neighbourhood grocery shop or kirana shop were more popular and much before the supermarkets or malls came into existence. The grocery shopkeepers would know every customer by their name, what was usually purchased by them, their preferred brands and so on. Through his friendly interactions with the customer, he could offer customers the products of their choice and in this way run his shop more efficiently. However, today with organised retailing shops having come to stay in India, retailers have to develop an understanding of the customer's needs, perceptions, attitudes and intentions. Current trends indicate that the retailers have to be sensitive to the changes in the customers' needs, demographic profile and lifestyle pattern in order to workout effective marketing strategies. There have been three significant changes involving the customers which could have an impact on the retailers' marketing strategies.

- Customers today are more price sensitive and attach more value to quality products.
- With media penetration in almost every home, customers are more aware and self-assured shoppers, having greater accessibility to information on products through home shopping channels, infomercials (commercial advertisements), and extensive advertising campaigns.
- Their greater sophistication, accessibility to additional (or more) information and concern for value have led customers to be engaged in a buying behaviour seeking outlets which sell more customised products.

This means retailers will have to work at customising their services and develop relationships with their customers. Through customer relationship management practices, the retailer tries to:

- Identify or find customers.
- Try to understand them (and their needs).
- Keep in touch with them.
- Make all efforts to ensure that they get all they want from them (retail outlets) in all aspects of their interactions with the outlet.
- Continuously strives to ensure that the customer is getting what has been promised.

From the retailers' perspective, the *benefits of CRM* can be seen in the form of:

- Customers stay longer, buy more, and more often at the outlet.
- Higher customer profitability because each customer buys more and a steady flow of customers will ensure a definite volume of business.
- Reduced cost of sales when existing customers continue to be more responsive to the outlet's attempt at satisfying their needs.

IMPORTANCE OF THE CRM PPROCESS

Retailers must try to understand that the essence of CRM must be extended to *customer retention management.* They have to leverage their data base in order to convert potential customers into actual customers and then make all efforts to build a long-term alliance with them through a range of insightful, customised programmes. Retailers have to accept that they will be able to penetrate the market better if they have loyal customers. This is possible if they treat each customer as unique and make product offerings to suit his/her need requirements without compromising on the quality aspect.

The CRM process can be understood better if one were to take a look at some of the critical issues affecting the relationship management chain with the customers.

- Non-availability of merchandise on the shelf.
- Try to increase the number of contact points with the customer.
- Use the concept of 'Loyalty Card Management' to create the desired loyalty among the customers.

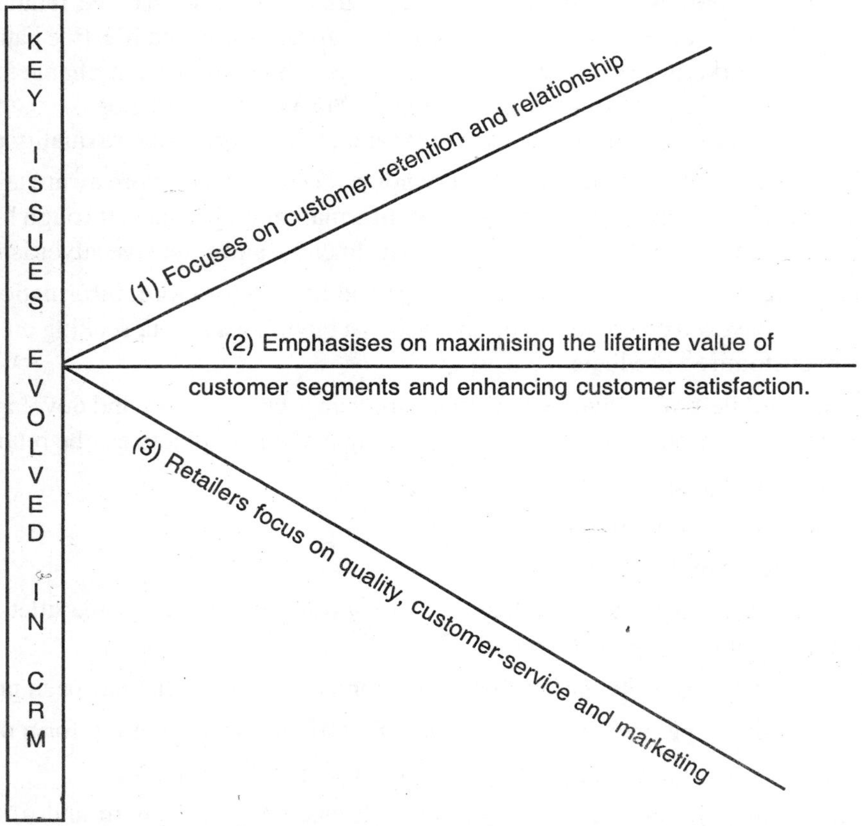

Figure 12.1: The key issues evolved in CRM process

Retailers have realised that the marketing approach to consumers is workable more on a *'one-to-one'* and *'customer focused'* basis, unlike the earlier practice of 'mass marketing' which was more product focused. This perspective implies that retailers have to use customer profiles more effectively to identify customer (or consumer) behaviour at different times and different situations and workout a CRM programme accordingly. Table 12.1 makes a comparison between relationship management chain and the CRM process.

Table 12.1: A comparison between issues relevant to CRM and Relationship Management Chain

Issues Relevant to CRM	Issues in Relationship Management Chain
• Trying to control and manage *out-of-stock* situations.	• Identify the appropriate customer value segments.
• Work on concepts like *self-service* kiosks and *self-checkouts* to take care of consumer needs such as paucity of time, purchase choice linked to quality and value, accessibility to internet (on-line) and mobile phone, etc.	• Designing of customer value delivery system.
• Be more customer-oriented and understand their buying behaviour and focus on working out a 'Customer Loyalty Card Management Programme'.	• Managing and maintaining of customer delivery of desired goods – all leading to customer satisfaction and delight.

Managing Out-of-stock Situations

The control of out-of-stock situations mentioned in Table 12.1, although, a part of supply-chain management, has more to do with CRM. For instance, if a particular product which the customer wants to purchase is not available at the retail outlet, this may frustrate him/her and also cause a loss of sale for the retailer. If such instances of non-availability of merchandise on the shelf occurs frequently, it could lead to losing the customer forever. Most of the customer satisfaction surveys have revealed customers complaining about the non-availability of merchandise at the outlet. To handle such situations, the retailer needs to re-engineer the end-to-end processes and combine it with suitable IT tools.

To illustrate this aspect we can take the example of *Procter & Gamble* (P&G) and the efforts made by them to reasonably improve their 'retail out of stock' situations. They, first at the system level, reviewed the business processes to identify real time data at the point-of-sale (POS). This helped them to automatically get a view of the required restocking, resupply and manufacturing responses in the supply-chain. Then a revised system was introduced with the help of Microsoft BizTalk Server 2000 adopters, which enabled the firm to become connected to the various point of sale systems used by the retail stores.

Such data collected from the POS is aggregated and processed by using algorithm so as to identify the possibility of out-of-stock items on a store-to-store basis. This information is forwarded to the concerned store using customised content rules. Thus, BizTalk Server 2000 has helped P&G to manage the POS data information as well as the customised retailer notification process.

Adopt Concepts such as Self-service Kiosks

Retailers will be able to achieve, their marketing objectives only if they adopt 'click and master' strategies and use the new technology concepts such as self-service kiosks and self-checkouts. Such concepts apart from proving to be a profitable service will also be useful in increasing the number of contact points with the customer. This is all the more necessary because of the 'new consumer trends' visible at the marketplace such as – want of time, desire for entertainment, purchase linked with quality and value, information technology facilitating easy access to internet (on-line) and mobile phones and so on. The benefits of such self-service kiosks are many:

- Electronic catalogues without increase in retail space can be used for *range expansion.*
- Expansion to other service areas like travel and financial services without increasing traffic.
- Enables customer to spend more shopping time.
- If customers go for preordering and selecting, it will result in reduced attendant services time.
- Increase in sales points for the retailer without adding fresh retail space.
- Shopping becomes a pleasurable experience when sufficient in-store assistance is provided to customers to select the desired merchandise from the store.
- At times, especially when shopping for personal accessories, customers may prefer to browse in private in the kiosks, before making the final purchase. In such cases, while customers browse, the kiosk systems can also track each one's trends.
- Supermarket retailers and established branded retailers can set up on-line kiosks for customers to place order for merchandise from them.
- With retailers having come to accept the selling of their merchandise through malls, kiosks will be useful and help customers to save time and purchase the goods they want by shopping in several stores together.

Branded retailers like *Big Bazaar* are considering using kiosks attached to other stores to take customers' orders for their daily shopping without even stepping into their store.

The concept of 'kiosks' have gained acceptance by retailers in other countries also. Personal accessory chain *Boots* and a well- known books and stationery chain in Europe came to know that every customer had to spend a lot of time looking around or needed a lot of assistance. To tackle this issue, the NCR range of kiosk systems helped these chains to provide in-store assistance to their customers in order to make the right selection of products from the stock available in the store. Another large lifestyle store in Colombo, *Odel*, is planning to setup kiosks over the net at seaports and airports so that sailors and tourists are able to shop at their store in a limited time.

Try to Implement Customer Loyalty Card Management Programmes

Although many retail businesses welcome this concept of Loyalty Card Management, they are unable to make the best use of it to create the desired loyalty. This could be partly because they are not able to deliver the value promised by them through the card. And at times, they fail to take proper care to capture customer buying behaviour and plan their merchandise to make it more customer-oriented. Moreover, the international brands of CRM are not only very costly but being generic in nature for all businesses, require a long lead time for implementation purposes. Thus, ideally, each retailer should opt for a 'Customised Development Model' suitable to their businesses. One such attempt was made by *Pantaloon Retail Group* with the help of *Seacom Solutions, Pune.*

Seacom integrated and delivered a specific POS software for Pantaloon (Dual Screen Module). This module helped to:

- Give detailed billing information to the customer such as details of items with images, loyalty points gained, etc.
- Indicate to the customer all the schemes, promotional events, display vendor advertisements (thus, offering an additional source of revenue) and also keeping her entertained at the checkout counter.

In the next phase, Pantaloon's existing Green Card System was reviewed. Then it was found that this system was not customer -friendly (as it was linked to the existing POS TIlls), there was no provision to monitor customer loyalty across the chain or group of chains and it did not offer global options to the customer. Based on this feedback a new server-based system was thought to be introduced so as to provide:

- An online integration with the POS system which would not only credit the loyalty points to the customer immediately but also enable him to redeem loyalty points at any of the chain of stores.
- Stores can create their own schemes, events, etc., for loyalty card customers.
- As and when required, immediate upgradation of loyalty customer status from one level to another.
- A common loyalty card for customers across all PRIL store formats. Arrangements for issue of temporary card to walk-in customers and obtain their data.

It was felt that once the system was fully implemented it would be linked to the company's enterprise system in order to gather information on each customer's buying habits. And this information could be used to optimise the inventory level at each store.

Planet M Stores had worked out a loyalty programme, *M-Xtasy World* which has become one of the largest clubs of music lovers in the country with the number of members touching even more than one lakh. The members of the club are given exclusive offers such as special invites to workshops, musical gatherings and international acts, discounts at prominent restaurants, hotels and high profile retail stores and many other offers round the year, apart from regular e-mails and newsletter updates.

So as to celebrate the hallmark of one lakh *loyalty membership*, Planet M had run a *special promotional* programmes for its members:

- Members with the highest purchases per city received free gift vouchers from Planet M.
- The member with the highest purchase amongst all 25 stores in India was gifted a sleek Akai DVD-TV set.

Thus, as seen from the above examples, retailers have to use unique CRM programmes, keeping in mind their customers' profile, identify the consumer behaviour and use this information to work at customer retention management.

STEPS INVOLVED IN THE CRM PROCESS

Broadly, the CRM process can be said to be comprising of four interactive activities, as shown in Figure 12.2.

(*a*) Gathering customer data and constructing a customer database.

↓

(*b*) Analysing customer data and identifying target customers.

(*c*) Develop CRM programmes for the different customer segments.

(*d*) Effective implementation of CRM programmes.

Figure 12.2: Steps in the CRM process

Let us study each of the above steps in detai:

(A) Collecting Customer Data and Constructing a Customer Database

The first step in the CRM process is building or constructing a *customer database*. This database would comprise of all the data, the firm has collected about its customers and will be the foundation based on which all the future CRM activities are planned and implemented.

Ideally, the customer database must contain the following information:

- ***Transactions:*** A brief history of the purchases made by the customer in terms of: date of purchase, the price paid, the goods purchased and whether or not the purchases made had been in response to any specific promotion campaign or marketing activity.
- ***A Record of Customer Interactions with the Retailer or Retail Outlet:*** This could include information on how many times the customer had visited the retailer's website, inquired through in-store kiosks (if any), made telephonic inquiries or if the retailer themselves had sent catalogues or direct mail to the customer.
- ***Customer Preferences:*** Information related to what was the customer's choice in terms of colours, brands, materials, sizes, etc. For instance, research had revealed that in the paint

industry, consumers considered the process of painting troublesome and do not have much technical knowledge about the different categories. They usually look for total solutions for painting and a package in terms of tools to help them in choosing the right products and correct shades for their homes and reliable painting contractors who would deliver a quality job at a reasonable price. This information inspired *RAMMS India,* a Bangalore-based retail management company to help *ICI* to open the first of its kind paint brand experience centre *'Colour Inspirations'* at the Metropolitan Mall, Gurgaon, offering to consumer's a 'complete painting solution'.

- ***Descriptive Information:*** More information describing the customer, especially demographic and psychographic data. Such information can be used to plan and develop various market segments.
- ***Feedback on Customer's Response to Marketing Activities:*** The analysis of the transaction and contact data will help the retailer to understand about the customer's response to marketing activities.

The retailer may require a complete detailed information on the customer to construct a customer data warehouse. India's first and largest food retailer *Foodworld* had found it difficult to meet their customers' needs to quote cheaper (or economical) price for certain consumption commodities like vegetables, fruits, rice, dal, etc., at the outlets. This problem was more prominent, during *Foodworld's* infancy stage as an organised retailer.

In order to meet the customers this requirement *Foodworld* setup two consolidation centres at Hoskote in Karnataka and Ooty for sourcing various vegetables directly from farmers. For procuring rice it tied up with 6-7 millers to supply specified grades, while dal is sourced directly from Latur, Maharashtra.This back-end consolidation reduced the role of intermediaries in the supply- chain and also ensured better quality of the commodities, vegetables and fruits. Today, *Foodworld* claims to have reached a stage that it can sell rice, dal and several fruits and vegetables at a much lesser rate when compared to the traditional kirana stores. *Foodworld* was able to obtain this information on the customers' requirement based on feedback questionnaire presented to their customers at their various retail outlets. And an analysis of the customer database enabled them to have important insights and plan for merchandise assortment.

Identifying Customer Information

It will be easier for retailers to construct database if the customers are online shoppers or catalogue shoppers or even use the retailer's credit card for buying merchandise in-stores. Most of the retailers provide 'free home delivery' of the merchandise ordered by the customer. In such instances, it will be easier for the retailer to have access to their (customers) contact information, names and address.

Similarly, when retailers issue their own credit cards, they can obtain the contact information for billing when customers apply for the card. In the above instances, the identification of the customers can be linked to the transaction.

But, nowadays when most of the customers are involved in in-store transactions, they may make payment for the goods purchased either through cheque, cash or using a third party credit card such as Visa or Master Card or Corporate Card (issued by some firms to the employees). In such cases, it may be difficult for the retailer to identify information on the customer. To overcome this problem, the retailer can opt for any of the following approaches:

(a) ***Ask Customers for the Identifying Information:*** Some retailers like *KSIC* ask their sales personnel to ask customers for specific information such as their name and address, their phone number, etc. This information is then used to create the transaction database for the customer. However, this approach has got some reservations:
   - Customers may be reluctant to reveal the information fearing that their privacy will be disturbed.
   - During peak hours when there are many customers to attend to, the salespersons may not find sufficient time to note down the relevant information from all the customers.

(b) ***Offer a Frequent Shopper Card to those customers who regularly patronise their retail outlet.***

When customers enroll themselves for such programme, they will be required to furnish some descriptive information about themselves and/or family to the retailer and will be issued a card with an identifying number. Retailers like *Shoppers' Stop* have incentive programmes for their frequent shoppers which could take the form of points awarded for money spent in the shop. At times the points (depending on the scheme in vogue) can be redeemed for items in a gift catalogue.

The benefits under the frequent shopper programme are:

- Customers provide demographic and other information about themselves to the retailer, when they sign up for the programme.
- Through frequent shoppers programme, customers are motivated to identify themselves at each transaction.
- The customer gets motivated by the awards offered to increase the frequency of visits to the outlet and also spend more amount on the merchandise purchased on each visit. Read Box 12.1 on 'Customer is the King'.

One of the major problems faced in using frequent shopper cards for identification is that today when most of the shoppers have access to more than one credit card, such 'frequent shoppers card' may not always be carried by the customer in his wallet. So, the customer might forget to bring it to the retail outlet or may decide not to use it if he is in a hurry.

Of course, another way of obtaining information by the retailer could be to check the account numbers from the credit card used by a customer to link the transactions to that person. But this could result in the issue of invading the customer's privacy.

Box 12.1. Customer is the King
Customer relationship management and marketing alliances have made furniture retailing a more marketing-oriented business. Partnerships are being used to integrate on-line shopping with furniture retailing. Furniturefan.com (an internet furniture directory) and Best Brands Plus (an organisation that specialises in furniture, appliance and electronic retailers), for example, have made plans for an on-line alliance. Furniturefan.com provides Best Brands Plus stores with a web presence designed to lead shoppers to a brick-and-mortar store. The combination of customisation through the web and convenience by the help of an accessible physical store location makes the alliance a major hit with the consumers.
(***Source:*** *Retail Biz,* May, 2004, p. 13.)

So, retailers while trying to gather detailed information about individual customers must be careful about not going to the extent of violating their privacy and objections are raised. They (retailers) must disclose to the customer the purpose for which the information was being collected and used it for that specific purpose only.

(B) Analysing Customer Data and Identifying Target Customers

The next step in the CRM process is to analyse the customer database and use this information to help retailers develop programmes for building customer loyalty.

Retailers make use of certain approaches to obtain such information. These include:

- ***Data Mining Technique:*** This technique identifies patterns of customer behaviour which the analyst is unaware of prior to searching through the data.

- ***Market Basket Analysis:*** This type of analysis focuses on the composition of basket or bundle of products purchased by the customers or household during a single shopping occasion. Such analysis can help the retailer to identify where to place merchandise in a store.

Audio Stream Solutions, an organisation which positions itself as a marketer of in-store radio stations is working on the concept of selling airtime to media buyers on behalf of companies who have customised music. For this purpose it had carried out pilot projects with *Barista, McDonald's Talwalkar's, Giant, Lifestyle* and *Health & Glow.* In the global market, *Audio Streams* works closely with *Image Sound,* UK., which is one of Europe's biggest in-store messaging service provider for organisation's such as *McDonald's, Ikea Adidas* and *Quick Save.* So, in India also, *Audio Stream* wanted to sell the concept of positioning itself as an in-store radio station and work as a medium through which organisations can advertise their brand and thereby become an alternative revenue system for the formats.

To quote another example – *Homeland, India's first home solutions mall* is a ₹ 50 crore venture of the Merlin Group of real estate developers and is exploring a new sector in home solutions through organised retailing. Homeland as a mall is proposing to offer the whole range of products needed to built a house. These gamut of products include everything – tiles and flooring materials, fittings and fixtures to a variety of furniture, consultancy services on interiors, *Vaastu* and *Feng Shui.*

For customers looking for good bargains, home loan facilities and property dealers would be available on the premises. This mall in Kolkata is able to provide for adequate space for loading and unloading, have separate good elevators, free office space for big showrooms, ATMs located at convenient corners, information kiosks, an art gallery and a library filled with the latest publications on homemaking. Merlin's role has been that of a facilitator to bring together a whole group of vendors under a single roof, who would cater to the requirements of the home-office segment. There would be customers comprise of architects, builders, interior decorators and small-time contractors.

Identifying Specific Market Segments

In the above two examples, we have seen how *Audio Stream Solutions,* and *Homeland* have used information to identify specific target market needs. These organisatons have realised that through organised retailing and customer data analysis they are (or will be) able to cater to the similar needs of their group of customers, purchase similar merchandise or services and respond in a similar manner to marketing activities.

In the course of time the information in the customer database can be used by the retailers to identify their 'Loyal Customers Target' and work towards developing customer loyalty programmes. Retailers can use some of the **following measures** to understand how valuable the customers are to the firm.

- ***Determine the Lifetime Customer Value (LTV):*** Lifetime customer value can be said to be the expected contribution to the retailer's profit from the customer, during his or her relationship with the retailer. LTV can be obtained by using the past behaviours to forecast the future purchase behaviours, the gross margin from such purchases and costs associated with servicing the customers. For a retailer, the costs associated with servicing the customer would include advertising and promotion costs, processing costs involved when merchandise is returned by the customer to the retailer and so on.

Hence, a customer who purchases provisions and grocery worth ₹ 1,000 from a supermarket every month is likely to have a lower LTV for the supermarket when compared to a customer who purchases goods worth ₹ 50 on every visit and shops at the neighbourhood kirana shop thrice in a week. Similarly, a customer who purchases merchandise only during discount sale programme period would have a lower LTV when compared to a customer who would pay the full price and purchase the same amount of merchandise from the company showroom.

- ***Working on the Customer Pyramid:*** Customers also differ in terms of their profitability to the retailer. This realisation is because of the *80-20 rule* which says that 80 per cent of the sales or profits usually come from 20 per cent of the customers. Thus, the retailers can categorise their customers into two groups based on their LTV score, as per the above 80-20 rule. Then, customers with the highest LTV scores would be a part of the 20 per cent of the customers group while the other group would include the rest (80 per cent) of the customers. But such groupwise distinction of customers may not always work. Valerie Zeithaml, Roland Rust and Katherine Lemon have used the "The Customer Pyramid" segmentation for dividing customers into various segments as shown in Figure 12.3. A brief description of each segment is given below.

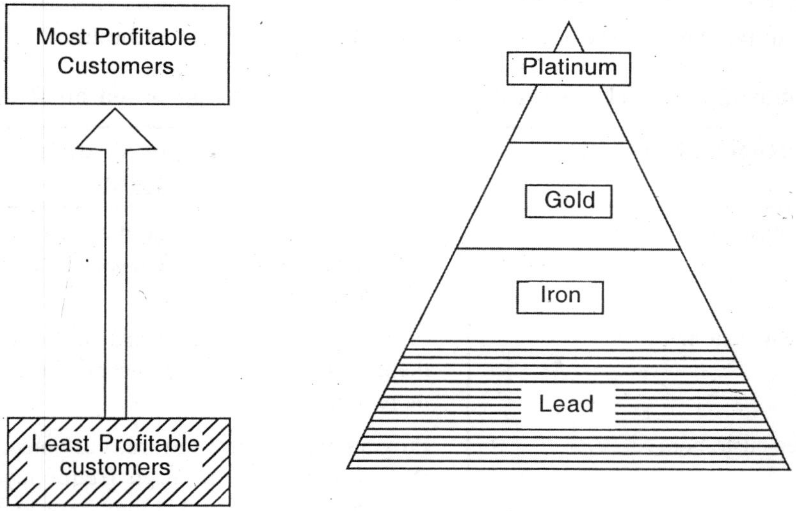

Figure 12.3: The customer pyramid

(***Source:*** Valerie Zeithamal, Roland Rust and Katherine Lemon, "The Customer Pyramid: Creating and Serving Profitable Customers", *California Management Review,* 43 (Summer 2001, p. 125.)

- ***Platinum Segment:*** This segment comprises of the retailers' most loyal customers with the top 25 per cent LTVs. These loyal customers are not much concerned about the price of the merchandise but give more importance to the 'Customer Service' aspect at the retail outlet.
- ***Gold Segment:*** The segment comprises of the next 25 per cent of the customers in terms of their LTV. The lower LTV when compared to platinum customers is because they are more price sensitive. They may not be as loyal as platinum customers and if price benefit is offered elsewhere may switch loyalty to the retailer's competitors. Although they may continue to purchase a significant amount of merchandise from this retailer.
- ***Iron Segment:*** Customer falling in this segment cannot be given much attention from the retailers' point of view due to their modest LTV.
- ***Lead Segments:*** Customers who fall in this category are those who, though spend a considerable time at the retail outlet demanding a lot of attention, do not buy much.

There is another segment scheme called *decile analysis* where customers are segmented into 10 deciles according to their LTV rather than in terms of quartilers. Of course while using decile analysis, the 10 per cent of the customers with the highest LTV would fall in the topmost category.

- ***Recency, Frequency, Monetary (RFM) Analysis:*** At times, retailers (catalogue retailers, direct marketers, etc.), make use of the RFM analysis for segmenting customers. This scheme segments customers based on how recently they have made purchases, how frequently they make purchases and the quantity (how much) of the purchases are made by them. The RFM analysis is typically a method of estimating the LTV of a customer on the basis of the recency, frequency and monetary value of past purchases made by them.

Retailers will be interested in having a continuous flow of *high value customers*. This is where RFM analysis can be used to develop strategies for different target customers.

Table 12.2: Development of customer target strategy based on RFM

Category of customer	Customer target strategy as per RFM
1. First time customers	Try to convert this segment of customers to 'early repeat customers' by offering schemes which motivate them to purchase more frequently.
2. Early repeat customers	Programmes directed towards customers to motivate them to maintain loyalty, increase retention and spend more amount repeatedly.
3. High value customers	Programmes directed towards customers who fall in the high value segment (high frequency, recency and monetary value) such that they (customers) continue to maintain loyalty, increase retention and gain bigger share of the wallet by selling more quality merchandise to them.

Customers who have made infrequent, small purchases in the recent past are considered to be *first time customers.* The objective of CRM programmes targeting this type of customers will be to convert them to early repeat customers and eventually to high value customers. Whereas, the objective of CRM directed towards *high value customers* will aim at ensuring continued loyalty, increase retention and gain bigger share of wallet by selling more merchandise to them. Designing of CRM programmes for identifiable target customers will be discussed in the next step of the CRM process.

(c) Develop CRM Programmes for the Different Customer Segments

After having segmented customers according to their future profit potential, the next step in the CRM process would be to develop programmes for different customer segments. Usually, the retailers will workout programmes to *retain their best customers,* make efforts to *convert good customers into high LTV* customers and try to *get rid of unprofitable customers.*

Retain Best Customers: For retaining the best of their customers, retailers try to reward their valued customers through frequent shopper programmes, offering special customer-service, personalised rewards or benefits and develop a sense of community among customers. Although, the following apprehensions could exist, which the retailer may have to deal with:

- Frequent shopping programmes can be very expensive involving a lot of costs towards developing marketing programmes, IT infrastructure, maintenance costs, etc.
- It will be difficult to make corrections or modifications in frequent shoppers programmes when problems arise, due to the fear of customers reacting negatively to any perceived "take away" after the programme is in place.
- Retailers are not very clear and also draw conclusions on the likelihood of customer spending behaviour and loyalty towards the retailer because of such programmes.

- It is difficult to gain a competitive advantage because such programmes can easily be duplicated by competitors.

In order to avoid some of these problems, retailers, try to offer personalised benefits (based on their unique knowledge of the customer) to their privileged customers.

Special Customer-services**:** Retailers provide very high quality customer-services so as to ensure the continued support or loyalty of its elite (platinum) customers. For instance, *Jet Airways,* allows its Business/Executive class customers to report for check-in at the airport just 15 minutes before the departure of the particular flight (after they telephonically confirm their booking status to the Jet Airways officials).

Such privileges are being offered by retail bankers to its 'Chosen Few' customers.For instance, *State Bank of India* had issued a range of tempting offers and discounts on some of the best selling brands (such as *India International Golf and Tennis Pvt. Ltd., Indian Terrain,* etc.), only to its SBI Gold Card users.

Personalisation: A big challenge before retailers is to workout strategies which would appeal to a majority of customers belonging to a particular segment of customers in the customer pyramid. Nevertheless, today with the availability of customer level data and analysis tools, retailers are in a better position to workout economically unique benefit offers and target communication to individual customers. Retailers are, thus able to workout packages/deals targeted at individuals as well as specific group of customers. For instance, it is only in the last few years that retail banking is being viewed seriously by all the nationalised banks. In the late 90s when private banks such as *HDFC Bank* and *ICICI Bank* had taken to retail banking in a big way, not many in the banking sector had taken them seriously. But all the efforts put in by them has paid-off.

These banks realised that customers were getting tired of waiting in endless queues to withdraw money from the nationalised banks. This resulted in setting up automated teller machine (ATMs) networks along with expanding the branches. The result was the customers now flocked to these ATMs to withdraw money. Thus, it was the combination of physical and electronic channels which helped ICICI Bank to widen their reach as well as service to the customers in a remote manner. But after sometime instead of trying to compete with the public sector banks by building branches, they opted for a combination of ATMs and branches. The 24×7 feature of ATMs have helped banks to attract customers.

Till the late 90s, foreign banks such as *Citi-bank* and *Kotak Mahindra* were considered to be leaders in auto loan market, but the trend changed after *ICICI Bank* came to the market. *ICICI Bank* began offering 4.5% to direct sales agents (DSAs), much above the norm at that time. This resulted in many DSAs switching over to ICICI Bank. Such high commissions meant that the DSAs began to pass on commissions to the customer to gain market share. This meant that although the official interest rate in the market for auto loans was around 13-14%, effectively the customer paid only around 11% on his loan, while the rest was borne by the agent. Thus, customers, felt benefitted with such offers.

State Bank of India (SBI) in order to reduce the risks inherent in retail banking had started offering specific services by leveraging its corporate banking relationships with almost 80% of corporate India. For instance, *Telco,* even though it has its own home loan scheme, was not in a position to meet the entire demand. SBI then made presentations to Telco's employees highlighting about its home loan packages with specific built-in advantages. The result was SBI getting a concentrated bunch of customers from one organisation (Telco) and these customers could easily be tracked down by the bank.

Working out retail programmes for small groups or individual customers is referred to as *1 to 1 retailing*. This is being practised by many local, small, kirana and neighbourhood provision shops. Such retailers make it a point to know each of their customers – by greeting them by their name as soon as they enter the shop and even recommend merchandise knowing the customers taste and preferences. Most often all this information is stored in the retailer's head. But for the big organised retailers or chain of stores, the CRM process helps to efficiently develop relationships with the customer. Today, online or internet is one medium through which big retailers are given an opportunity to automate and practise 1 to 1 retailing.

For instance, if a customer has purchased Marketing and Branding books from *indiatimes.com* in the past, the latest books from the same area are presented to him when he visits this website again. This is because the retailer and its sales associates are in possession of this customer in their database, when he earlier had accessed their website, based on which they are able to pass on the personalised benefits or information. Thus, effective use of the information can result in the creation of a positive feedback cycle in the CRM process utilised by the retailer. Another way of building customer retention and loyalty can be through the *feeling of community* among the customers. On-line media enables customers to exchange information using bulletin boards and thereby develop more personal relationships with one another as well as with the retailer.

- ***Converting Good Customers into Best Customers:*** Retailers are interested in converting iron and gold customers (as per the customer pyramid) into platinum customers. Retailers to try to innovative ways in order to encourage their existing customers to purchase more goods and services and thereby increasing the retailer's share of wallet with them.

Retailers usually go for a mix of *cross-selling* and *add-on selling. Cross-selling* by the retailer means selling a complementary product or service as a part of a specific transaction. For instance, banks such as *HSBC* or *Citibank*, to their existing credit card customers offer add-on or additional credit card which can be used by their spouse, parents, brothers/sisters or children (above 18 years). *Add-on selling* involves selling additional new products and services to its existing customers. A savings bank accountholder with cheque book facility with *Corporation Bank* may be approached by the bank to also go for a housing loan from the bank.

To Tackle Dealing with Unprofitable Customers: Very often retailers may have to deal with customers who may be having negative LTV, and they (retailers) may actually be losing money on the sale transactions they have with the customers.

For example, in the 80s, when State Bank of India (SBI) got into retail banking for the first time, it launched the 'Big Buy Scheme', a consumer finance scheme for consumer durables like televisions, refrigerators, VCRs and music system. But this scheme landed SBI in major recovery problems. Since these were small ticket items, SBI did not bother to tie-up with the manufacturers. Moreover, in order to meet their target of ₹ 7-10 lakh a month, the branches chased a large number of borrowers. The result was that the branches were saddled with a large number of accounts which were widely spread. Further, the follow-up attempts by the bank to recover the dues was also working out to be too costly. If the bank was following up on a ₹ 5,000 advance, they may have to send a person 10 kms away. Moreover, due to systems where diligence was weak, dealers and consumers, cheated the bank, often taking loans on paper transactions. Finally, the bank had to do away with the scheme.

(d) Effective Implementation of CRM Programmes

The purpose of having CRM programmes is to increase sales and profit of the retailer. The effectiveness of the CRM programmes will depend upon the coordination of different functional activities in the retailer's organisation. Thus, the MIS department has to collect, analyse and make the relevant information easily accessible for employees to implement the programmes. Finally, successful implementation of the CRM programmes will depend upon store operations and human resource management, *i.e.,* hiring, training and motivating employees who will be using the information to deliver personalised services.

SUMMARY

Customer Relationship Management (CRM) can be said to be a business philosophy, set of strategies, programmes and systems which focuses on identifying and building loyalty with a retailer's most valued customers. Today, with growing awareness among customers about various products, their usage, availability at outlets, *etc.*, retailers have realised the need to leverage their databases in order to convert potential customers into actual customers and then put in all efforts to build a long-term alliance with them through a range of insightful customised programmes. The CRM process can be said to be comprising of four interactive activities namely: *(a)* gathering customer data and constructing a customer database, *(b)* analysing customer data and identifying target customer segments, *(c)* develop CRM programmes for the different customer segments, and *(d)* effective implementation of CRM programmes.

CHAPTER QUESTIONS FOR DISCUSSION

1. Define Customer Relationship Management.
2. Discuss why is it necessary for retailers to focus on Customer Relationship Management today?
3. Analyse the various steps involved in the CRM process.

ACTIVITY

Select a department store and a supermarket each in your city and try to find out about the CRM methods used by each of them. What similarity and differences do you find in the CRM processes followed by each of them?

❑❑❑

UNIT VI

CASES

CASE I

BHARAT KHADI ELITE (HYDERABAD)

The journey of the company in brief

The relationship with Khadi was started by Ambala Narsimhan in Nizamabad when he opened the store named "*Khadi Kharkana*" in 1930. Having been a freedom fighter, he had a lot of attachment with 'Khadi' which is called the fabric of freedom, the pride of India. Mahatma Gandhi had promoted Khadi to boycott imported foreign goods. During pre-independence period, the movement of Khadi manufacturing and wearing started so as to discourage the Indians from wearing foreign cloths. Ambala Narsimhan ran the business for forty years. After him his son Ambala Satyapal, setup the "*Bharat Khadi Bandar*" in 1960 in Nizamabad. Thereafter came up the "*Khadi Bharat and Handloom House*" in Nizamabad, setup by Sataypal's son Ambala Muralidhar. Thereafter in 1987, they expanded to Hyderabad with a showroom "*Bharat Khadi Kendra*" next to Ravindra Bharati in Saifabad. And in 2010 came up the '*Bharat Khadi Elite*' and '*Indo Fab International Linen Club*', at Saifabad.

Khadi

Khadi has the unique property of keeping the wearer warm in winter as well as cool in summer season. Since the fabric has coarse texture it can get easily crumpled but starch is added it keep it firm and stiff. Khadi does not get easily worn out and can last for 4-5 years. During spinning of Khadi the threads are interwoven in such a manner that it provides passage of air circulation in the fabric. It is eco-friendly and people-friendly and is mainly manufactured in rural areas of India.

Long back Khadi was considered as the fabric for the poor rural wovers and farmers. But now it is no more for the poor. In fact, many high profile personalities and economically well off people also wear clothes made of Khadi. Even very attractive and designer apparel are made by doing handwork on the garments made of them. Today, Khadi is considered as the most beautiful Indian fabric.

The store – "Bharat Khadi Elite and Indo Fab International"

The Ambala Muralidhar family felt that even after 63 years of our independence, Khadi is still not preferred by many consumers, to be on par with ready-made clothes and designer wear offered by the MNCs. So, in order to bring back glory to Khadi, this family setup the 'Bharat Khadi Elite' a 4,000 sq.ft. a two floored air- conditioned showroom at Saifabad. This showroom is on par with many MNCs showrooms in décor, ambience and range and setup with huge investments.

Along with Bharat Khadi Elite, Indo Fab International, a linen club, exclusively ready-made lenin garment is also setup. This outlet showrcases never seen before sparkling Khadi, linen, super bright, stripes,white, dark, fluorescent and pestal colour garments. It also has a separate division for dignified Dr. A.N.R. Khadi and Kashmirshawls.

Ambala Muralidhar's aim is to bring about a revolution in wearing Khadi garment and clothes in the state. He wants to give a facelift image for Khadi from a freedom fighter's identity fabric to that of a fashion garment. He wants to convey through the products offerings in his store that the person who wear Khadi gets a royal and distinguished look due to its fall and style and it symbolises luxury and uniqueness.

Khadi has gained worldwide appreciation as it is hand-made, durable, long-lasting and organic in nature. But in India it is still not preferred by many Indian youth. The full potential of the Khadi fabric is yet to be achieved. It is produced by the masses for the masses. Khadi is even popular in the Indian fashion circle. Through the medium of Khadi weaving, the weaver expresses art and designing by the spindle and loom. Leading fashion designer now present their clothes with collection of designer wear made with Khadi Material. There is a huge demand of Khadi in international market, especially in the Western countries.

Via their store 'Bharat Khadi Elite', the promoters want to make Khadi the much soughtafter clothes material, even overtaking the Western ready-made clothes. They would also like to encourage usage of Khadi clothes among the college-going youth as well as school-going children also.

Questions

1. What is the product range that the 'Bharat Khadi Elite Showroom' should stock so that it is able to appeal to the young and youth of today?
2. Can you suggest the various promotional inputs which can be used by the store, so that it becomes a destination store for its target market?

CASE II

'SMART KIDZ TOYS' (HYDERABAD)

The store

Dubai's Worldwide Traders, one of the biggest branded toy distributors in the GCC based in USA (Oman and Qatar) opened an exclusive toy store in Hyderabad during July 2010. This toy store "Smart Kidz Toys" is said to be the sister concern of the Dubai's Worldwide Trade and the biggest exclusive toy store as well as the first flagship store in India.

The store is fully air-conditioned with a floor space of 4,000 sq. feet area adjacent to Bhavan's School in Jubilee Hills, Hyderabad. It is the biggest dedicated toy store in the twin cities of Hyderabad and Secunderabad with a full range of branded toys. Apart from toys, gift, etc., there is a special gaming corner where kids can try their gaming skill using PS3, Wii Vmotion, etc.

Product (Toys and brands)

The 'Smart Kidz Toys Store' has many products under a single roof related to gifts and accessories for any occasion along with greeting cards, books for kids, stationery, CDs, party items, gift wrapping, etc. The store promoter feel that toys are children's best friends making them happy on receiving one but it can also help to develop their various skills.

Smart Kidz Toys' products are which help children develop sensory skills, creative skills, linguistic skills, social skills, motor skills, etc. The store has on display famous international brands such as *VTech* (renowned for Electronic Educational toys). New *Bright* (popular for its radio control and remote control vehicles, train sets and electric toys and accessories) *Lotus* (Electronic function dolls) *Imperial* (Boys/Girls activities sets), *Crayola* (artistry suppliers including, Crayons stationery, etc. MJX brand of Ferari Remote controlled Racing cars, *Megcos* (Pre-school and educational toys). The store also offers other major brands, products such as *Fisher-price, Barbie Hot Wheels, Funskool, Zapak,* etc., as well as quality soft toys and cycles.

The price range of the products available at ' Smart Kidz Toys' are from ₹ 99 to ₹ 9,999 and thus very much affordable. The store's aim is to make it a kids paradise with branded toy which are best at the three E's: – Educating, Entertaining and Enriching kids as well as adults.

Questions

1. What do you think most have been the factors considered by the promoters of "Smart Kidz Toys" store before setting up such an exclusive kids toys and games quality store at Hyderabad?
2. Can you suggest few ways of promoting the idea of motivating the target market (both adult and kids) to visit and make purchases from such an exclusive quality kids toys outlet ?